THE CRAFT
OF
TUBAL CAIN

Traditional Witchcraft and the
Legacy of Robert Cochrane

T0375905

ABOUT THE AUTHOR

KENNETH JOHNSON was quite literally born and raised in "Surf City USA"—he grew up in Southern California during the 1960s. He obtained his B.A. in Comparative Religions at California State University Fullerton and his M.A. in Eastern Studies at St. John's College in Santa Fe, NM.

For some years a staff writer for The Mountain Astrologer, Kenneth also participated in Project Hindsight, a colloquium of astrological scholars dedicated to restoring and interpreting the earliest known texts on horoscopic astrology.

Kenneth has published many books. His best-known works are *Mythic Astrology* (co-authored with Arielle Guttman), a vast reference work on the archetypal symbolism which lies behind all the planets and signs used in astrology (and still in print after 29 years), as well as *Jaguar Wisdom: An Introduction to the Mayan Calendar*—carried through Latin America by gringo travelers for many years now, right next to their Lonely Planet guidebooks. His works have been translated into German, Portuguese, Japanese, Czech, Russian, and Bulgarian.

An inveterate world traveler, Kenneth is currently ensconced in a remote Mayan town in the mountains of Guatemala where, after ten years of study, he was initiated into the Indigenous Mayan priesthood as an aj q'ij (keeper of days) in November of 2017.

For more on his work with the Maya, see www.JaguarWisdom.org, or follow him on Facebook at Jaguar Wisdom.

THE CRAFT
OF
TUBAL CAIN

Traditional Witchcraft and the
Legacy of Robert Cochrane

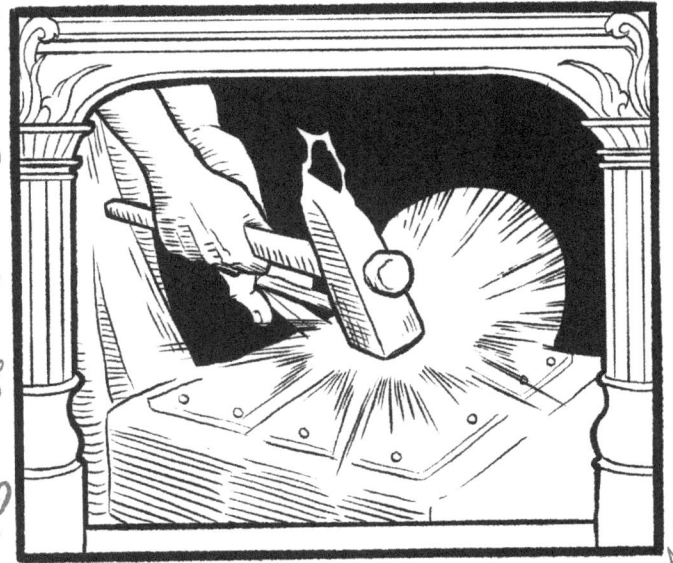

KENNETH JOHNSON
Foreword by Shani Oates

Chicago, Illinois

Paperback ISBN: 978-1-959883-64-7
Hardcover ISBN: 978-1-959883-76-0
Library of Congress Control Number on file.

Published by:
Crossed Crow Books, LLC
6934 N Glenwood Ave, Suite C
Chicago, IL 60626
www.crossedcrowbooks.com

Printed in the United States of America.
IBI

OTHER TITLES BY KENNETH JOHNSON

This work is dedicated to Nicole Combes

Forever the Muse

CONTENTS

PART I
LIVES

PART II
MYTHS

"If he [Cochrane] did compose the rituals and their underpinning ideas himself, then the word for him is surely not 'charlatan,' but genius."

—Ronald Hutton, *The Triumph of the Moon:*
A History of Modern Pagan Witchcraft

FOREWORD

Tubal Cain, a name evocative of mystery and menace, conjures intrigue and fascination, and as a figure of historical myth, he is herewith explored by the author, Kenneth Johnson, who exposes all his vainglorious guises. For my own part in this venture, I was first sought out regarding the relevance of this "mighty man of old" to The Clan of Tubal Cain, and to its founder Robert Cochrane, who died tragically at Midsummer in 1966.[1] Both Cochrane and his relationship with this enigmatic figure have been the subject of considerable speculation ever since. As Matriarch of The Clan of Tubal Cain, the author felt I was uniquely placed to provide an authoritative voice to his own musings, and thus engaged me initially as consultant on all things of consequence between Robert Cochrane, his Clan, and its Tutelary spirit—Tubal Cain. To be thus considered is a singular honour, a precedent I hope others will follow. After all, there is no-one better placed to speak of the beliefs and histories of a tradition than those who bear its torch as living exponents of that tradition; so, for this profound courtesy I am extremely grateful. Getting the information right from the onset helps better inform the people interested in this distinctive avenue of old British Craft and avoids the errors and misrepresentations that have afflicted countless other commentaries on Robert Cochrane and our tradition. With this knowledge secure, the author now has a unique opportunity to publish genuine material for the first time outside the Clan, yet sourced from within it. Truth is, after

---

1   Paraphrased from the nineteenth-century poem "Tubal Cain" by Charles Mackay.

all, the primary tenet of our tradition, a principle Robert Cochrane was moved to place above all other aspects of the Faith.

Describing himself as "a scholar in the fields of mythology and folklore," Kenneth Johnson explores the fundamental beliefs that inform the various practises of Traditional Craft. To that end, he sets his essential core subject—Tubal Cain—within the greater context of the Occult world, where some aspects only bear close connections to the Craft of CTC. Because Cochrane favoured not the path of the eastern star, his choice of Tubal Cain as his Tutelary spirit has led to considerable speculation in that regard.

As disclosed by its title, this is a book that explores the wider myths and legends associated with the biblical figure of Tubal Cain, whose associations range from Freemasonry to the Horsemen's Word. Johnson's compilation nevertheless ties them together, offering a sound and inspiring basis for others to explore further, should they wish to. It is very much a presentation of his own perspective on matters of the Craft, and as noted above, not all of them relate to Robert Cochrane and CTC. Having laid the bare bones of our tradition before him, the provision of certain pertinent facts has enabled Johnson to mold a body of work around that structure which captures something of the mystery of Robert Cochrane the man, his work, and, most importantly, his relationship with the mythical figure of Tubal Cain.

Kenneth Johnson speaks candidly on this lore, informally, and, some might say, with an assumed familiarity, for which I played no small part. Working closely with him through all versions of the manuscript, it is unsurprising it should seem so. Followers of CTC and Robert Cochrane will therefore recognise here many elements, rites, allegories, and myths from my own work in various tomes and articles published over the past twenty years, but will find a different voice in their expression, which is the point—otherwise this would just be a regurgitation of our work. For instance, Johnson has blended in much Celtic and Classical lore, which, though very popular in the 60s, has become less so in our own times, and is, strictly speaking, outside CTC's cosmology, yet Johnson has engagingly offered it up as supplementary yet compatible knowledge.

Johnson is also very keen to emphasise Cochrane's own obsession with mysticism and the divine and, in particular, with the mysteries of communion and individuation. Cochrane certainly understood the cyclic nature of wisdom, asserting how its discovery "creates the alchemy that brings forth an answer."[2] He asserted how "[h]uman beings are alchemical metals—and we change from dross to gold slowly…it is the work of godhead on that person, and the gold increases according to how it is cherished…it is the gold of spirit, sometimes dulled by foolishness—other times shining bright. It is only bought by our personal search for the Grail, the Holy Cauldron."[3]

Alchemy is the science of God, our gift of transmutation from matter into spirit or the body of light and bliss, and to initiate this process, we engage a quaternary of rites initially devised by Cochrane and Evan John Jones, though not fully realised until after Cochrane's death, when his Tanist confederate Evan John Jones became the next Magister of the Clan. EJJ writes: "Before his death, Robert Cochrane spoke more than once of breaking with the past and moving on in what he called his personal 'magical argosy.' Had he lived, there is no doubt he would have re-created the [tetradic rites known in the outer as] *'Cave of the Cauldron,'* the *'Chapel of the Grave,' 'The Castle of the Four Winds,'* and *The Stone Stile,* designing his own ritual for each of them."[4] The Clan of Tubal Cain today continues to revise and develop these works.

These cyclical rites of transmutation within the "Great Work" have previously appeared in print, published by Evan John Jones and myself, where they are solely expressed in the context of the Clan.[5] Kenneth Johnson has reproduced them here in their wider form to highlight the theme of mystical elevation associated with Tubal Cain as the expounder of Wisdom within the Mysteries of the Faith and the Craft proper. In that regard, Robert Cochrane recognised three basic ritual forms fundamental to the "True Faith" which he believed were focussed on Divination, all acts of Magic, and, most importantly, of (mystical) Communion.

---

2   Letter #4, Robert Cochrane to Joe Wilson. In Oates, Shani, *Star-Crossed Serpent III: The Taper that Lights the Way* (Mandrake of Oxford, 2016); Oates, Shani, *Tubelo's Green Fire* (Mandrake of Oxford, 2010).

3   Letter #10, Robert Cochrane to Norman Gills. *Ibid.*

4   Direct quote from a manuscript by Evan John Jones, entitled *The Cave and The Castle: The Witchcraft Tradition of Tubal Cain* (2000), later edited and published as Jones, Evan John and Shani Oates, *Star Crossed Serpent I: Origins* (Mandrake of Oxford, 2012).

5   Oates, Shani, *Tubelo's Green Fire* (Mandrake of Oxford, 2012) and *Star Crossed Serpent Series I–IV* (Mandrake of Oxford, 2010–2017).

The Faith is finally concerned with Truth, total Truth. It is one of the oldest of religions, and also one of the most potent, bringing as it does Man into contact with Gods and Man into contact with Self.[6]

EJJ also explained the Clan's stance on working outside, in the midst of nature, amongst the wild spirits of the land. "Yes, the Faith is rooted in nature as well as in the interplay between the natural and the supernatural. So, by working our magic where the deadening hand of the urban dweller has only lightly touched, we are linking up with the spiritual genius from whence the Craft first sprung."[7] This comment very much reflects Cochrane's position as a radical reformer of the Craft, and his aspiration to lead a revival of the arcane mystery traditions rooted in north European culture in opposition to that of the Mediterranean, which dominated the newly emerging and popular "Wicca." Such was his dream.

For twenty years after Robert Cochrane's death in 1966, William Gray and Evan John Jones climbed Newtimber Hill every Midsummer to the *oak* tree that featured in so many Clan rituals. Based in the basic structure of the rite of *The Stone Stile*, they would approach their old site by stepping over a large stone that formed a "stile" separating it from the surrounding area, whence each would place a small stone they had carried with them upon a memorial cairn erected for this purpose. Lighting a candle, they first poured a libation to times past and absent friends, then to the elemental spirits and land wights in recognition of it as a hallowed place. Before leaving, they tied tokens to a clump of *holly* in remembrance of Cochrane's association with this virtue of the waxing King.[8]

Every year at Midsummer, we (the Clan) continue to commemorate this gesture still, and as I write this, it is with a nod to Fate and to

---

6   "The Faith of the Wise" by Robert Cochrane, *Pentagram*, vol. 6, August 1965. In Oates, Shani, *Star Crossed Serpent III: The Taper That Lights the Way, op. cit.*

7   Jones and Oates, *Star Crossed Serpent I: Origins, op. cit.*

8   These are key themes relating to CTC cosmology that feature in *Tubelo's Green Fire* and the *Star Crossed Serpent Series, I–IV,* and may also be observed throughout this book.

Providence that I am called upon to comment upon his work and mysteries at such a time.[9]

> *The real mystery is only uncovered by the individual and cannot be told, but only pointed to. Any occultist who claims to have secrets is a fake—the only secret is that which man does not understand—otherwise all wisdom is an open book to those who would read it. One is discreet about certain things because of blank incomprehension or misunderstanding, but wisdom comes only to those who are ready to receive it—therefore much of the nonsense believed by gardnerians [sic] and hereditary groups alike is concerned with secrecy. There is no secret in the world that cannot be discovered, if the recipient is ready to* listen *to it—since the very air itself carries memory and knowledge. Those men that speak of secrets and secrecy and not of discretion or wisdom are those who have not discovered truth. I personally distrust those who would make secrets, since I suspect their knowledge to be small. I was taught by an old woman who remembered the great meetings—and she took no terrible oath from me, but just an understanding that I would be discreet. She did not require silence, only a description of what I had seen and what I had heard and said when I was admitted. The Gods are truly wise—they know the future as well as the past and they admit not those who would abuse knowledge or wisdom.*[10]

Shani Oates, Clan Matriarch
Midsummer 2024

---

9   There is a further measure of synchronicity here too, as a book by Shani Oates on the early works and rituals of Robert Cochrane and CTC, *Tubelo's Forge,* is due to be published this winter by Anathema Publishing Ltd.

10   Letter #4, Robert Cochrane to Joe Wilson. In Oates, *Star Crossed Serpent III: The Taper That Lights the Way, op. cit.*

AUTHOR'S PREFACE

UPON SEVERAL OCCASIONS during its history of nearly sixty years, the Clan of Tubal Cain has experienced difficulties regarding its leadership and the correct interpretation of the Mysteries contained within its doctrines, so it is just as well to state my own position here at the very beginning.

I am not a member of the Clan of Tubal Cain, nor do I make any claim to have special information, secret revelations, or anything of the sort. I am a scholar in the fields of mythology and folklore, and as the influence of Robert Cochrane and Traditional Witchcraft grows stronger at the present time, I have set out to explore the myths and legends which lie behind the practice of Traditional Witchcraft.

I owe a debt of gratitude to Shani Oates, the Maid of the Clan of Tubal Cain, who has so generously provided comment and correction to the book, and who made materials from original sources available to me as my journey of exploration through the writing of the book continued.

This exploration has been a marvelous journey indeed. Robert Cochrane was a modern mythmaker of extraordinary talent, and the lore which lies behind his Clan of Tubal Cain ranges from the Bible to Greek mythology to Norse and Celtic legend. Seldom have I encountered another individual who spun the ancient stories in a new and creative way to the degree that Cochrane did.

This ought not to be taken as a claim that I possess any secret knowledge relating to the Clan or its practices, or that my own interpretations of the mythic background upon which Cochrane fashioned his vision of Traditional Witchcraft is the one and only truth of the matter, or even that current leaders of the Clan agree with me. (It is entirely possible that they may not.)

I am just one more wanderer upon the Crooked Path, one who is in agreement with the quotation from Ronald Hutton given above and whose journey on the Path has been deeply rewarded.

Kenneth Johnson
October 14, 2023

 xx

PART I

LIVES

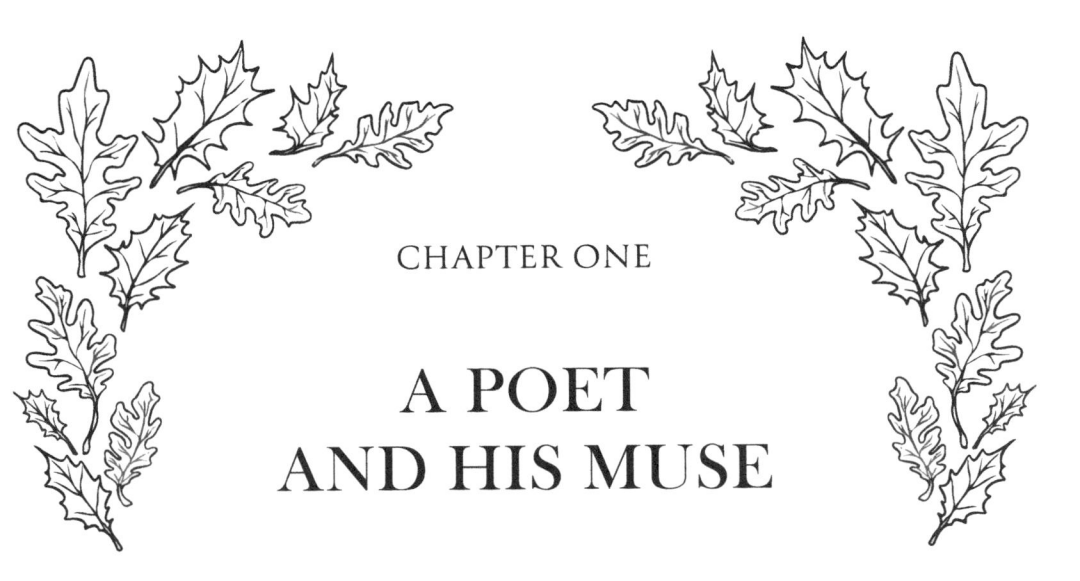

CHAPTER ONE

A POET AND HIS MUSE

ACCORDING TO THE RECORDS of the Third Battalion of the Royal Welsh Fusiliers, Captain Robert Graves was dead, having been struck by shrapnel in the lung during the Battle of the Somme in 1916. This was an exaggeration. Young Captain Graves, already gaining a literary reputation for a volume of poetry which depicted the First World War with unusual realism, was actually alive, albeit in the hospital. Soon he would be sent home to England, where his real life was about to begin. There he would marry Nancy Nicholson and begin to attend Oxford in 1918, where he would study English Language and Literature as well as the Greek and Roman classics—an interest which would prove to be of great significance in the development of contemporary Neopaganism.

Graves' wife Nancy was a committed feminist. She rode round the countryside on a bicycle and preached contraception to gatherings of women, despite the fact that it was still illegal at the time. By 1926, she even went so far as to accept a marriage situation which was, in fact, a *ménage à trois*. The other woman who had charmed Graves' imagination was an American, born Laura Reichenthal, who had already gone by many names but was now calling herself Laura Riding. Her poetry was attracting a great deal of attention. Unknown to anyone at the time, the relationship between Graves and Riding was to play a key role in the origins of modern witchcraft.

When Riding met the Irish poet Geoffrey Phibbs in 1929, she invited him to join the household that already contained herself, Graves, and Nancy. The *ménage à trois* became a *ménage à quatre*. This arrangement, which the participants initially called "The Holy Circle," was by no means holy, nor was it an equal partnership; everything revolved around Laura Riding. Graves and Phibbs were both sleeping with her. But after a few months, Phibbs changed his mind and returned to his wife, referring to the abrasive and controlling Riding as "a virago" in a letter to a friend. When Phibbs attempted to leave the relationship, Riding sent Graves to track him down. With some difficulty, he brought Phibbs back into the circle—and a split occurred. Phibbs continued to dislike Laura Riding and strongly preferred to make love to Nancy. On April 27, 1929, a furious argument took place. The melodramatic Riding easily progressed from histrionics to hysterics and leapt out the window. Some sources say it was a fourth-floor window, others merely a second-floor window. In any case, she was hospitalized with life-threatening injuries. During the chaos, Graves followed Laura's lead by jumping out a window himself, though he apparently first removed himself to a lower floor since he was uninjured by the fall.

Not surprisingly, the incident caused a major scandal in literary London. Nancy filed for divorce. Graves and Laura Riding retreated to Majorca in the Balearic Islands, where they set up a small press publishing house until Graves entered the big time in 1934 and 1935, first with his historical novel *I, Claudius,* and then with a sequel, *Claudius the God.* He had become a successful professional writer.

Graves and Riding left Majorca in 1936 at the outbreak of the Spanish Civil War. After a period of wandering, they moved to the United States in 1939, and there the tempestuous relationship between them finally came to an end. They parted in 1941. Laura Riding soon married an American and lived quietly in Florida until her death in 1991.

Graves returned to Britain and began a relationship with Beryl Hodge, though they did not marry until 1950. In 1946, they moved back to Graves' beloved Majorca, where he lived for the rest of his life.

It was in Majorca that Robert Graves finally sat down and wrote his book about Laura Riding—or, more accurately, his book about her ideas and her influence upon his own thinking. In 1948, he published it. His tribute to Laura Riding became one of the principal cornerstones of Neopaganism and modern witchcraft: *The White Goddess: A Historical Grammar of Poetic Myth.*

Graves had made his initial reputation as a poet and had achieved fame as the author of historical novels. But though he had written many a love poem for Laura Riding over the years, it was neither poetry nor fiction that he chose for his ultimate homage to his most important muse. Instead, he created a work of non-fiction which appeared to be a scholarly stew of Greek and Celtic myth, the Irish Ogham alphabet, goddesses various and sundry, and kings who fought seasonally for the land and the Goddess who ruled it. There was to be a great deal of controversy about how scholarly the book really was.

Robert Graves

To Graves, the worship of an all-powerful Goddess underlaid the mythology of ancient Europe. Though one, she often appeared in triple form, and therefore he designated her as a Triple Goddess. She ruled over "birth, love, and death." Her life cycle was linked with the phases of the moon, and therefore she was a "white" goddess indeed.

Graves saw the "language of poetic myth" as a magical language originally created to honor and worship the Goddess, the ultimate Muse; this language of myth and magic was the language of "true" poetry. He postulated ancient Europe as a matriarchal society that had been laid waste by the growth and eventual dominance of patriarchal mythologies, and then by patriarchal monotheistic religions. This idea was to have an almost incalculable influence over the development of feminism and modern Paganism.

But Graves didn't stop there. He went on to argue that the names of the Ogham letters in the alphabet used in parts of Gaelic Ireland and Britain contained a calendar that was founded in an ancient liturgy involving the human sacrifice of a sacred king. The idea of a ritually sacrificed king was one that Graves had gleaned from the enormous multi-volume work entitled *The Golden Bough* by Sir James George Frazer. Graves postulated that a Summer King and a Winter King, also known as the Oak King and the Holly King, fought—and killed—each other twice a year to mark the changing of the seasons and to honor the Great Goddess.

Though *The White Goddess* strikes most readers as a very scholarly (and sometimes difficult) read, the experts in Classical and Celtic studies at Oxford and Cambridge disagreed. The Celtic specialists sneered at Graves' linguistic errors and unconventional interpretations of Ogham. The Classicists groaned in pain over Graves' insistence on re-interpreting all Greek mythology in terms of Frazer's notions about the sacrifice of sacred kings.

But perhaps the most vicious commentary came from the Muse herself, whose remarks cast her as the "virago" that so many believed her to be when she sounded forth on the way Graves had poetically re-envisioned many of her own ideas. "Where once I reigned, now a whorish abomination has sprung to life, a Frankenstein pieced together from the shards of my life and thoughts."[11]

She also vented her vitriol in a longer statement: "As to the 'White Goddess' identity: the White Goddess theme was a spiritually, literarily and scholastically fraudulent improvisation by Robert Graves into the ornate pretentious framework of which he stuffed stolen substance of my writings, and my thought generally, on poetry, woman, cosmic actualities and the history of religious conceptions."[12]

---

11   Cited in Lindop, Grevel ed., *Robert Graves: The White Goddess: A Historical Grammar of Poetic Myth* (Carcanet Press, 1997).

12   Cited in Jackson, Laura (Riding), *The Person I Am: The Literary Memoirs of Laura (Riding) Jackson* (Trent Editions, 2011) p. 70.

In 1967, however, her comments were a bit kinder:

In my thinking, the categorically separated functions termed intellectual, moral, spiritual, emotional, were brought into union, into joint immediacy; other conceptions put the sun and moon in their right rational places as emblems of poetic emotionalism, and lengthened the perspective of Origin back from the skimpy historical heavens of masculine divinity through a spacious dominion of religious symbolism, presided over, for the sake of poetic justice, by a thing I called mother-god.[13]

Graves died in Majorca in 1985, but *The White Goddess* was not forgotten, and, in fact, it is still popular—at least among certain readers. Though academics sneered and Riding raged, there were many who found *The White Goddess* a fascinating text which spoke to them in a deeply personal way. The Swiss scholar Johann Bachofen in the nineteenth century and the French writer Robert Briffault in 1927 had already postulated a matriarchal Neolithic utopia, but it was *The White Goddess* that brought such theories to popular attention. When similar ideas were embraced by Marija Gimbutas, Dean of Old World Archaeology at UCLA in the 1980s and 90s, the concept of a matrifocal paradise in ancient Europe became a mainstay of feminist thought, spawning a host of popular books by authors such as Merlin Stone and Riane Eisler.

Though the social structure of Neolithic Europe remains a topic of debate in academia, the idea of a utopian matriarchal epoch brought to grief by vicious patriarchal invaders had become enshrined in the popular imagination. After the fall of the Soviet Empire allowed archaeologists from the Western and Soviet blocs to communicate freely, Marija Gimbutas acknowledged that the European Neolithic cultures were brought to an end by climate change rather than invasion. Her recantation of the invasion thesis was buried deep in literary obscurity, since publishers were making a fortune from authors who raged against the drooling, mutated patriarchs that had carved a trail of blood as they rode through Europe. The truth is that they made their trail through the continent without violence in big clunky wagons, and it is not clear as to whether they could actually ride horses at that time.

---

13   "A Letter to The Editor" [On Michael Kirkham on Robert Graves] (Minnesota Review, 1967) 7(1) pp. 77–9.

Graves' portrait of a goddess-centered civilization in ancient Europe also appealed to practitioners of the occult sciences and to students of witchcraft and magic. Most importantly for our purposes, *The White Goddess* served as inspiration for two antagonists who stand at the forefront of the modern witchcraft revival. Gerald Gardner, the founder of Wicca, was an ardent fan, and even traveled to Majorca to visit with Graves. The individual who would become known as Robert Cochrane began a correspondence with Graves in the early 1960s. The letters from Cochrane to Graves are both revealing and frustrating. They are not dated, though Cochrane still signed himself as "Roy Bowers," which was his birth name, so he seems not yet to have adopted the name Robert Cochrane. Even more frustrating than the uncertain timing is the fact that Graves's replies—which Cochrane sometimes mentions—have not survived.

Cochrane writes: "I sometimes feel when I am wandering around in the marshes of the old knowledge, that the dam upstream is going to burst and the whole of humanity is going to be submerged by fifty thousand years of pre-history, swamping the neat subtopian conventions of the last thousand years."[14]

These words, written before the turmoil of the 1960s and the return of witchcraft under the influence of Cochrane and Gerald Gardner, proved to be powerfully prophetic. They bear witness to the occasional insights that sometimes leap forth from a plethora of confusing and contradictory statements.

Here is one more quote from Cochrane's letters to Graves:

> *I was interested in your description (one of the difficulties of communication interested!) of the physical appearance of the Goddess symptons [sic] (Gawd, my spelling). I am not biased towards the poetical aspect but more towards the Black Goddess, so my knees do not shake or eys [sic] run, but I do get a sudden feeling of intense pressure, something like an approaching storm.*

The storm was indeed approaching, and Robert Cochrane was one of the individuals who was to raise the winds and send the rains.

---

14   All the quotes from Cochrane's letters to Robert Graves are from docplayer.net/526 12115-Robert-cochrane-s-letters-to-robert-graves.html, retrieved June 4, 2023.

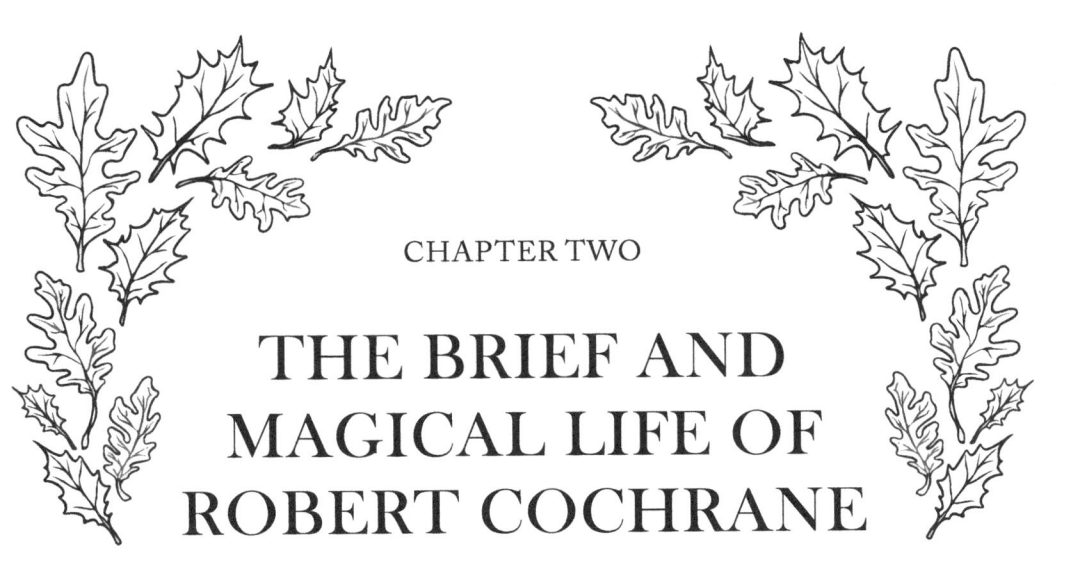

CHAPTER TWO

THE BRIEF AND MAGICAL LIFE OF ROBERT COCHRANE

A FIRE HAS BEEN LIT in a clearing in the woods. The participants in the ceremony, each of them clad in black robes, shiver in the midnight chill.

The magister, a young man, barely thirty, holds a forked staff called a stang in his hand as he intones his chant—an invocation to a seemingly random colloquy of ancient deities—Odin, Diana, Hecate. Mixed in among the gods of times long past are paeans to folkloric figures such as Robin Hood and King Arthur.

And one name resonates again and again—that of Tubal Cain.

The magister's countenance, transfigured by the firelight, shines with an Otherworldly glow. Some of the participants perhaps find him a little bit frightening.

No one knows what will happen next.

While some contemporary witches such as Gerald Gardner used a Book of Shadows with rituals carefully noted in precise detail, a book that could be studied until all his followers in the Craft knew exactly what to do, Robert Cochrane never used a book. He *had* no book. His rituals were improvisations, which is why no one ever knew what was coming next, there in the firelight on a cold night in the forest.

As Marian Green, editor of a magical publication called *Quest Magazine*, once remarked:

> *The rituals were often very long with stamping dances, invocations and prayers, building up a powerful and magical atmosphere. They were far louder, wilder and more primitive than anything I have ever*

 9

written down...It was the feeling of raw and ancient energy and the visions of things halfseen [sic] by firelight that stuck with me, almost half a century later.... I have never come across any other situation where the elemental forces and the wild beings of the land, both visible and invisible, were brought into the fire-lit circle to be experienced for healing, knowledge and power.[15]

Bill Gray, another participant, stated that "Cochrane possessed real power and he had seen him transfigured by 'supernatural energy' during the rituals he attended."[16]

Robert Cochrane

The seminal figure in what is now known as Traditional Witchcraft was born in London under the name of Roy Bowers on January 26, 1931. He described his childhood neighborhood as a slum, though other family members have called it a respectable working-class district. With eight children in the family, it must have been a lively, vigorous, and noisy home. During his childhood, the Nazis bombed London on an almost nightly basis; Roy Bowers grew up with the sound of bombs exploding outside the window at night, and adults as well as children

---

15 Marian Green, quoted in Howard, Michael, *The Children of Cain* (Three Hands Press, 2011) p. 83.
16 Howard, *op. cit*, p. 82.

huddled together with fear. Many sought comfort in sex—thus was John Lennon conceived.

Roy grew up to be a brawler, and one could see that his nose had once been broken. In the early 1950s, he served his mandatory two years in the British army, but military life did not suit him, and he was sent to prison for going AWOL. His father, a military hero from the Battle of the Somme (like Robert Graves), was angry and supremely disappointed.

After he got out of the army, Bowers worked as a blacksmith in the foundry of a company called London Transport. Since the Industrial Revolution, ironmasters in England had been fond of naming their foundries after Vulcan, the blacksmith of the gods in Greek mythology, or Tubal Cain, named in the Bible as a primordial blacksmith and craftsman. Bowers no doubt heard such tales, and perhaps even knew individuals who had worked in foundries named for these mythic figures. This may well be where he acquired the name of the witchcraft coven (Cochrane himself often wrote it as "covine" or "cuveen") he would found not long afterwards: the Clan of Tubal Cain.

Still known as Roy Bowers, the incipient magister of Traditional Witchcraft married his girlfriend Jane and the two of them took jobs as "bargees." In those days, coal and other goods were still transported by water rather than overland, especially through the complex system of canals that traversed the British Midlands. The narrow boats were called barges, and the workers were known as "bargees." Many of the barges were decorated with paintings of various symbols such as a rose or a castle—images which became important in Cochrane's mythos later on. Indeed, some barge workers had a reputation as "water witches," and barge symbols such as a sun wheel with six spokes were almost certainly esoteric. Was this where the future Robert Cochrane first became acquainted with esoterica?

That is a question which perhaps will never be answered. His aunt claimed that he became interested in occultism after attending a Society for Psychical Research lecture, to which she apparently introduced him. Cochrane himself claimed to have been born into a family of traditional witches that had been practicing the magical arts for centuries. Other family members fiercely denied his claims, asserting that they had "always" been Methodists and had nothing whatsoever to do with witchcraft.

It was also around the same time that Bowers discovered *The White Goddess* and began his correspondence with Robert Graves, mentioned in the previous chapter.

Cochrane writes: "Dear Robert Graves, I have read and re-read your book, *The White Goddess,* with admiration, utter amazement and a taint of horror."[17]

It is clear, then, that the influence of Graves' work went deep with Cochrane, since he had "read and re-read" the book. It is easy to understand why he speaks of "admiration" and "utter amazement," but mysterious as to why he speaks of "a taint of horror." As we become familiar with the breadth and scope of Cochrane's mind, as well as his eccentricities, the statement may seem less unusual.

Apparently, Graves expressed an opinion that Sufi philosophy was a strong influence on witchcraft in the British Isles, or at least upon occult philosophy, for Cochrane writes in return:

I fail to see that Islamic practice or belief had reached so far, since, as you will know, the Sufi and kindred societies did not enact the part of God; Thier [sic] aim was to achieve a mystical state vide various practices.[18] To the best of my knowledge, that was not the aim of the Staffordshire and Warwickshire witches. Flags, flax, fodder and Frig

---

17 Robert Cochrane's letters to Robert Graves, docplayer.net/52612115-Robert-cochrane-s-letters-to-robert-graves.html, retrieved June 4, 2023.

18 Graves was deeply connected with the famous Sufi teacher Idries Shah, and even wrote an introduction to his best-known work, which was entitled simply *The Sufis.* Shah takes things somewhat to extremes in claiming a Sufi origin for almost every facet of medieval mysticism in the West, though he certainly makes some strong and accurate points. The most famous book of magic in the Middle Ages was the *Picatrix,* which had its origins in Islamic Spain. How did Sufi influence reach a Europe so powerfully controlled by the medieval Catholic Church? For that, we may thank one of history's most remarkable women, Eleanor of Aquitaine, who ruled the south of France and kept the borders with Islamic Spain open for trade—and for the trade of ideas as well. Eleanor was the patroness of the Provencal troubadours, whose complex rhyme schemes appear to be based upon Arabic models. Her daughter, Marie de Champagne, was the patroness of Chretien de Troyes, the author who gave us our first version of the medieval era's most important contribution to world mythology—the Quest for the Holy Grail. There is some evidence that Cochrane later came to acknowledge the influence of Islam on medieval magic.

was their total aim, good crops, healthy children and some power to strike back at the oppressor was the aim, and in my opinion they succeeded. There was poetry, there was mysticism, but these were either side effects or something that belonged to the individual rather than the group.[19]

Cochrane often spoke of "Flags, Flax, Fodder, and Frigg," which he frequently abbreviated as "FFFF" and with which he often signed off his letters. *Flags* represents the hearth or home, *flax* is clothes, *fodder* is food, and *frigg* is sex, so Cochrane was wishing the person an abundance of all these.

At the time that he was discovering *The White Goddess,* Cochrane was living with Jane and their son in a council house in Berkshire. He wasn't happy there. He described his neighbors as "the biggest load of monkeys there have been trained since the Ark."[20] He didn't like his job, either. He was working as a typographical draughtsman and complained that he would rather be working outdoors.

Yet, it was at this time that Roy Bowers chose to launch himself into the world of witchcraft.

The modern revival of witchcraft had already begun some years before Cochrane entered the field. Beginning in 1949 with his novel *High Magic's Aid,* Gerald Gardner had begun to propound his philosophy of magic and witchcraft, which he named "Wicca" and which now forms a Neopagan religion with a number of branches, by far the best-known manifestation of contemporary witchcraft. Gardner, originally from a wealthy family, had led a somewhat checkered life in Ceylon (modern Sri Lanka) before retiring from various foreign jobs in 1936 at the age of fifty-two and returning to England.

Gardner was interested in Rosicrucianism and often attended Rosicrucian meetings. He became disillusioned with the group itself and sought out the company of other disaffected members, notably Edith Woodford-Grimes, Susie Mason, her brother Ernie, and their sister Rosetta Fudge. These were the individuals who, in September of 1939, allegedly took Gardner to a large house owned by "Old Dorothy" Clutterbuck, where he was made to strip naked and then guided through

---

19   Robert Cochrane's letters to Robert Graves, docplayer.net/52612115-Robert-cochrane-s-letters-to-robert-graves.html, retrieved June 4, 2023.

20   Howard, *op. cit.*, p. 43.

 13

a ceremony of initiation into a group he called the New Forest Coven. According to Gardner, this group was one of the few remaining covens of the ancient pre-Christian Pagan religion of Britain, its adherents long ago condemned as "witches" but surviving nevertheless.

The idea of witchcraft as an organized Pagan religion that survived "underground" throughout attempts during the late medieval and Reformation periods to destroy it had its origin—or at least its most authoritative statement—in Egyptologist Margaret Murray's *The Witch-Cult in Western Europe*, first published in 1921. Though elements of Pagan worship clearly survived into medieval Europe, Murray's idea of an organized Pagan religion subsisting beneath the surface of medieval Catholicism has been shown by almost all interested scholars to be inaccurate.[21] Research undertaken by Gardner's biographer Philip Heselton and academic scholar of Paganism Ronald Hutton strongly suggests that the New Forest Coven was founded in the mid-1930s by Gardner's friends, who had been inspired by the writings of Margaret Murray, and that it was only a few years old when Gardner was initiated into it.

In 1945, Gardner moved to London, intent upon promoting his new "religion" of Wicca and garnering as much media attention as possible—and indeed, he had a talent for doing so. Gardner's Wiccan groups worshiped a Horned God and a Mother Goddess. They believed that these had been ancient deities who had commanded devotion ever since the Paleolithic and whose cult had been secretly passed down to the present. This concept was based directly on the work of Margaret Murray, who asserted that this eternal witch cult had venerated a Horned God at the time of the Renaissance and Reformation witch trials but had also worshiped a Mother Goddess in earlier times. The Horned God is most often associated with animals, the natural world, and the afterlife, while the Mother Goddess is linked with life, fertility, and springtime. Wicca's God and Goddess have been compared to the Taoist system of yin and yang. In the early 1960s, such concepts were just becoming popular bywords among the adherents of the counterculture. Gardner was nothing if not timely.

Other Wiccans have perceived the God in terms of the Oak King and the Holly King, a favorite concept of Cochrane's as well as of Robert

---

21 Johnson, Kenneth, *Witchcraft and the Shamanic Journey* (Crossed Crow Books, 2023).

Graves, though Cochrane acquired his own concepts of the Oak and Holly Kings from the Old Craft tradition of Evan John Jones, who became Cochrane's successor as Magister of the Clan of Tubal Cain, rather than from Graves. The God has also been seen—once again by Cochrane as well as Gardner—as the Leader of the Wild Hunt. The Goddess is often portrayed as a Triple Goddess, usually as Maiden, Mother, and Crone, though, as we shall see, Cochrane re-envisioned the triplicity of the Goddess with dramatic and powerful differences.

Gardner stated that beyond Wicca's two deities was a "Supreme Deity" or "Prime Mover," which no mere mortal could ever understand. Cochrane also envisioned a power beyond the gods, though once again we shall see that his ideas were radically different from those of Gardner.

While some Wiccans are thoroughly polytheistic in their outlook, there are some, especially in the United States, who accept the view that all gods are simply aspects of one god, and all goddesses of one goddess. Thus, Odin, Aphrodite, Kuan Yin, Dionysus, and a host of others may be perceived as manifestations of the God and the Goddess espoused by Gardner.

Reincarnation is the dominant afterlife belief within Wicca, and Gardner taught that the human soul rested for a time between death and reincarnation in a place pleasantly known as the Summerland.

Perhaps the most controversial—or at least the most sensational—aspect of Gardner's Wicca was the practice of working in the nude, known as *sky-clad*, a practice drawn from Charles Leland's *Aradia, or the Gospel of the Witches*, a well-known work on Italian witchcraft. Ritualized sex magic was performed in the form of the Great Rite, whereby a High Priest and High Priestess invoked the God and Goddess to possess them before performing sexual intercourse to raise magical energy for use in spell-work. However, this union was almost always performed symbolically rather than in actuality, with the *athame* or witches' knife symbolizing the penis and the chalice symbolizing the womb. Gardner himself believed strongly in sex magic, and much of Wiccan practice in its early days centered around the power of sex and its liberation.

Though Gardner died in 1964, his vision of witchcraft seemed specially designed for the emerging psychedelic counterculture with its passion for Eastern religions, meditation, and sexual freedom, and, indeed, Wicca grew in popularity during the middle and late 1960s, cheerfully embraced by the counterculture.

By the early 1960s, Cochrane had already founded one coven, which consisted of only a few people and quickly disintegrated. He had then launched another group, the Clan of Tubal Cain, which is still alive and well today, and, at first writing anonymously (to prevent his "monkey" neighbors from throwing bricks at his window and perhaps harming his wife or son, as he said), he entered the field of modern witchcraft.

Unfortunately, we have few actual publications by Robert Cochrane; he wrote very little. In addition to several articles in obscure magazines, we also have his letters.[22] His first written work (authored anonymously) was an article in a spiritualist newspaper entitled *Psychic News*, which was published in November of 1963.

Cochrane begins by announcing that he is descended from a long-standing family of witches; this, as we have already seen, is one of his most controversial claims. He goes on to launch intense criticism at the two doyens of emerging modern witchcraft—Margaret Murray and Gerald Gardner—by asserting that "witchcraft is not paganism, though it retains the memory of ancient faiths."[23] He goes on to argue with Gardner's sky-clad, "free love" ideas by describing witchcraft as "mystical in approach and puritanical in attitude."[24] To Cochrane, a witch is a mystic who practices the last of the ancient mystery cults, and he takes yet another swing at Murray and Gardner by claiming that witchcraft has numerous similarities with Christianity, and that one can be a witch and a Christian at the same time.[25]

---

22 Cochrane's works and letters have been published in Oates, *The Star Crossed Serpent III: The Taper That Lights the Way*, *op. cit.*

23 Quoted in Howard, *op. cit.*, p. 45.

24 *Ibid.*

25 Though this may be an uncomfortable assertion to many modern Neopagans, Cochrane is on firm historical ground here. Surviving records of the European witch trials amply illustrate the complex and sometimes bizarre mixture of Christian and Pagan practices which formed the mystical reality of medieval and early modern witches. Many examples can be found in Johnson, *Witchcraft and the Shamanic Journey*, *op. cit.*, and the present author has witnessed Eastern European folk healers practicing a similar Pagan/Christian syncretism as recently as the winter of 1994–1995. (See Johnson, Kenneth, *Flight of the Firebird* [Crossed Crow Books, 2023]).

Though Cochrane expressed skepticism regarding Islamic influence in his private letter to Robert Graves, he acknowledges it in the *Psychic News* article. And despite the fact that *Psychic News* was a spiritualist publication, he denies any direct link between witchcraft and spiritualism.

In 1964, an individual calling himself "John Math" (and thereby concealing his true identity as an important British aristocrat) founded the Witchcraft Research Association (WRA). The new society launched its own periodical called *Pentagram*. The first issue was published in August of 1964 and featured a welcoming article by Doreen Valiente, one of the most important figures in the development of modern witchcraft. Ms. Valiente had been initiated into Wicca by Gerald Gardner in 1953, but dropped out of his movement in 1957 because of her frustration with Gardner's publicity-seeking personality. In the first issue of *Pentagram*, she voiced her hope that the WRA would serve as a forum where all those interested in witchcraft could reach an understanding with each other and practice tolerance toward each other.

Her optimism must have turned into disappointment very quickly. *Pentagram's* first issue had announced a special dinner to be held at a London hotel in October of that year; participants in various different schools of witchcraft were all invited, hopefully to interact in peace with each other. This was not the case. The followers of Gardner sat at one table, though Gardner himself had passed away while traveling in Tunisia in February of that year; Cochrane and his friends sat at another. The rivalry between the two camps was already evident.

Doreen Valiente had already met Robert Cochrane on Midsummer's Day of 1964 at a gathering in Glastonbury. She was impressed by his charisma—so impressed that she became initiated as the sixth member of the still rather small Clan of Tubal Cain. But though Valiente, like so many others, found Cochrane's personality charismatic and truly magical, it is questionable as to whether this proponent of peace and harmony between witches would have been pleased by his article for the November issue of *Pentagram*, entitled "The Craft Today." It would drive an even stronger wedge between the Gardnerians and the followers who were beginning to collect around Cochrane's Clan of Tubal Cain.

Taking direct aim at Gardner's followers, Cochrane—now writing under that name—spoke disdainfully of those who regarded witchcraft as an escape from modern society and an embrace of a utopian past. Rather than a return to a simple, goddess-worshiping religion of nature, witchcraft was to Cochrane a form of Gnosticism, and the true witch was a seeker of gnosis, of esoteric knowledge. Cochrane believed this quest for gnosis had been driven underground during the witch persecutions and, hidden among the common people and mixed with their folklore, these esoteric mysteries had evolved into what Cochrane called "Traditional Witchcraft"—which was a long way from what he perceived as Gardner's "happy hippie" misinterpretation of the art.

He exercised his vitriol on those who rejected the modern world and followed rituals with no relevance to present political circumstances and the ongoing social revolution (Cochrane was something of an anarchist in terms of politics).[26] He went on to write that, although witchcraft remained a haven of the ancient pre-Christian Mystery Religions, it was doomed to failure and a quick extinction if it failed to address the issues of the modern age.

In August of 1965, another article by Robert Cochrane appeared in *Pentagram,* this one entitled "The Faith of the Wise." Taking aim once again at both Margaret Murray and Gerald Gardner, Cochrane re-asserted his view that witchcraft was not an ancient Pagan religion that had been sustained by country folk throughout the centuries. Instead, he characterized it as a mystical religion dedicated to the experience of transcendent states of consciousness. He named a number of spiritual practices by which these states of consciousness could be attained. First,

---

26 This may seem puzzling to younger readers. In 1964, the counterculture was focused primarily upon politics, notably opposition to the Vietnam War and support for the US Civil Rights movement. Demonstrations at universities were tempestuous affairs which frequently became violent. Anarchism was popular, and counter-cultural anti-war sentiments mixed freely with the ideas of contemporary socialist writers like Frantz Fanon and Regis Debray, with some associations (such as the Students for a Democratic Society) openly describing themselves as "socialists." The shift to experiments in utopian lifestyles by those among the counterculture, generally called "hippies," did not become well-known until 1966 or reach international fame until the so-called "Summer of Love" in 1967. Nevertheless, as a veteran visitor to Haight-Ashbury in the summer of 1967, I have taken the liberty of describing Gardner's outlook as "happy hippie" because, as many other writers have noted, his philosophy shares much in common with the hippie utopian ideals which were only beginning to emerge at the time of Gardner's death in 1964.

there was "Poetic Vision," which used the symbolic imagery experienced in dreams. Then there was "The Vision of Memory," in which the aspirant achieved memory of one's past lives. Here, Cochrane went so far as to claim that no one could be a serious practitioner of the Craft unless they were in fact able to remember previous incarnations.

Cochrane also postulated a spiritual practice he called "Magical Vision," somewhat vaguely described as a method by which the student reached "certain levels." He went on to speak of "Religious Vision," in which the witch experiences oneness with God, as well as "Mystical Vision," in which the union with God became deeper and more permanent.

The precise techniques that Cochrane used to access such states of consciousness are, unfortunately, unknown. He seemed to have had his moments of uncanny foresight; for example, he predicted in a letter to the well-known British occultist William Gray that one of the Beatles will come to a "bloody and untimely end."[27]

Gerald Gardner's ethos was simple enough, and fit beautifully with the "happy hippie" outlook of his burgeoning crowd of followers: "Do as thou wilt, an it harm none." What could possibly be a more amenable rule of living by which to dance a ring dance in the nude on a glorious summer day?

Cochrane's stance on the ethics inherent in witchcraft was harsher than Gardner's. "Do not do what you desire," he declared. "Do what is necessary." And another precept: "Take all you are given; give all of yourself." And another: "What I have, I hold!" And finally: "When all else is lost, and not until then, prepare to die with dignity."

The last precept is one which Cochrane may have taken a bit too seriously.

Cochrane's vision of witchcraft was unquestionably more complex and more mystical than the simple, joyful Pagan nature religion expounded by Murray and Gardner. To Cochrane, witchcraft was a relentless search for absolute Truth—and Truth, as Cochrane once noted, can be ruthless. From Cochrane's point of view, Gardner was anything but ruthless. Writing to Bill Gray, Cochrane mocked Gardner's "Blessed Be" by wishing Gray "Brigitte Bardot" instead, remarking that it made a much better greeting or farewell.

---

27 Cochrane, Robert, "Letters to Bill Gray," clanoftubalcain.org.uk/the_letters/letters_Bill_Gray_lk.pdf, retrieved June 18, 2023.

 19

But even though Cochrane may have seemed out of step with the utopian dreams of his era, a following had begun to gather around him. These were the days of the firelight rituals, the invocation of ancient gods and heroes, and the sense of authentic magic mentioned by so many visitors to Cochrane's ceremonies, created largely by the intense charisma of Cochrane's personality.

And yet charisma works both ways; it can be either positive or negative. The darker side of Robert Cochrane was beginning to emerge. One issue was his use of hallucinogenic drugs. Another writer for *Pentagram,* who called himself Taliesin after the Druidic bard, spoke of using the fly agaric mushroom, *Amanita muscaria,* in witchcraft ceremonies, claiming that the psychedelic mushroom was sacred to the Goddess. Cochrane himself favored belladonna, commonly known as "deadly nightshade," over *Amanita muscaria.* In a handfasting ceremony held for Evan John Jones (who later became the leader of the Clan of Tubal Cain) and his wife, Cochrane administered a dose of the broom plant to them, which made them quite sick.

His personal life was becoming questionable as well. Cochrane began having an affair with a member of the covine, and in May of 1966, his wife Jane—always a powerful and important force in the Clan of Tubal Cain, a gifted magical personality, and a better organizer than her husband—walked away from it all and filed for divorce. Lacking Jane's authoritative voice, the covine began to disintegrate. John Math shut down *Pentagram,* disillusioned by the continual infighting between various factions within the witchcraft community.

Cochrane contributed to the antagonism between the various groups of witches. His hostility toward the Gardnerians grew more and more bitter. At one point, he even suggested that it might be useful if someone were to perform a "Night of the Long Knives" against them. This reference to an infamous purge by Adolf Hitler in 1934 was too much for Doreen Valiente. She had already lost a great deal of her trust in Cochrane due to his nonchalant outlook on hallucinogenics (of which she disapproved) and his adultery: she found it unacceptable that Cochrane elevated his new mistress, Audrey, to a status which rightfully belonged only to Jane, and he treated Audrey as the Maid of the Clan. Even though his suggestion of a purge against Gardner's followers may not have been serious, it was too much for Valiente. "I told him that I was fed up with listening to all this senseless malice, and that, if a 'Night of the Long

Knives' was what his sick little soul craved, he could get on with it, but he could get on with it alone, because I had better things to do."[28]

Doreen Valiente left the Clan of Tubal Cain. Things appeared to be falling apart for Robert Cochrane, and there was worse to come. In April of 1966, he told his friend Norman Gills that he was now entirely without friends, and that he was "at the bottom of a well with little or no hope for the future."[29]

Beyond that, Cochrane had become possessed by a myth.[30]

The myth of the Oak King and the Holly King, an important cornerstone in Cochrane's thought, was a concept well known in both folklore and mysticism. The mythic battle of the Oak King and the Holly King marked the annual shift in polarities that occurs in the seasons of the year. The Oak King and the Holly King are engaged in an endless battle with each other, for they represent the opposite polarities of summer and winter respectively. Summer and winter may also be said to represent the polarities of growth and harvest, of male and female, of summer light and winter darkness. Such, at least, was the traditional view of the Oak King and Holly King, though Cochrane had once again developed his own creative twist upon the mythic paradigm: the Oak King was aligned to the Waning Solar Tide, from Midsummer to Yule, while Holly was conversely aligned to the opposite or Waxing Solar Tide—Yule to Midsummer. On Midsummer's Day, it is the Holly King's eternal destiny

---

28 Valiente, Doreen, *The Rebirth of Witchcraft* (Robert Hale, 2007) p. 129.

29 Howard, *op. cit.*, pp. 71–2.

30 Carl Jung would have said "possessed by an archetype." While establishing a strong connection with the archetypes (Pagans would call them "the gods") is a positive thing, it is not healthy to lose one's human individuality and become so deeply identified with an archetype that one can no longer separate one's own personality from the archetypal force. After visiting a few scholarly conferences in Germany during Hitler's rise to power, Carl Jung warned the world that Germany, as a nation, was becoming possessed by the archetype of Wotan (Odin), the god of battle and sacrifice. Jim Morrison, the lead singer of The Doors, was sufficiently well read to understand that he was becoming possessed by an archetype—in his case, that of Dionysus—but though he cried out for help, no one seemed to understand what he was talking about. It has been suggested that Marilyn Monroe, in similar fashion, was possessed by Aphrodite.

to wither and transform along with the season. The Oak King will then reign as Lord of the Waning Solar Tide, until a new Holly King will return again. This time it is the Oak King who retreats and the Holly King who will take prominence.

The summer solstice of 1966 was swiftly approaching. It is said that Cochrane was hinting to his friends that he might no longer be with them after Midsummer. No one took him seriously, as he was prone to making wild, exaggerated statements on a regular basis.

There was evidence that Cochrane was depressed and possibly bipolar. His doctor prescribed tranquilizers and sleeping pills. On June 19, he told Evan John Jones that he would soon be "hunting from the Other Side"—a reference to the Wild Hunt, one of Cochrane's most important myths and one founded upon the pan-European myth of the hosting of the spirits of the dead.

June 23 was Midsummer's Eve. On that night, Cochrane wrote notes to the local coroner, his wife's lawyers, and Doreen Valiente, whom he told that, by the time she received his letter, he would be dead. He then allegedly ingested a mixture of Librium and belladonna.

When his wife's attorneys received his letter, they called the police, who broke into his house and found him on a sofa in the living room, wrapped in a sleeping bag. He was in a coma but still alive. The police called an ambulance, but it was too late. Robert Cochrane died in the hospital nine days later. Though the police questioned several of his associates, they found no evidence of foul play, and his death was ruled a suicide.

The King had passed. He was buried in an unmarked grave. His sister-in-law consigned all his private papers to the fireplace.

PART II

MYTHS

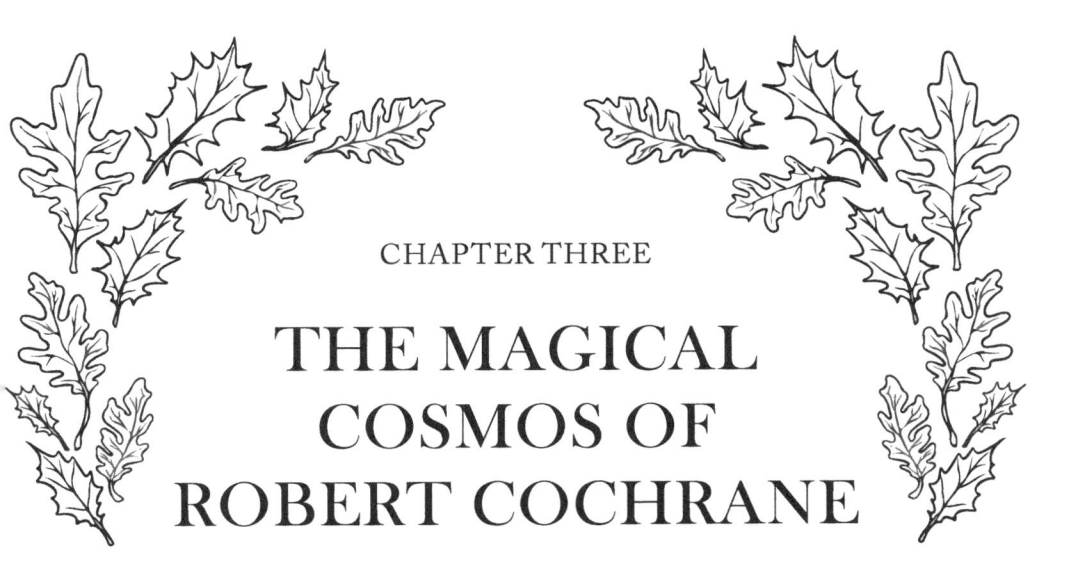

CHAPTER THREE

THE MAGICAL COSMOS OF ROBERT COCHRANE

ROBERT COCHRANE WAS A MYTHMAKER.

It should be understood that when I say "myth," I do not mean it in the sense of "an untrue story," a legend to be debunked or disproven. I mean it in the sense of "a higher truth."

Truth may be expressed in many ways and many forms. Some great truths may be expressed in terms of simple statements. "All human existence is suffering. The cause of suffering is desire. The way to eliminate suffering is to eliminate desire. The way to eliminate desire is the Eightfold Path." Here is a simple truth, simply expressed in simple words. And here is another one:

"If therefore thine eye be single, thy whole body shall be full of light."[31]

But there are some truths too complex to be expressed in a single phrase, no matter how pithy and perfect it may be. Such truths require a story. And such stories are myths.

When we walk down the beach, we must believe that shining Aphrodite may come to us, laughing through the sea foam. When the old man with a white beard and a gray cloak begs for a place by the fire, we must believe that this might be Odin, and magic might be afoot. We must learn to close our ears when the sirens sing.

---

31   Matthew 6:22. Even if you have a general distaste for Christianity, do not dismiss these words too quickly, for in them lies the key to the creation of a great deal of magic.

Every woman is Psyche, the Soul, in search of Eros, the Divine Madness that elevates us to the gods.[32] Every man is a weary knight in search of the Holy Grail, which shall bring him to enlightenment.

As Joseph Campbell said: "Myths are public dreams, dreams are private myths."

Researchers have suggested that we may very well be in the process of dying when we are no longer able to dream. The same has been suggested for civilizations and cultures, with the knife-edge proviso that our own civilization has lost its myths, and, therefore, soon must die.

At times, it does indeed seem as if our modern culture has lost its myths. Protestantism has always abhorred image and symbol; Islam allows no images at all. On such straight paths, we shall find no glorious Sistine ceilings or sacred icons upon which to meditate.

And yet, even in our secular civilization, devoted as it is to cell phones and the Internet, myth survives along what traditional witches would call a "crooked path"—a term that describes the complex roads and spiritual byways an individual typically explores before finding their way to the path of Traditional Witchcraft.

It was in the turbulence of the 1960s—which, let us remember, was Robert Cochrane's era—that the literati began to suggest that science fiction writers were our new mythmakers. Robert Heinlein's *Stranger in a Strange Land,* Philip K. Dick's *Do Androids Dream of Electric Sheep?,* Frank Herbert's *Dune*: these were our new myths.

It could also be said that the making of new myths for our secular society began much earlier, with comic books in the 1930s. Superman was the new Apollo; Spider-Man was another Lancelot whose performance of heroic deeds is partly inspired by his love for Mary Jane Watkins, his Guinevere. And it is hard to imagine a mortal closer to a goddess than Wonder Woman.

The new archetypes that continue to emerge from science fiction and comic books have the same distance from us mere mortals as did the

---

32 See Plato's *Phaedrus* for the idea that there are various types of madness, all brought on by the gods. Apollo brings us the madness of prophets, the Muses bring us the madness of poets, Dionysus brings us the psychological problems that arise from what we now call dysfunctional families, and Aphrodite brings us the love madness, Eros, the erotic power which, according to Plato, is the only madness that elevates us to the consciousness of the gods.

Olympians or the Aesir of ancient myth. There is something inhuman about them and therefore unreachable. Though many might fall under the spell of Harley Quinn, an intelligent person will know that it wouldn't be a good idea to date her.

The tales spun by writers of comic books and science fiction have been further spun into a new world of legend by that factory of dreams called Hollywood; we watch our myths parade across a giant screen.

And there are, of course, unique mortals who are able to consciously design new myths, to create new worlds of magic and mystery. These are the writers of high fantasy. J. R. R. Tolkien rewove the skeins of ancient legends to create a mythic world with relevance to our own contemporary condition; his private myth became a public dream.

If a mere mortal proves incapable of bringing their vast, intricate mythos to fulfillment as a public dream, the Hollywood dream factory will gladly do it for them. The body of Daenerys will be carried away to the east by her dragon whether the creator of her mythic world has finished his series or not.

Though Robert Cochrane, arguably the most extraordinary mythmaker in modern magic, worked largely with older myths in the Greek, Norse, and Celtic traditions—while re-envisioning them in a way entirely his own—he also created his own theogony, an origin myth of his goddesses and gods and the magical universe in which they lived:

In the beginning, there was only Night and She was alone. Being was absolute. Movement was there none. Being force without form, and since She desired that form was desired. Woman being woman, She desired union, and Created Man from her North side. Having Created Man, She discovered Love and so all things began. Here was the first of all sins, Desire. From Desire sprang all movement, all Life, all Time, all Death, all Joy and Sorrow alike. From the Gods came seven children, who Created Seven Worlds to Rule over, and they formed a Great Halo about the Great Gods as Seven Stars. They also Created Earth, Air, Fire, and Water, and gave these lands to four of the Seven Gods. These Gods each lived in a separate Land, bounded by the Great Gulf Anwen which is the Land of Chaos, and unredeemed souls.[33]

---

33 Oates, *The Star Crossed Serpent III: The Taper That Lights the Way, op. cit.*

Cochrane's myth of origins clearly owes a great deal to the creation myth of the ancient Greek cult of Orpheus.

In the beginning, there was Nyx (the Greek word for Night). She was a bird with black wings, and she mated with the Wind and produced a silver egg in the primal darkness. From the egg was born a child, sometimes known as Eros, a god of love with golden wings, and sometimes known as Protogonos, which means "first-born." Above him was the void of Sky, below him the quiet immensity of original Chaos. Deep within the egg were the children of Nyx—Okeanos (the Ocean) and Tethys (fresh water). They too mated, and from them all the gods began to be born.[34]

Though Cochrane omits the silver egg, the debt to the Orphic cult is quite clear: in the beginning is Night, who produces the firstborn, whom the Greeks called Eros or Protogonos but whom Cochrane calls simply Man. From this primal creation, all the other goddesses and gods come to birth, though, unlike the Greeks, Cochrane postulates a single divine entity, whom he calls Truth. Neither does the Orphic myth include the four castles, which are a feature of Western magic and, according to Cochrane, one of the principal decorative features on the old transport barges where he once worked, and whose keepers (again, according primarily to Cochrane, though there are other sources) were sometimes adept in magic. Here, then, is Cochrane's interpretation of the four castles.[35]

THE CASTLE OF THE EAST

The Castle of the East was the Castle of Fire, for it was fire that surrounded that edifice. Its ruler was called Luci. On an archetypal level, Luci and Lucifer are one and the same, a fiery god with wings of flame who appears to us as a bright golden light with wings. He moves quickly and can be both a mischief maker and a thief, yet at the same time, he

---

34 Kerenyi, Karl, *The Gods of the Greeks* (Pickle Partners Publishing, 2016) pp. 36–9. The book was originally published in 1951. Karl Kerenyi was a friend and occasional collaborator of Carl Jung.

35 Oates, *The Star Crossed Serpent III: The Taper That Lights the Way, op. cit.*, pp. 267–9.

is the king of light, of love and of fire, king of the intellect, of birth, and of joy. In Cochrane's clan, the Magister was called "the Divil," and assumed the mantle and the archetype of Lucifer during ritual.

In an interview with Michael Howard, Shani Oates, the present Maid of the Clan of Tubal Cain, was asked: "Is there a Luciferian element in the present-day Clan of Tubal Cain?" She replied: "Unreservedly."[36] Thus, in order to understand the role of Lucifer in Cochrane's magical cosmos, we must understand what he meant by the mythic figure of Lucifer. It has nothing at all to do with the Christian devil. The worship of Lucifer is partially inspired by the teachings of Gnosticism (and let us remember that Cochrane regarded witchcraft as a quest for gnosis), which reveres Lucifer not as the devil, but as a savior, guardian, or instructing spirit.

Lucifer is the Latin name for the morning appearances of the planet Venus. His name means "light bearer," and he is most often depicted as a beautiful, androgynous, and ageless being with long hair, violet eyes, and golden wings. He is sometimes considered a son of Aurora (the dawn).[37] This Roman god of light is regarded as a god among certain witches in his aspect as "light bringer"—a guide, enlightener and teacher of humankind.

In the Abrahamic religions, Lucifer appears as a rebellious angel who challenges the supremacy of Yahweh and is cast down to Earth to become the planetary regent. This fall from Heaven into the Underworld may have its ultimate origins in the Sumerian myth of the descent of the goddess Inanna (Babylonian Ishtar) into the Underworld. Inanna is associated with the planet Venus, who is the morning star and a goddess

---

36 Howard, Michael, "An Interview with Shani Oates." clanoftubalcain.org.uk/shani-interview.html, retrieved June 26, 2023.

37 Lucifer's mother Aurora corresponds to a plethora of goddesses in other cultures. The name "Aurora" is cognate to the name of the Vedic goddess Ushas, the Lithuanian goddess Aušrinė, and the Greek goddess Eos, all of whom are also goddesses of the dawn. They are all regarded as having their origin in the Proto-Indo-European stem word *h₂ewsós* (later *Ausós*), "dawn," a stem that also served as the origin of Proto-Germanic *Austrō*, Old Germanic *Ōstara*, and Old English *Ēostre/Ēastre*—whence also Modern English "east" and "Easter." Cochrane seems to have been on solid mythological ground when placing Luci's fiery castle in the East.

of battle when she descends (when Venus becomes invisible), and a love goddess when she rises again as the evening star.

In Leland's *Aradia, or the Gospel of the Witches,* the old Roman god of light, Lucifer, plays a prominent role as both the brother and consort of the goddess Diana, and the father of the witch goddess Aradia. In the myth recorded by Leland, Diana pursued her brother Lucifer across the sky. After dividing herself into light and darkness:

> *…Diana saw that the light was so beautiful, the light which was her other half, her brother Lucifer, she yearned for it with exceeding great desire. Wishing to receive the light again into her darkness, to swallow it up in rapture, in delight, she trembled with desire. This desire was the Dawn. But Lucifer, the light, fled from her, and would not yield to her wishes; he was the light which flies into the most distant parts of heaven, the mouse which flies before the cat.*[38]

Here, the actions of Diana and Lucifer correspond to the celestial motions of the Moon and Venus, respectively.

The "crooked path" by which the ancient Roman god of light became transformed into the Christian Satan is a long and convoluted tale. Inasmuch as it has nothing to do with Cochrane's vision of the cosmos, the present author shall spare his readers the details.

THE CASTLE OF THE WEST

The Castle of the West was the Castle of Water, whose ruler is called Node. In Cochrane's mythos, Node is the God of Paradise, of rest, sleep, achievement, and the fruition of one's endeavors. He is the god of spiritual growth and the king of wisdom. He fights always for righteousness, and Cochrane compares him with King Arthur. His castle lies beneath the sea. He appears as a mature man who shines with a golden light. His eyes are wide and sad, and a lion rests at his feet.

---

38 Leland, Charles Godfrey, *Aradia, or, the Gospel of the Witches* (Global Grey eBooks, 2023) p. 14.

THE CASTLE OF THE NORTH

The Castle of the North was the Castle of Air. It is a castle surrounded by clouds. Cochrane bestowed the name of Tettens upon its ruler. He is the waning sun, a master of mysticism, of magic, powers, and death. He can be the Destroyer. Though he is a god of war, he is also a god of justice and ruler of the winds. He is a god of magicians and witches, an adept in sorcery, yet capable of nobility, a symbol of Truth. He is a tall man, dark, shadowy, and unpredictable, sometimes cold and even deadly.

Tettens was strongly linked in Cochrane's imagination with any number of mythic figures, including Cain himself as the "Man in the Moon," of whom we shall hear more a bit later on. He was also associated with Hermes or Mercury, and the Norse master of wisdom and the runes, the god Odin. Odin was sometimes called the leader of the Wild Hunt, and is a wanderer upon the earth. Dressed in a long cloak of gray and carrying a staff, he walks through the world, his face half hidden by the hood of his cloak, and a long white beard concealing the lower half of his face. He is likely to appear at your home with a seemingly shy knock at the door. He may ask for a bite to eat and a place by the fire to sleep; if he does so, one may anticipate that magic will happen. King Volsung's palace was built around a mighty tree; one day, an old man with only one eye, garbed in a cloak of gray and sporting a long white beard, came into the palace with a sword, thrust it into the tree, and declared that it would belong to whoever could pull it out of the tree again. The man who accomplished that feat, Sigurd son of Volsung, became a great hero. The white-bearded old man who first thrust the sword into the tree was, of course, Odin.[39] By now, a number of readers will have recognized that J. R. R. Tolkien, a master scholar of Norse lore, modeled the character of Gandalf the Gray upon wandering Odin.

Odin's wanderings are not limited to this Earth. He hung, like a human sacrifice, upon the World Tree for nine days and nights. The

---

39 Crawford, Jackson, trans., *The Saga of the Volsungs: With the Saga of Ragnar Lothbrok* (Hackett Publishing Company, 2017).

old sagas say that he "sacrificed himself to himself." He undertook this painful venture for the sake of knowledge—specifically for knowledge of the runes. Having crossed the threshold of sacred wisdom, he was able to travel through all the worlds: the heavenly world of Asgard, where he lived among the gods; the human world of Midgard, which quite literally means "Middle Earth"; and even the dark Underworld, the home of the Dead, ruled by the goddess Hel.

As noted, Odin also figures in Cochrane's cosmology as one of the leaders of the Wild Hunt, and he has remained a prominent figure in the Clan of Tubal Cain. He is the subject of several books by the Maid of the Clan, Shani Oates.[40]

THE CASTLE OF THE SOUTH

The Castle of the South was the castle of Earth, also known as the Castle of Life. Its ruler was a figure that Cochrane named Carenos. He was said to be the "Lord of the Animals" and of joy and passion. He is a god of the forests, as well as a tutelary deity of happiness, fruition, and fertility. He has the horns of a ram. Cochrane saw him as a young Dionysus. He is an archetype of Life, Growth, and Strength.

It is not clear how or from what resources Cochrane developed his personal cosmos. His four castles and their lords are drawn from idiosyncratic but cumulative folkloric traditions with origins which can be traced back to Roman, Christian, Celtic, and Norse myths, while his creation myth is similarly founded in the teachings of the ancient Greek cult of Orpheus.

Cochrane's visionary world was also in perfect alignment with mythic themes from all over the globe, for it was founded on the number four, and a fourfold world is a universal concept.

---

40 See also: Oates, Shani, *Wolf's Head: Odinn, The Ecstatic God of Tethers and Skin-Turning* (Anathema Books, 2020); *The Hanged God: Odinn Grimnir* (Anathema Books, 2022); and *The Search for Odinn: From Pontic Steppes to Sutton Hoo* (Anathema Books, 2022).

There are four directions, and in the Western world, there are four elements.[41] One could easily have designed an outlook on physics that included more than four elements—for example, the Chinese recognize five—but the Greeks settled upon four. They followed up with a vision of humanity as a microcosm of the universe in which the human constitution was comprised of four temperaments or "humors," and they all had their correlation with the elements. There was also a mystical "fifth element," which could not be logically defined but was a kind of quintessence of all the other elements.

Nor was the fourfold universe confined to Europe. In North America, Native Americans designed a universe based on four directions, which constituted a Medicine Wheel. Farther south, the Maya likewise postulated a world view of four directions, expressed generally as a cross. (Such crosses can be found all over the Mayan territory.) Even today, in villages in the Guatemalan highlands, the Maya often think of themselves as "living between four sacred mountains." The author lived in such a community with a hill in the very center of town, which was perceived as the "central mountain" or universal center.

Yet farther south, we find the Inca Empire divided into four parts, with the city of Cuzco as a mystical fifth at the center. The city's name is based on the word *qosqo*, meaning "navel" or "umbilicus," regarded among Peruvian shamans as the most important center of power in the human body.

If we wonder whether Cochrane's fourfold universe also had a mystical fifth, the answer is yes. There is a fifth castle, sometimes bearing the Celtic name of *Caer Sidi*, but also known in the Clan of Tubal Cain as

---

41 Cochrane used a compass composed of many rings, but the correspondence of the quarters to the four elements was different from that generally used in the Western Mystery Tradition, namely Air at the East, Fire at the South, Water at the West, and Earth at the North. Cochrane kept the convention of the Four Castles or Watchtowers, but regarded the East as the place of Fire, the West as the place of Water, the North as the place of Air, and the South as the place of Earth. Doreen Valiente points out that Cochrane's scheme of the four directions matches that of the "eccentric" but gifted scholar T. C. Lethbridge. If Cochrane and Lethbridge were in contact with each other, Cochrane was certainly in good company.

the "Castle of the Rose."[42] (Castles and roses were common symbols painted on the barges where Cochrane and his wife Jane worked as bargees.) It is the Underworld home of the Goddess, the place to which the souls of witches travel after death, crossing a moat to reach this magical castle which cannot be described because each witch formulates their own vision of the Otherworld, woven from the collective strands of the beliefs of all one's ancestors.

Carl Jung hypothesized that the fourfold universe is in fact modeled upon the human psyche—we are the universe and the universe is us. The psyche is comprised of four functions, which have their correspondences to the four elements: intuition to Fire, feeling to Water, thinking to Air, and sensation to Earth. Since all of us possess these four functions of the psyche, human beings tend to see the world around them in groups of four, regardless of their homeland or ethnicity.[43]

It is unlikely that Cochrane got his ideas directly from Jung, whose psychology he regarded as "a rehash of mysticism." If he used any model other than his own visionary experience, he probably drew upon the same models that Jung did—the four elements of classical Greek philosophy and the magical world view of alchemists and astrologers.

---

42 Higley, Sarah, trans., "Preiddeu Annwn: The Spoils of Annwn." d.lib.rochester.edu/camelot/text/preiddeu-annwn, retrieved Oct 18, 2023.

43 Jung actually claimed that Christianity as a religion was "incomplete," since its essential premise was a divine power, God, perceived as three—Father, Son, and Holy Spirit. The fourth component, which would have made it a complete religion, one of wholeness, was lacking. As an early student of Gnosticism (and a collector of Gnostic manuscripts), Jung was aware that the original conception of the Holy Spirit had been the creative feminine energy of God, and that this creative feminine power was sometimes embodied in the Gnostic writings as Sophia and sometimes as Mary Magdalene. Knowing that Mary the Mother had taken over all the attributes of the numerous Mediterranean Mother Goddesses, Jung boldly suggested that the Catholic Church should find some clever way to make Mary into a Goddess, thereby rendering Christianity fourfold and complete—a male father, a male son, a female mother, and a female incarnation of God as pure energy. Cochrane promoted this view as well, hence his expression that "woman is the lesser moon."

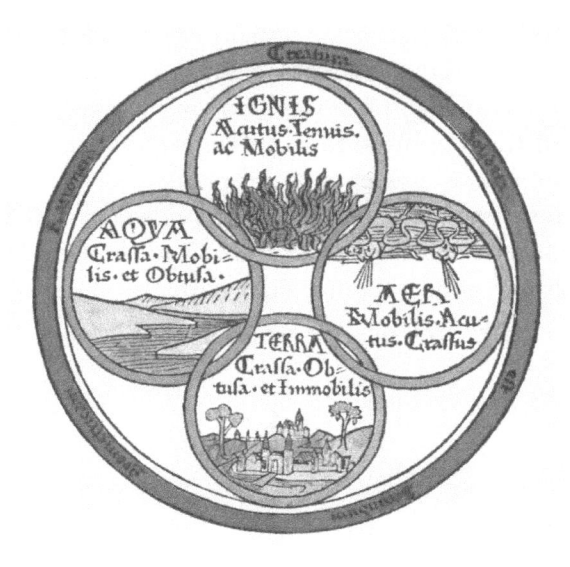

Cochrane populated his fourfold cosmos with a plethora of gods and humans. But beyond these numerous goddesses and gods, a power or energy existed that we might well describe as God in the monotheistic sense of the word. Cochrane believed that this Supreme Cosmic Creator was feminine in nature, and though she was said to be nameless, Cochrane was inclined to name her Truth. She could not be approached through prayer or ritual, but only through the grace of the Mothers—tutelary spirits of the elements who are both eternal and celestial, though they too are ultimately absorbed into Fate. Light and Darkness and Good and Evil were relative, limited terms that did not greatly matter. The only thing that really mattered was the gnostic quest for Truth, the Divine, not the illusion of the material world, although absolute Truth could be "ruthless."

Cochrane also taught that in primeval times there had been a union between Gods and humans. In Genesis 6:1–4, we learn: "…there were giants in the earth in those days, and also after that, when the sons of God came in unto the daughters of men, and they bore children to them; the same were the mighty men that were of old, the men of renown."

The Hebrew word for "giants in the earth" is *Nephilim*. This mysterious term has produced a vast literature of New Age speculations about UFOs and alien origins for humanity. Still, inasmuch as Cochrane died long before Zecharia Sitchin and David Icke began to publish their works or assert that our political leaders are actually lizard-like aliens in disguise, we can be certain that this was not Cochrane's vision of the Nephilim.

While Mr. Gardner and Mr. Cochrane would almost certainly take umbrage with the present author for suggesting that some of their ideas were similar or even identical, it is rather clear that both Gardner and Cochrane postulated a single Divine Power, manifested in two polarities—male and female—as the God and the Goddess, and that all other gods and goddesses may be regarded as various incarnations of this essential polarity.

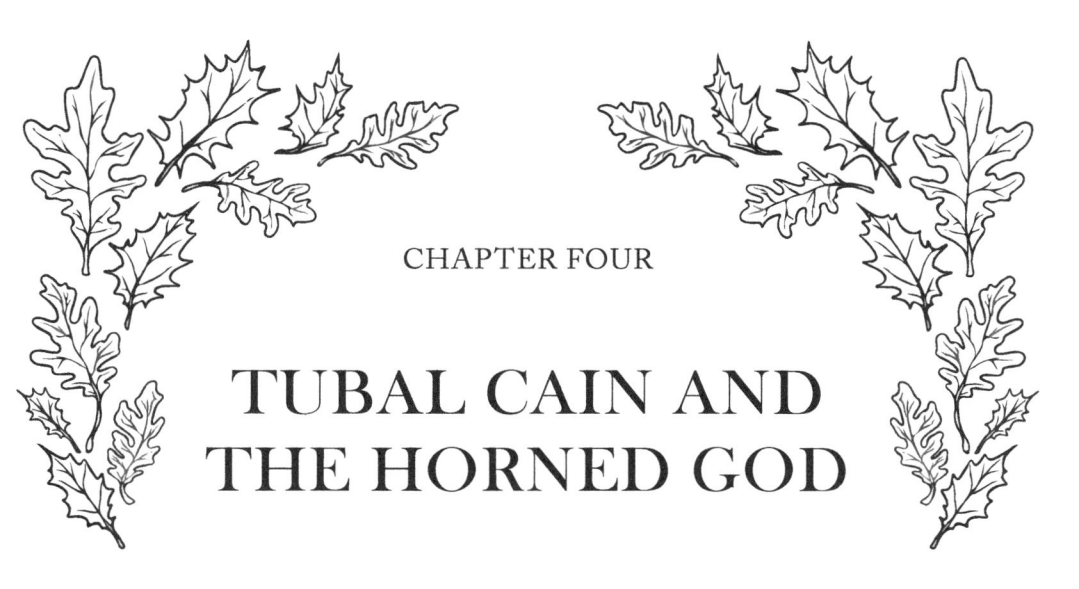

CHAPTER FOUR

TUBAL CAIN AND THE HORNED GOD

ONE THING THAT APPEARS to be commonly agreed upon is that the Witch God sports a pair of horns or, sometimes, antlers. It is also agreed—at least among witches—that the horns of the God have nothing to do with the Christian concept of Satan.

During the epoch of the witch trials, both Protestant and Catholic witch hunters affirmed that the leader of the witches was the Devil, Satan himself, and that Satan had horns. But nowhere in the Bible is it said that Satan sports such a rack, and religious scholars have debated the notion of which particular horned Pagan deity served as the origin for a horned Satan. Of all the available candidates for transformation from god into demon, the most commonly accepted and admired by witches is the Celtic deity Cernunnos.

Despite the popularity of Cernunnos in modern witchcraft, the earliest depictions of Satan with horns dates all the way back to c. 900 CE, a time during which the name of Cernunnos had been forgotten altogether. It is most likely that the horns of Satan are based upon those of the Greek god Pan. To the Clan of Tubal Cain, this figure was a nameless woodland spirit; Cochrane called him Pan only with certain reservations, for he believed the name to be only an approximation. He mocked Pagan followers of Pan for their primitive understanding of this spirit of the wild.[44]

---

44   Shani Oates, personal communication, January 2024.

In ancient Greek religion and mythology, Pan was the god of the wild, of shepherds and their flocks, of rustic music played upon the pipes, and was an eternally lustful companion of the nymphs. He has the hindquarters, legs, and horns of a goat, in the same manner as a faun or satyr. With his homeland in rural Arcadia, he was also recognized as the god of fields, groves, wooded glens, and often affiliated with sex; because of this, Pan is connected to fertility and the season of spring. As a rustic god, Pan was not worshipped in temples or other built edifices, but in natural settings, usually caves or grottoes.

It may well be relevant that Pan was famous for his sexual prowess and often depicted with a phallus. Cochrane had no patience with the 1960s-style "free love" outlook that characterized Gardner's Wicca. And yet the Horned God was known among members of the Clan of Tubal Cain and the Traditional Witchcraft groups which followed Cochrane's works and teachings as "Old Horny," who carried a raw, ancient potency. Cochrane was contemptuous of Pagans who mistook this energy for sexuality.[45]

In essence, Pan was perceived as one of a trinity of mythic figures, including Hermes and Hecate—all of them regarded by Cochrane as "close approximations" only, and nothing more—who therefore represented the metaphysical virtues inherent within Clan cosmology and who inform the People of Goda.[46] Tubal Cain is the Tutelary Spirit who is seen as a guiding figure at the core of the Clan.[47] As noted earlier in his letters to Bill Gray, Cochrane mocked modern-day worshipers of Pan (although only inasmuch as they underestimated his potential) with as much gusto as he mocked the Gardnerians, for he believed that witchcraft was definitely not a peaceful Pagan nature religion.[48]

To Cochrane, Tubal Cain was capable of taking on a number of different identities, as we shall see. Within the Clan of Tubal Cain, this arcane figure is associated with fire, the Underworld, and time, and has been described as a goat god of fire, craft, lower magic, fertility, and death.

But what was Tubal Cain himself like?

---

45 Shani Oates, personal communication, January 2024.

46 "The People of Goda" is another name for the Clan of Tubal Cain, though it has its own specific meaning which will not be addressed herein.

47 Shani Oates, personal communication, January 2024.

48 Cochrane, "Letters to Bill Gray," *op. cit.*

Shani Oates, the current Maid of the Clan of Tubal Cain, says:

Tubal Cain, the "Hairy One," is a mythical progenitor and benefactor of the human race, heir to an unknown and non-human race, archaic and primal. He is embodied in all things wild and all things tame, he is the master of the animals, yet the tiller of the earth. He forges metal for the community and killing fields. He is the ancestral priest-king imbued with the generative spiritual fire of the Elder Gods, he is the hunter and the hunted, the lover and the beloved. He is the alchemical serpent-king of wisdom and the sacred horn(ed) goat of enchantments, mighty warrior, and the champion of the individual, the pioneer, the recluse, the mystic, and the mage.[49]

Considering the important role played by Tubal Cain in Traditional Witchcraft, the reader may be surprised to learn that he is mentioned only once in the Bible, in Chapter Four of the Book of Genesis.

And Adam knew Eve his wife; and she conceived, and bare Cain, and said, I have gotten a man from the Lord.

And she again bare his brother Abel. And Abel was a keeper of sheep, but Cain was a tiller of the ground.

And in process of time it came to pass, that Cain brought of the fruit of the ground an offering unto the Lord.

And Abel, he also brought of the firstlings of his flock and of the fat thereof. And the Lord had respect unto Abel and to his offering:

But unto Cain and to his offering he had no respect. And Cain was very wroth, and his countenance fell.

And the Lord said unto Cain, Why art thou wroth? And why is thy countenance fallen?

---

49 Howard, "An Interview with Shani Oates," *op. cit.*

If thou doest well, shalt thou not be accepted? and if thou doest not well, sin lieth at the door. And unto thee shall be his desire, and thou shalt rule over him.

And Cain talked with Abel his brother: and it came to pass, when they were in the field, that Cain rose up against Abel his brother, and slew him.

And the Lord said unto Cain, Where is Abel thy brother? And he said, I know not: Am I my brother's keeper?

And he said, What hast thou done? The voice of thy brother's blood crieth unto me from the ground.

And now art thou cursed from the earth, which hath opened her mouth to receive thy brother's blood from thy hand;

When thou tillest the ground, it shall not henceforth yield unto thee her strength; a fugitive and a vagabond shalt thou be in the earth.

And Cain said unto the Lord, My punishment is greater than I can bear.

Behold, thou hast driven me out this day from the face of the earth; and from thy face shall I be hid; and I shall be a fugitive and a vagabond in the earth; and it shall come to pass, that every one that findeth me shall slay me.

And the Lord said unto him, Therefore whosoever slayeth Cain, vengeance shall be taken on him sevenfold. And the Lord set a mark upon Cain, lest any finding him should kill him.

And Cain went out from the presence of the Lord, and dwelt in the land of Nod, on the east of Eden.

And Cain knew his wife; and she conceived, and bare Enoch: and he builded a city, and called the name of the city, after the name of his son, Enoch.

And unto Enoch was born Irad: and Irad begat Mehujael: and Mehujael begat Methusael: and Methusael begat Lamech.

And Lamech took unto him two wives: the name of the one was Adah, and the name of the other Zillah.

And Adah bare Jabal: he was the father of such as dwell in tents, and of such as have cattle.

And his brother's name was Jubal: he was the father of all such as handle the harp and organ.

And Zillah, she also bare Tubal Cain, an instructor of every artificer in brass and iron: and the sister of Tubal Cain was Naamah.

And Lamech said unto his wives, Adah and Zillah, Hear my voice; ye wives of Lamech, hearken unto my speech: for I have slain a man to my wounding, and a young man to my hurt.

If Cain shall be avenged sevenfold, truly Lamech seventy and sevenfold.

And Adam knew his wife again; and she bare a son, and called his name Seth: For God, said she, hath appointed me another seed instead of Abel, whom Cain slew.

And to Seth, to him also there was born a son; and he called his name Enos: then began men to call upon the name of the Lord.[50]

These few phrases from Genesis are all we possess of the original mythology of Cain and his family, including Tubal Cain, who receives only this single mention in the entire Bible. Yet, the mythos of Traditional Witchcraft as envisioned by Robert Cochrane—and of many others who both preceded him and followed in his footsteps—cannot be separated from the legend and lore surrounding Tubal Cain. Indeed, it is all about the folklore rather than Hebraic theology, and to this very day, the

---

50 Genesis 4:1–26.

 41

association that Cochrane founded still bears the name The Clan of Tubal Cain.

From these few brief words in Genesis 4:22, legends have been birthed and the art of magic has found one of its most powerful and important archetypes.

After Cain had killed his brother Abel, a mark was put upon him so that no one would kill him. Medieval theologians debated endlessly about what that mark might have been. They argued: Why should one not kill him? After all, he was the first murderer. No conclusions were ever reached upon that matter. The word for "mark" (*'oth*) as given in the Bible could mean "a sign," "an omen," "a warning," "a motion," "gesture," "miracle," "wonder," or, most commonly, "a letter." Therefore, some have speculated that the mark was a Hebrew or Sumerian letter placed on either Cain's face or arm.

In the Kabbalah, the *Zohar* states that the Mark of Cain was one of the twenty-two Hebrew letters. Some commentators on the *Zohar* suggest that it was the letter *vav*. Another rabbinical commentator writes that God gave Cain a dog, while yet another claimed that God made a horn grow out of his head. It was also a very common belief that the Mark of Cain was some sort of wound or injury, most commonly in the leg.

The horn and the injured leg are of importance to the Cain and Tubal Cain of Traditional Witchcraft, for they appear again and again in the various mythic figures whom Cochrane regarded as avatars or incarnations of Tubal Cain. The Clan of Tubal Cain, however, does not regard the Mark of Cain as a physical sign, but rather as a "state of mind," a dormant gene present within the "children of Cain," which is "seen and acknowledged by those who share that path."[51]

It is said that Cain wandered and ended up in a place called the land of Nod, east of Eden, often identified with India. Since Cain and Abel were the first children of Adam and Eve, it has mystified readers of the Bible as to how there could have been a flourishing population of human beings in the land of Nod—but Genesis is a book of myths, and myths always have their mysteries.

---

51 Oates, Shani, *The Star Crossed Serpent IV: The Devil's Crown* (Mandrake of Oxford, 2017).

THE FAMILY OF CAIN

Tubal Cain was one of three brothers and had one sister, Na'amah. He and Na'amah's two older brothers were born of a different mother. Writer Ian Chambers notes that the names Jabal, Jubal, and Tubal all originate from the same Hebrew root word *yabal* יבל, the definition of which is given as "being led," "to carry," "to conduct," or "to convey and bear along."[52]

Shani Oates notes that in the Clan of Tubal Cain itself, the name Tubal Cain is seen as a composite of nouns meaning "world," "earth," "stream," "to lead," "carry," and "crafter [of Metals, and Industry, Music and the Arts; Law and Justice]."

> *He is the civilizing force of evolution, the progressive, the challenger of the status quo…. This force mediates the Promethean spirit of Lucifer, who is perceived as the inherent indwelling spark, the light within, that by certain bridges, gateways, and keys may be realized as the outer light and drawn into exalted states wherein gnosis profoundly accelerates our being in awareness of itself, humanity, and all things divine. He is therefore the Guardian of the Hidden Treasures of the Mysteries.*[53]

As Chambers speculates, all of these definitions suggest a moving force that transmits, although it is not the source of its own drive or motion. While this opens a number of possible applications in ancient Hebrew, it allows us to generally draw some small conclusions regarding the names Jabal, Jubal, and Tubal. For example, *yabal* יב suggests a watercourse (as in "conveys water"), while *yobel* implies a wind instrument ("carrying sound or air"). Both would appear relevant to the brothers Jabal and Jubal, who are Biblically described as wandering nomads and fathers of musicians, while their half-sister Na'amah is credited as the inventor of the lament and, some say, of music itself.

The name Cain has received much attention over the years. Cain and Abel are known in the original Hebrew as Qáyin and Hével. Cain was the first born in Genesis 4:1. Abel is born in the very next verse. In British

---

52 Chambers, Ian, "Tubal Cain and the Dolorous Spear." clanoftubalcain.org.uk/spear.html, retrieved July 1, 2023.

53 Shani Oates, personal communication, April 2024.

folklore, Abel's name was believed to be derived from the words *ab* and *el*, which mean "source of God." But since his original Hebrew name was Hével rather than Abel, this cannot be accurate. Abel's name is also said to derive from a hypothetically reconstructed word meaning "herdsmen," which has the Arabic cognate *ibil*.[54]

The etymology of Cain's name is derived from different sources. The original Hebrew word for Cain was *qanithi*, which means "to get," although some speculate that the name comes from the Assyrian *aplu*, meaning "son." The name Cain is identical to the Hebrew word *qyn*, meaning "spear." Cain's name is also said to derive from the mid-first millennium BCE South Arabian (present-day Yemen) *qyn*, which was a word applied to a metalsmith. It has also been asserted that the names Cain and Abel were merely descriptions of the roles they play in the Genesis narrative—their real names never really being known, they were given the names Cain and Abel (Qáyin and Hével) over the millennia when Genesis was reconstructed, altered, and mistranslated.[55]

There are some Biblical scholars who take the root meaning of the first part of Tubal Cain and that of the second and equate the name to mean "bring a strike." This title is indicative of the role Tubal Cain plays in the demise of his progenitor Cain by means of an arrow launched from Lamech's bow.[56]

It is said that Cain's tribe increased as one generation followed another, though we must remember that these were the days when the "begats" of the Bible often ascribe hundreds of years to the age of these patriarchal figures. So it came to be that Cain himself, the first murderer, was still living when his descendant Lamech, the father of Tubal Cain, was old and blind. In early medieval times, the highly influential Talmudic scholar Rashi gives us this story:

Tubal Cain was the maker of many things in metal and in iron. Especially, it is said, he was a maker of weapons. He was of the tribe of Cain, and he shared in the darkness that surrounded them. Since Tubal Cain had forged many implements and weapons, Lamech asked his son to take him out hunting to demonstrate Tubal's new creation,

54   Shani Oates, personal communication, April 2024.

55   *Ibid.*

56   Chambers, "Tubal Cain and the Dolorous Spear," *op. cit.*

a bow and arrow, even though Lamech could only hear their intended prey; he couldn't see it. Being blind, Lamech needed Tubal Cain to help him by pointing his arrow toward the prey before he released it.

And he cried out, "is that an animal over there?" And Tubal Cain answered, "yes, yes it is," though in fact it was no animal but Cain himself. And Lamech, following the sounds of his intended prey, let loose an arrow that killed Cain.

Thus Lamech, a descendant of Cain, broke the Lord's command and murdered the first murderer, which caused him grief.[57]

And all because of his son Tubal Cain.

Tubal Cain's dreadful mistake in ridding the world of his progenitor Cain transformed Tubal into an outcast, and thus, in the mythos of Traditional Witchcraft, he stands at the head of a society of outcasts as well as a society of adepts.

Nor does he stand alone. As we shall see, his sister Na'amah also has a place among the world's more colorful outcasts. But it is the figure of Cain himself, the first murderer, the original outcast and wanderer, who will make his appearance time and again in the theology of Traditional Witchcraft. Sometimes, it will be difficult to distinguish him from his descendant, Tubal Cain.

If we translate Tubal as "to bring," and the word for Cain as "spear," we can perceive Tubal Cain as a name denoting one who creates the weapon of murder or implement of death. Tubal Cain is said to have forged weapons and brought these to mankind, while he also brought the death of Cain with a small spear or arrow. The name can also mean "brought by the spear" or "spear bringer."

In one legend of the Horseman's Word, Tubal Cain was taught half of the secrets of the horse by a woman (some say Lilith) while he was crossing a river. Lilith offered Tubal Cain the choice of learning the knowledge of horses or the knowledge of women, and Tubal, being

---

57 Ben Isaiah, Rabbi Abraham and Rabbi Benjamin Sharfman, *The Penta-teuch and Rashi's Commentary, A Linear Translation into English*, "Genesis 4:22" (1949).

cunning, chose to learn one half of each. Consequently, Lilith was swept away in the river before she could complete her teaching, and thus Tubal acquired only half of the knowledge of horses and none of the knowledge of women. Here, we can see an Old Craft tradition regarding lost knowledge, especially that which pertains to the female mysteries. Robert Cochrane claimed in his letters that the Craft has three traditional mysteries relating to men, women, and priests or priestesses. He claimed to have complete knowledge of the male mysteries but not of the female mysteries, which is reminiscent of the story of Tubal Cain and the lost knowledge of women carried away by the river.

Cain and Tubal Cain are both cited in some material from the Guild of the Horseman's Word (whom we shall meet soon) as the first ploughmen. The Bible asserts that Cain was the first agriculturist, as opposed to his brother Abel, who was the patron of shepherds.

The Hebrew Tubal, although originating in the same root words as the names of his brothers, is also related to the Hebrew *tebel* תבל and is a feminine noun that simply means "world." Thus, Tubal Cain can be literally translated as "world spear," the meaning of which could be expanded to include "King of the World." Here, we can see the magical image of the spear brought to the cauldron, the maypoles, and the *axis mundi.*

To early nomadic peoples, the central tent pole was regarded as a symbol of the World Tree or *axis mundi;* it looked toward the sky. In accordance with the Hermetic axiom "as above, so below," we can perceive the world center or omphalos as the North Star—the destination of the shamanic journey—above us.

Tubal Cain is rendered in Hebrew as *Tuwbal Qayin* (תובל קיק). The symbol of the spear could be seen as a ray of sunlight that shines forth from and returns to the cosmic axis at the heart of a six- or eight-spoke wheel. Like the mystic spear of so many myths and legends, the solar ray, whether it be a spear or golden arrow, is launched at its target but ultimately returns to its owner.

The mythic spear is prevalent in many traditions spanning the globe—Chambers mentions the Spear of Longinus, the Spear of Lugh, Odin's Gungnir, Arthur's Rhongomyniad, and the Gáe Bulg of Cuchulain, which could be translated as "lightning spear," linking it to the lightning bolts of other mythological gods, such as Zeus and Thor.[58]

---

58 Chambers, "Dolorous Spear," *op. cit.*

The Spear of Longinus is purported to be the spear that pierced the side of Christ at the crucifixion, causing blood and water to flow from his side, where it was captured in the cup that became the Holy Grail. The blood and water brought forth by the spear and gathered into the cup bestows grace upon us. The Spear of Longinus later developed an occult significance as the Spear of Destiny, which unfortunately became associated with the Nazis and Hitler.

Robert Cochrane wrote to his American friend Joe Wilson of what he called the "Cauldron Mystery," which he claimed was in a single line taken from the *Song of Amergin,* a mythic poem from ancient Ireland that played a large role in Robert Graves' *The White Goddess*: "I am a spear." According to Cochrane, the cauldron, the "original Holy Grail," was activated by a priest bearing a spear who, like Sir Gawain, may be said—at least in my own opinion—to have performed the sacred marriage or *hieros gamos* of the Goddess and the God by thrusting the spear into the cauldron. The Clan of Tubal Cain, however, perceives the symbolism rather differently. The spear and cauldron represent a conjunction of elements, a union not *of* love but *as* love, a love which ought not to be mistaken for sex in any way, but is "a meeting or fusion of duty and devotion, a sacred act, a needful process that desires a specific outcome, one of sacrifice in fact. This is the true significance of the spear piercing the cauldron, a vessel that represents Time, the Spear, and Motion. The dynamic of death is a union with whatever lies beyond it through love. Love is the vehicle, death the force."[59]

As for Cain himself, theologians have never known what to do with him.

Cain is the first son of Adam and Eve, the first human conceived and born rather than independently created. He is said to be the murderer of his brother Abel, the first human to die. How could a child of the deeply reverenced Adam and Eve grow up to be a killer—committing fratricide, no less—as well as an outcast (though protected by God himself) and a rootless wanderer? Some thinkers, especially during the Middle Ages, asserted that Cain was not the son of Adam at all and that Eve bears the blame for fouling things up, as usual, having committed adultery with various unpalatable figures, including the notorious Serpent of Knowledge and the fallen angel Samael.

---

59 Shani Oates, personal communication, January 2024.

Such speculations have given rise to more speculation. If Cain was indeed a mix of a mortal and a divine (albeit fallen) being, then he might well be classified among the Nephilim mentioned in Genesis 6:1–4.

Though the word Nephilim is most easily and simply translated as "giants," there is a long-standing tradition that the Nephilim were fallen angels (which would include Luci, ruler of the Castle of the East), and another tradition asserting they were the descendants of Cain, the first murderer. Cochrane regarded them as the semi-divine ancestors of a priestly caste of mystics and seekers of gnosis.

Another medieval Christian belief claims that the Man in the Moon is Cain himself, marked by God and left to mourn over his wrongdoing for all eternity. The Christian European tradition says that Cain is unable to settle or forgive himself, troubled by his weariness and sorrow for all eternity, wandering with a dog and a thornbush.

And yet there is a tradition that Cain has wandered far beyond the Moon into the deep void of the sky, where he appears as the constellation Boötes, the Ploughman (and here we see, once again, Cain's role in the origins of agriculture). In conventional starlore, Boötes is said to be a ploughman driving the oxen in the Ursa Major or Big Dipper constellation, followed by his two dogs, represented by the constellation *Canes Venatici*, the Hunting Dogs. The ploughman's oxen are tied to the polar axis and their movement keeps the sky itself in motion. Boötes is usually said to be Arcas, a son of Zeus and Callisto (an ancient Greek queen angrily transformed into a bear by Zeus' wife Hera, but then placed in the sky by Zeus as the Great Bear itself, Ursa Major).

Robin the Dart, former Magister of the Clan of Tubal Cain, associates Boötes with Cain.[60]

Boötes rises during the darkest days of winter, and he is accompanied by a meteor shower that falls profusely in the northern skies, seeding the earth to make it ripe for the first ploughing. Up to 101 meteors per hour may fall between December 28 and January 7, with the apex of the meteor shower usually occurring around January 3 or 4. Myths regarding this celestial phenomenon are often concerned with castrated fertility gods from Greece and the Near East, and perhaps include the Egyptian Osiris as well.

---

60 Robin the Dart, "Cain: An Agricultural Myth?" clanoftubalcain.org.uk/cain _ag.html, retrieved July 3, 2023.

Seen from this point of view, the progress of Boötes through the sky is, according to Robin the Dart, a kind of ritual gnosis:

- At Yuletide, Cain begins to rise, symbolizing the rebirth of the sun and the renewal of life.
- By Twelfth Night, Cain has fully risen. His arms extend outwards, pushing the plough. A shower of meteors bursts forth from the east, where Cain is rising, filling the universe with light and power for the ritual "ploughing" of the earth.
- By Candlemas (around February 2), Cain has fully risen in an arc across the sky, symbolizing the return to Earth of the powers of nature and growth.
- At the spring equinox, Cain is close to the zenith of the sky, a mythic symbol of the *hieros gamos,* the Sacred Marriage when humankind first knew the gods.
- At Beltane, Cain reaches the azimuth and is at the height of his power, an incarnation of the powerful and virile Green Man of Spring. He is male essence and giver of life.
- At Midsummer, Cain begins to descend, dropping into the western half of the ecliptic, like the sun or Son becoming the Father.
- By the time of the autumn equinox, only half of Cain remains visible above the ecliptic, but the seven elders of the Corona Borealis remain in clear view, watching over the mythic descent

into the Underworld as experienced by Inanna (Babylonian Ishtar) as she searches for her lover, Dumuzi (Babylonian Tammuz).

- By Samhain, Cain has almost sunk on the ecliptic, and only his head can be seen. Symbolically, he dies. This is the time for rituals of prophecy and oracular pronouncements.[61]

In the Cultus Sabbati and some Cochrane-inspired Traditional Witchcraft groups, Cain is the first witch and the sire of all the other witches that followed him.

Daniel A. Schulke, a Magister of the Cultus Sabbati, suggested that the cunning men assimilated Tubal Cain's archetype with that of the Horned God as represented by the "coal black smith" in the popular folk song "The Two Magicians."[62] In some forms of modern Traditional Witchcraft, the

---

61 According to Robin the Dart, this celestial event slips neatly into the Craft Mythos of the Council of Seven who chose Cain to bring forth agriculture to benefit mankind. The Council appears in the sky as the Corona Borealis, which goes by many names in many different cultures, including the Crown of the North, the Silver Wheel, and Caer Arianrhod (a Welsh goddess who will make an appearance in the next chapter). Boötes includes Arcturus, the fourth brightest star in the sky. It is worth noting that the Egyptians called this star *Bau*—"the Coming One."

62 The folk song entitled "The Two Magicians" or "The Coal Black Smith" tells the story of a woman who is pursued sexually by a "coal black smith." Smiths were often regarded as magicians in the old days, so the smith pursues the woman by changing from one animal to another. Yet the woman is magical too, and she manages to transform herself into animal form, even as he does, and thus remains one step ahead of him. An easily accessible version of the song is performed by the Scottish folk group Steeleye Span.

The story of shape changing during the magical pursuit of a woman by a man is universal. In the legends surrounding the poet Taliesin, he is pursued by Ceridwen, the keeper of the magical cauldron of inspiration from which Taliesin has acquired his bardic gifts. The oldest version of the story known to the author can be found in the Hindu *Upanishads* (c. 500 BCE), in which the creator god Prajapati becomes enamored with his own daughter and pursues her across the sky. In the *Upanishads* she is known as Sandhya, but in Hindu astrology, she is known as Rohini, the red star Aldebaran. Prajapati is the constellation of Orion.

dark and bright twins Cain and Abel are represented by the Oak and Holly Kings (see Chapter Five) and by the Green Man and the Lord of the Wild Hunt (see Chapters Seven and Eight) who rule summer and winter. In the Sabbatic Craft tradition, Cain is seen as an aspect of the European folk figure known as the Green Man or Green Jack, the Lord of the Wildwood or Greenwood, or the God of the Forest, and the corn spirit John Barleycorn who is sacrificed at harvest time.

Both Andrew Chumbley, another leader of the Cultus Sabbati, and Schulke have compared Cain with the Sufi saint Al-Khidir, the "Green One." Schulke says that this saint is similar to both the Green Man and the vegetation god Adonis. Like the exiled Cain, Al-Khidir wanders the earth and only returns to the same place every five centuries. The linking of this patron saint of Islamic mysticism with Cain also connects the Sabbatic Craft with the Arabic influence, which, according to Robert Graves and Idries Shah, permeated the medieval witch-cult and helped to create the Traditional Craft as we know it today.

TUBAL CAIN IN THE MASONIC TRADITION

Tubal Cain was an important figure in magic, or at least in occult speculation, long before Robert Cochrane. He was a man of skill, a maker of things in metal—and since he is said to be the first blacksmith, he stands first among those who make it possible to build. Thus, he occupies an important position in the mythology of Freemasonry, which the Masons themselves assert is descended from doctrines taught by the builders of the great Gothic cathedrals and, even earlier, by Hiram Abiff, the architect of the Temple of Solomon.

While it is not known precisely when Tubal Cain made his mark in the rituals of speculative Masonry, it is said in the Masonic tradition that he introduced many arts into society that tended towards its improvement and civilization. In Masonry, Tubal Cain is often compared to or even identified with the god Hephaestus or Vulcan, the master craftsman of Greek and Roman mythology who forged not only the most famous weapons of the great heroes, but even archetypal creations such as the winged helmet of Hermes. The Masonic tradition asserts that Tubal Cain was not only a worker in metal but an adept in the Mysteries; he is often regarded as the hierophant of a mystical order or lodge dedicated to the improvement of the physical pursuits of humanity. As such, he is often looked upon as a Masonic ancestor.

Tubal Cain mastered working with metals and forging tools and was the first instructor of workers in those metals, affording him a place of honor and respect in Freemasonry as a forefather of all master craftsmen. To complete the third degree, a Mason must learn to use the working tools of Tubal Cain's Craft to fulfill the plans of the Divine Artist.

The first stage of becoming a Freemason is completing the first degree of the Entered Apprentice. In this degree, the candidate is inexperienced and lacks knowledge of the craft, like the rough stone from the quarry that needs to be shaped and polished before it can be used in building. He is handed a common gavel, the tool workers use to shape the stone or rough ashlar. He is challenged to strike off the vices and distractions in his life that may lead him astray, away from what is essential to a meaningful and satisfying life.

The twenty-four-inch gauge represents time. The apprentice learns that we must use our time well, and he is instructed to divide the day into three parts: time for God, our neighbors, and ourselves. Exercising self-control, making good decisions, taking action, understanding, and fulfilling duties, whether as employees, husbands, fathers, or believers, are all addressed by implication in the management of time.

The tools of the second degree or Fellow Craft are the square, level, and plumb. The square teaches a Fellow Craft to ensure that he is right and just in his actions. It is among the most essential tools in Freemasonry, serving as a daily reminder for Masons on how to live their lives and treat others. The level represents equality, teaching that all Freemasons are equal, share in one goal, and receive God's same judgment. The plumb is the tool of integrity, teaching a Mason the virtues of being just, honest, and upright through actions big and small. This degree cements a Mason's commitment to the core values of brotherly love, relief, and truth.

By the third degree—that of the Master Mason—one has learned to use all the tools of his craft to fulfill the plans of the Divine Artist, and he is then introduced to the trowel. The trowel is used by stonemasons to spread the cement that binds the stones of the building into one common structure.

Masons are bound together by certain common values and experiences. They share the knowledge they have learned in their progress through the three degrees, and their lives are thereby improved in physical, moral, and spiritual ways. They are united by brotherly love and friendship. Great ideas enrich the mind and common experiences inspire the spirit. Thus, it is fitting that the final working tool presented to the Master Mason is the trowel to spread the cement of Brotherly Love and Friendship.

One can only achieve the rank of Master Mason, living his life fully in the light of Freemasonry, by mastering the moral and philosophical lessons taught in the lodge by wise and experienced brothers who are walking in the footsteps of Tubal Cain.

It is as such a commanding and creative figure that Tubal Cain appears as a legendary practitioner in the arts of high magic.

In addition to the Masons, British iron masters made use of the archetype of Tubal Cain to present themselves as the masters of useful things fashioned from metal. During the Industrial Revolution—which was also the heyday of speculative Freemasonry—they often named their foundries for either Tubal Cain or the Roman god Vulcan, perhaps simply as a matter of pride, but in other ways as a move that established one's place of business as a kind of lodge or esoteric society. Interestingly enough, as previously mentioned, Robert Cochrane spent his youthful working days employed as a blacksmith at the foundry of London Transport. This may have been where he first encountered the name of Tubal Cain as a magical archetype.

THE GUILD OF THE HORSEMAN'S WORD

A British secret society called the Guild of the Horseman's Word traced its origins back to Cain.[63] In folklore, Cain is sometimes called the first horseman, and it was said that his descendants inherited a knowledge of horsemanship. Some of the Romani claimed an ancestry that dated back to Cain and asserted that this is why they have always traditionally been horse dealers. In the Guild of the Horseman's Word, the candidate for initiation is told the story of how Cain was wandering in the deserts of Arabia when he came upon a mare drinking at an oasis pool. Being a cunning fellow, he managed to catch her, fashioning a collar for her neck and horseshoes for her feet. In this particular piece of folklore, the roles of Cain and Tubal Cain are, as often occurs, interchangeable; here, it is said that Cain was not only the first horseman, but also the first smith (though there were some in the Horseman's Word who claimed that Cain's traditional role as the first horseman and smith ought to be attributed to his descendant Tubal Cain).

Since ancient times, the blacksmith has been regarded as a natural magician. He worked with metal and fire and could transform them alchemically into tools and weapons. In some traditions of the Old Craft, the hammer and tongs as well as the anvil used by smiths are still regarded as ritual objects. British countryfolk sometimes muttered that good smiths must have sold their souls to the Devil in exchange for their esoteric knowledge, and there are many folk tales of blacksmiths outwitting the Devil himself.

Though the lore of the Horseman's Word began in the steppes of Central Asia and Ukraine, its "official" founding took place in southeast Scotland in the eighteenth century, though it has also been speculated that it began in East Anglia. British immigrants took it to Canada and parts of the United States such as Texas, Kentucky, and Wyoming. Author Michael Howard hints that the character played by Robert Redford in the American film *The Horse Whisperer* may have been based upon

---

63　For this summary of the Guild of the Horseman's Word, the author is in-debted to Michael Howard's *Children of Cain, op. cit.*

individuals who were connected in one way or another with the Guild of the Horseman's Word.[64]

Similarities have been noted between the rituals and ceremonies of the Horseman's Word and Freemasonry. This may not be mere coincidence, as the Grand Lodge of England was established in London in 1717, about the same time that the Guild of the Horseman's Word made its first appearance in Scotland. Some writers on the subject believe that the Horseman's Word originated in or connected with Pagan Britain. However, in his book *The Triumph of the Moon: A History of Modern Pagan Witchcraft*, Professor Ronald Hutton of Bristol University concludes that, although its rituals and initiations have certain magical attributes, the society cannot be convincingly shown to have had links with Pagan beliefs or witchcraft. Hutton compares the rituals and organizational structure of the Horseman's Word to Freemasonry, but once again, he is skeptical of any direct connection.

The membership of the Horseman's society was exclusively male and comprised entirely of individuals who worked with horses: stable boys, wagon drivers, blacksmiths and farriers, wheelwrights, ploughmen, and harness makers. Only those who showed unusual skill with handling horses were considered suitable.

As with other secret societies, and as with witchcraft, there was a hierarchy, a probationary period, secret passwords, and emotionally charged rituals that emphasized the transmission of secrets and arcane knowledge to new members. After initiation, the novice would learn the magical "horseman's word" that was used to control horses and other animals, along with practical techniques that allowed the initiate to

---

64 Howard, *Children of Cain, op. cit.*, pp. 135–6. Howard writes that the historical individual upon whom Redford's character was based was one Monty Roberts who, as of the time of writing, is still alive at the age of 88 and living in central California. To Californians (like the present author), Roberts is a controversial character whose veracity is not always to be trusted. Nicholas Evans, upon whose novel the film was based, has stated that his inspiration for the leading character was one Buck Brannaman and his teachers, Tom Dorrance and Ray Hunt, all of them still alive today. Mr. Evans does not mention the Guild of the Horseman's Word.

use it effectively. Initiates were promised control over horses—and over women. For a virile young lad setting out in life and hoping for success, this was an intoxicating combination. Few potential candidates refused initiation into the guild, for the Horseman's Word might treat such a reluctant young fellow harshly.

Initiations into the Guild of the Horseman's Word were typically carried out at the full moon closest to Halloween or Martinmas (November 11); the date must also be after the first frost. The ceremony took place at midnight and at a farm that was different than the one where the candidate typically earned his daily bread. This was important because the candidate was required to make a special journey to the place of initiation. He was blindfolded and led by several other guild members to the initiatory location by "crooks and straits," or in any case, by a path that was not a straight line. Here, as early as the eighteenth century, we find evidence of a "crooked path."

After reaching the destination, the candidate was led into a place where heavy curtains or a black cloth hid the windows to prevent any light from entering the sacred enclosure and to conceal it from others. An improvised altar was covered with a cloth. At the altar stood a Guild member called "the Devil," a long-time adept in the Horseman's Word. He wore a ritual costume of calf skin and a horned mask that resembled a ram or a goat. Once inside the initiatory place, which was usually a barn, various "ordeals" or tests were carried out to establish the candidate's dedication, courage, and trust in the Guild. After these initiatory tests, the blindfold was removed and the first thing the new initiate saw looming over him from the shadows was a shaggy figure with horns. Sometimes, the Devil's costume was smeared with phosphorus, glowing in the dark with an eerie green light.

A toast was made to Cain, the first horseman and therefore the patron of the society, and the initiate was told the story of how he tamed the first horse. Finally, the new member was given the Horseman's Word—the magical word that gave him mastery over any animal. (The "word" was also said to enchant women, and the Guild was actually blamed for the high rate of illegitimate births among unwed women in northeast Scotland during the 1800s.) The initiate was shown the secret handshake used to recognize a fellow member, then given an initiatory name from Greek mythology by which he would be known at meetings, and something called "the mark," said to be in the shape of a crescent moon, perhaps symbolic of Cain as the Man in the Moon.

The initiate then took an oath, parts of which were dark indeed. The oath of the Guild of the Horseman's Word was reminiscent of some of the bloodier Masonic pledges. The oath threatened the initiate with cutting his heart out, and his body dismembered and buried by the seashore (which, as Michael Howard points out, reminds us that the seashore was considered a liminal place between the worlds, and hence a gateway to the Otherworld).[65]

The new initiate was assigned a mentor who taught him the secrets, techniques, rituals, and legends of the guild. He was told that the initiation ceremony represented the Twelve Labors of Hercules and the Seven Deadly Sins, and that the Chief Horseman or "Devil" was symbolic of none other than Hercules himself. There were special names used in the Guild, all of them replete with mythic meaning: Gabriel was the angelic messenger; Selene was a Greek moon goddess who represented the night and the west; Perseus, the conqueror of Medusa, taught the guild members courage; Apollo had care over animals, especially horses; Lucifer, who was sometimes identified with the Devil, as he is in Christianity generally, symbolized winter; Helios, a sun god, represented daytime and the east. Even the secret "word" itself was related to Greek mythology, for it is said to have been linked with the centaur and healer Chiron, who was half man and half horse.

But it was not only the magic word that gave members of the Horseman's Word their power over horses. It was also a practical knowledge and experience of horses built up over many years. Most of the guild's techniques were founded in basic psychology and made use of the horse's acute sense of smell. The members of the Horseman's Word used to blow into the animal's nostrils so that it recognized the man by his breath. The horse would not forget him.

Various recipes for magical oils were known and used by the members. They were a guarded secret within the society and passed down through the generations orally from member to member. Ingredients included aromatic herbs, pig excrement, cat, badger and stallion urine, pepper, and dried stoat's liver. Horsemen were usually skilled herbalists and grew

---

65 Howard, *Children of Cain, op. cit.*, p. 144.

their own plants for use in the various oils. Aniseed, cinnamon, nutmeg, members of the *Origanum* family, thyme, fennel, and tincture of opium were all quite common, as were cumin seed, celandine, white bryony (the English mandrake), burdock, meadow rue, fenugreek, feverfew, and horehound. Sometimes, herbs were mixed into a kind of cake that was placed under a guild member's armpit to absorb his sweat. If it was then fed to a horse, the animal would follow him anywhere. The oils were also sprinkled on a handkerchief and then waved beneath the horse's nose.

The Guild of the Horseman's Word, which began in the eighteenth century, is believed to have survived until the 1930s. Some say that it survives still. In a letter to American witch Joe Wilson, Cochrane claimed that his father was a member of the Horseman's Word.

Though Cochrane's Clan bore—and still bears—the name of Tubal Cain, that legendary individual does not always appear as the divine smith and great craftsman. Instead, he appears in a number of guises. In a sense, all the god figures who play a role in this mythos seem to have been regarded by Cochrane as aspects of Tubal Cain. In Cochrane's Clan of Tubal Cain, some of the most important of the mythic figures who act as incarnations or avatars of the Horned God are the Oak King and the Holly King, and the Leader of the Wild Hunt.

CHAPTER FIVE

THE OAK KING AND THE HOLLY KING

THE MYTHIC BATTLE of the Oak King and the Holly King was a fundamental part of Cochrane's mythos, for it marked the annual shift in polarities that occurs both in the seasons of the year, and, in the interplay of microcosm and macrocosm—and the human consciousness as well—symbolizing the endless cycle of birth, death, then rebirth again, a cycle which Cochrane (like Buddhists and Hindus) believed we should abandon and transcend.

What I shall describe as the "standard" or "conventional" version of the myth is as follows. The Oak King and the Holly King are engaged in an endless battle with each other, for they represent the polarities of summer and winter. Summer and winter may also be said to represent the polarities of growth and harvest, male and female, and summer light and winter darkness. When the weather is warm and the crops are growing, the Oak King reigns supreme as the Lord of Summer. In the standard rendition of the myth, when his power reaches its zenith at Midsummer, the longest day of the year, the Oak King is confronted by the Holly King, the Lord of Winter, who appears at the precise moment that the days will begin to grow shorter. They battle with each other, and it is the Oak King's eternal destiny to lose the fight and die along with his season. The Holly King will then reign as the Lord of Winter, reaching the zenith of his glory at Midwinter.

Yet somewhere in secret, the Oak King has been born again at the autumn equinox, when the day and night are equal. When the winter solstice comes again, as it always will, he will be full-grown and ready

 59

to challenge the Holly King in combat once again, but this time it is the Oak King who will triumph and the Holly King who will meet his downfall, only to be born again at the vernal equinox.

The myth makes good astronomical sense. The Oak King is slain upon the summer solstice and the Holly King upon the winter solstice. Upon the longest and shortest days of the year, respectively, the sun appears to stop (the word *solstice* means "station") and then turn around to move in the opposite direction.

In some versions of the Oak King and Holly King tale—including the one preferred by Gerald Gardner—the two kings fight to win the hand of the Goddess of the Land. In myth and legend, she may first manifest herself as an ancient crone, for the earth—which, after all, is who she really is—has been present since the beginning, forever, and is older than all of us who walk upon her fruitful and wondrous body. And yet, over the course of the story, she transforms herself into a young and beautiful woman, for the Goddess of the Land is forever beautiful. The year will wane into the brief ancient days of winter, but blossoms again, a maiden still, into spring and the long, abundant days of summer.

THE SEASONAL KINGS IN THE CLAN OF TUBAL CAIN

We know that Cochrane was influenced by Robert Graves's *The White Goddess*. Graves devoted a great deal of time to the myth of the Oak King and the Holly King, and he gave us a list of stories from mythology (usually but not exclusively Celtic) that he believed to embody the myth of the Oak King and the Holly King.

Yet the version of the Oak King and Holly King mythos as understood by the Clan of Tubal Cain is quite different than what I have described as the "standard" or "conventional" version. The Clan perceives the Oak King as the one who is aligned to the Waning Solar Tide, from Midsummer to Yule, while the Holly King is aligned to the Waxing Solar Tide from Yule to Midsummer. Hence, the terms "Summer King" and "Winter King," so common in most forms of modern witchcraft and Neopaganism, are not used by the Clan of Tubal Cain, for they relate to seasons that encompass both the waxing *and* waning elements, whereas the Oak and Holly Kings as understood by the Clan are pertinently and singularly dedicated only to either the Waning *or* Waxing Solar Tides, respectively. These two figures pass to their successor the single crown—which is a shared icon that represents the rays of Lucifer's own crown—at Midsummer and back again at Midwinter. Oak, who in the Clan's mythos plays the role of the Old Horn(ed) King, relinquishes his crown at Midwinter to his younger "self"—the Young Horn(ed) Holly King, whose power waxes with the new sun. There is no pitched battle; the crown is given up, but they do not fight; each surrenders or submits to the other at the appointed time to "become" other—the face turned, unseen. The Clan's perception of the Oak King and Holly King polarity is more about true sacrifice, about surrender rather than the typical view of a "death" required or taken. Therefore, Shani Oates describes the Holly King as "youthful, vibrant and wild," in accordance with his seasonal tide in the waxing of the year, while the Oak King is described as a "wise, old 'father'" figure in accord with the waning cycle of the year.[66]

Nature accents the power of holly in winter, when all else lies sleeping, with its bright waxy leaves and its vibrant berries. Its light, full of solar power, lasts until late spring. Its red berries are the color of blood, and its totem bird is the robin, whose red breast also suggests blood, both in birth and sacrifice.

The Holly King can be seen as the spirit of growth itself, covered in holly and evergreen, giving his blessings of light, life, and fertility for the warm season to come. This erotic Holly God lies at the root of folkloric figures such as the Green Man, the May King, and Jack-in-the-Green. His dark yet shining leaves symbolize the immortal light of spirit within nature. Twelfth Night is traditionally known as Holly Night or Holy Night; fiery holly branches are carried as torches, bringing light from the darkness. Holly can be used in magical operations related to dreams, divination, and enchantments. Holly is also used to make highly concentrated charcoal for smithcraft and is thus associated with Tubal Cain. (In ancient times, smiths were commonly perceived as magicians, possessing all the wisdom and cunning of the gods.) Other mythic associations with the Holly King's reign are the Saturnalia, fertility, sex, magic, thunder, light, and power.

---

66 Shani Oates, personal communication, April 2024, and "12th Night: Hunting the Wren," in *Meanderings of the Muse*, clantubalcain.com/page/4/, retrieved January 13, 2024.

 61

As the leaves of the holly begin to fade, those of the oak begin to flourish in late May, growing in size and strength at the time of the summer solstice, fruiting in autumn, and keeping its leaves throughout most of the winter, but losing them, as one might expect, around the winter solstice. The oak is one of the most ancient trees on Earth. It is the wood of oracles and prophecy; the legendary Oracle of Zeus at Dodona was an oak tree. The oak is a channel through which the sky god can communicate with mortals. Its sacred mistletoe can be regarded as the sperm seed of God. The oak is a guardian of the threshold. Great fires of oak were burned at Midsummer, celebrating the power and the glory of its life-giving abundance in the season ahead. The oak also represents the presence of the Sun God, who draws back the veil between the worlds on Samhain and makes it possible for the living to communicate with the spirits of the dead. The wren is the totem bird of the Oak King.

The oak is symbolic of the ultimate power of nature, the Spirit of God which is within all life. The Druidic tradition of the robin and the wren, birds that were totemically linked with the Oak and Holly Kings, exemplifies dual themes of sacrifice and submission. The wren is sacred to the Celtic god Brân, as well as to Saturn.

On the metaphysical level, the Oak King and the Holly King are one; they are simply opposite manifestations of the same eternal polarity. "He is not a dying and resurrected god, but one who turns, shifts, morphs, becomes what he needs to be for the tide ahead, embodying the spirit and metaphysics of that tide."[67]

An ancient expression of this seasonal myth may be found in the Roman festival of Saturnalia and the celebrations for the two-faced god Janus, god of the year, both of which occurred during the winter solstice time and ran alongside the seasonal celebrations of the birth of the new son, sun, or aeon. The same idea can be found in many Mystery religions. Janus holds the key of life in his left hand and the scepter of death and judgment in his right hand. These two symbols stand for power and glory, wisdom and might, truth and revelation, past and future, and mercy and severity. These concepts symbolize unity and wholeness, not polarity, for all is within the one, and the one is within the whole.

Janus was represented astronomically by the constellation of Gemini, which appears at precisely the right time in the midwinter sky, and in the

---

67   Shani Oates, personal communication, January 2024.

 62

east, the direction of new beginnings. In ancient times, the Midwinter festivals honored the darker side of life in death—of sacrifice. Saturn, the dethroned Old King of the Gods and the Lord of Misrule for whom the Saturnalia is named, has a Celtic counterpart—Brân, who appears in the Welsh *Mabinogion* and functions as a symbol of oracular wisdom, prophecy, and necromancy. We shall have more to say of him later on.

The wren is Brân's sacred bird and was known to the Druids as the "King of Birds." Thus, we are led to a place where myth and folklore meet—as they so often do. The wren is killed by the robin, who then becomes king for a time. After it has been killed, the wren is then mounted upon a pole and paraded around by whoever has slain it. The robin is alive and king for his season. This event takes place during the midwinter festivals, and it was forbidden to kill the wren at any other time. The wren plays the role of the king who must shed his blood for the redemption of his people. The robin is the Holly King, and the wren is the Oak King.

This ritual activity is recorded in a folk song which, upon first hearing, sounds like a rhyme for children, but hidden within its deceptively simple lyrics is the killing of a mighty king:

> *"We hunted the Wren for Robin the Bobbin*
> *We hunted the Wren for everyone."*

The hunters depart for the forest to hunt the wren, but as the song goes on, it becomes clear that slaying the wren is no small task.

> *"How will you shoot him?...*
> *With bows and arrows...*
> *That will not do...*
> *What will do then?...*
> *Big guns and cannons!..."*[68]

---

68 In some ways, the song "The Hunting of the Cutty Wren" reminds me of "John Barleycorn Must Die," which begins and ends as a "protest song" against the banning of barleycorn whiskey but includes within it a song that describes the death and resurrection of the Harvest Lord. In much the same way, what sounds like a simple folk song carries within it the seasonal myth of the Oak King and Holly King.

The wren, after it has been killed, cannot be carried home by ordinary men, but must be transported in a big cart or wagon. It cannot be cooked in conventional pots and pans and requires a large cauldron (and therein lies a whole different myth).[69]

There are several stories that contain elements of the Oak King and Holly King myth. *Sir Gawain and the Green Knight,* a medieval English poem that preserves a great deal of ancient material, has often been cited, though the underlying myth is somewhat muddled due to later—and probably Christian—changes in the story. Gwyn ap Nudd, the old Welsh ruler of the Underworld, also exemplifies parts of the myth of seasonal kings. We shall meet him later on.

The closest match with the original myth that I have been able to locate is a story from part of the *Mabinogion,* a collection of Welsh tales written down in the eleventh or twelfth century but contains much mythology from more ancient times. Shani Oates describes it as an invaluable teaching text.[70]

Here, then, is the tale of Llew Llaw Gyffes.

LLEW LLAW GYFFES
(adapted from the 1845 translation of Lady Charlotte Guest)

While many stories have been attached to the *Mabinogion,* it is the group of stories called the "Four Branches" that constitute the original core of the work. The tale of Llew Llaw Gyffes is found in the fourth branch, entitled "Math, Son of Mathonwy."

Math, the son of Mathonwy, king of the Welsh realm of Gwynedd, asked Gwydion the Magician: "Tell me what maiden I should take to wife."

"That is an easy question," said Gwydion, "for you should take Arianrhod, the daughter of Don, your niece, your sister's daughter."

They brought her unto him, and the maiden came in, and Math said, "are you a maiden?" Arianrhod answered: "I know not, lord, other than that I am." But when he asked her to step over his magic wand, a chubby yellow-haired boy appeared. When the child cried, Arianrhod turned around and departed. And Math said, "I will cause this one to be baptized, and Dylan is the name I will give him." The boy was baptized in the sea, and he took its nature, and swam as well as the best fish that was therein.

---

69   Oates, "12th Night," *op. cit.*

70   Shani Oates, personal communication, January 2024.

One day, Gwydion walked forth and the boy followed him, and he went to the Castle of Arianrhod.[71] When he came into the Court, Arianrhod arose to meet him, greeted him, and bade him welcome.

"Who is this boy that follows you?" she asked.

"He is your son," answered Gwydion.

"What has come unto thee that you shame me thus and seek my dishonor?"

"Unless you suffer from a dishonor that is greater than my bringing up such a boy as this, your disgrace is very small."

"What is the name of the boy?" asked Arianrhod.

"He does not yet have a formal name," replied Gwydion.

"I lay this destiny upon him, that he shall never have a name until he receives one from me."

"You are an evil woman," replied Gwydion. "But the boy shall have a name, no matter how hard you object. And as for you, no one will call you a maiden any longer."

And Gwydion departed with the boy in anger.

Gwydion arose the next day and took the boy on a walk on the seashore. There, he saw some sedges and seaweed, and he turned them into a boat. And out of dry sticks and sedges, he made some Cordovan leather and colored it in such a manner that no one had ever seen leather more beautiful. Then, he sailed with the boy to the castle of Arianrhod. And he began forming shoes and stitching them, until he was observed from the castle. He then used magic to change his appearance and that of the boy so that they would not be known.

"What men are those in yonder boat?" said Arianrhod.

"They are cordwainers," was the answer.

"Go and see what kind of leather they have and what kind of work they can do."

"I will not make her any shoes until I see her foot," he said.

---

71 Arianrhod's Castle is in the sky as well as upon the earth. We know it as the Corona Borealis. Interestingly enough, the daughter of King Minos of Crete who was abandoned by Theseus and married Dionysus, sometimes known as the Queen of the Labyrinth, had a similar name, Ariadne, and is also identified with the Corona Borealis. The Clan of Tubal Cain, however, identifies the Corona Borealis with the Council of Seven, as related by Robin the Dart in Chapter Four above.

And this was told unto her.

"I will go unto him," she said.

So she went down to the boat, and when she came there, he was shaping shoes and the boy was stitching them.

"Heaven prosper thee," said she. "I marvel that you cannot manage to make shoes according to a measure."

"Now I shall be able," he replied.

Then a wren came and stood upon the deck of the boat, and the boy shot at it, and hit it in the leg between the sinew and the bone.

Then Arianrhod smiled. "Verily," said she, "with a steady hand did the lion aim at it."

"Heaven reward thee not, but now he has got a name. And a good enough name it is. Llew Llaw Gyffes be he called henceforth."[72]

"You will not thrive the better for doing evil unto me," said Arianrhod.

"I have done thee no evil yet," said he. Then he restored the boy to his own form.

"I will lay a destiny upon this boy," said she, "that he shall never have arms and armor until I invest him with them."

"By Heaven," said Gwydion, "let thy malice be what it may, but he shall have arms."

Gwydion raised Llew Llaw Gyffes until he could manage any horse and he was perfect in features, strength, and stature. And then Gwydion called unto him. "We will go on an errand together tomorrow," said he.

At the dawn of the next day, they arose. They equipped themselves with horses and went towards the Castle of Arianrhod. And they changed their form and pricked towards the gate in the semblance of two youths, but the aspect of Gwydion was staider than that of the other.

"Porter," said he, "go thou in and say that there are bards from Glamorgan here."

With great joy, they were greeted. And the hall was arranged, and they went to meat. When meat was ended, Arianrhod discoursed with Gwydion of tales and stories. Now Gwydion was an excellent teller of tales. And when it was time to leave off feasting, a chamber was prepared for them, and they went to rest.

---

72 *Llew Llaw Gyffes* means "Lion with a Steady Hand" in Welsh.

In the early twilight, Gwydion arose and called his magic and his power unto him. And by the time that the day dawned, there resounded through the land uproar, trumpets, and shouts. They heard a knocking at the door of the chamber, and Arianrhod asking that it might be opened. Up rose the youth and opened unto her.

"Ah, good men," she said, "in evil plight are we. We cannot see the color of the ocean by reason of all the ships, side by side. And they are making for the land with all the speed they can. What can we do?"

"We must close the castle upon us and defend it as best we may."

"Truly," said she, "here you may have plenty of arms."

And thereupon she went forth for the arms and returned with two maidens and suits of armor for two men.

"Lady," said Gwydion, "arm this stripling, and I will arm myself with the help of your maidens."

"I will do so, gladly."

So, she armed him.

"Have you finished arming the youth?" asked Gwydion.

"I have finished," she answered.

"I likewise have finished," said Gwydion. "Let us now take off our arms; we have no need of them. There is here no army. The tumult was but to break thy prophecy and to obtain arms for thy son. And now he has got arms without any thanks unto thee."

"By Heaven," said Arianrhod, "you are a wicked man. Now will I lay a destiny upon this youth," she said, "that he shall never have a wife of the race that now inhabits this Earth."

"Verily," said Gwydion, "a wife shall he have notwithstanding."

They went to Math the son of Mathonwy, and Math said, "we will seek, you and I, by charms and illusion, to form a wife for him out of flowers." So, they took the blossoms of the oak, the blossoms of the broom, and the blossoms of the meadow-sweet and produced from them a maiden, the fairest and most graceful that man ever saw. And they baptized her and gave her the name of Blodeuwedd.

After she had become his bride, and they had feasted, Math gave the young man the best land to hold, and there he dwelt and reigned, beloved by all.

One day, he went forth to visit Math the son of Mathonwy. On the day that he set out, Blodeuwedd walked in the court and heard the sound

 67

of a horn. A tired stag went by, with dogs and huntsmen following it. After the dogs and the huntsmen, there came a crowd of men on foot.

"Send a youth," said she, "to ask who yonder host may be." So, a youth went and inquired who they were.

"Gronw Pebyr is this, the lord of Penllyn," said they.

Gronw Pebyr pursued the stag, overtook it, and killed it. As the day departed and the night drew near, he came to the gate of the Court.

Then messengers went to meet him and invite him in. And he accepted her bidding gladly and came to the Court, and Blodeuwedd went to meet him and greeted him, and bade him welcome.

And Blodeuwedd looked upon him, and from the moment that she looked on him, she became filled with love. He gazed on her, and the same thought came unto him as unto her, so that he could not conceal from her that he loved her, but declared unto her that he did so. Thereupon, she was very joyful. And all their discourse that night concerned the affection and love they felt for the other, which in no longer space than one evening had arisen. And they spent that evening in each other's company.

The next day, he sought to depart. But she said, "I pray thee go not from me today." And that night, he tarried also. They consulted by what means they might always be together.

"There is no other way," said he, "but that you must learn from Llew Llaw Gyffes in what manner he can be slain."

The next day, Gronw sought to depart. "I ask you not to go from me today," said Blodeuwedd.

"At your request, I will not go," said he, "though there is danger that the chief who owns the palace may return home."

"Tomorrow," answered she, "will I indeed permit you to go forth."

The next day, he sought to go, and she hindered him not. "Be mindful," said Gronw, "of what I have said and converse with him fully under the guise of the dalliance of love, and find out by what means he may come to his death."

That night, Llew Llaw Gyffes returned to his home. They went to rest, and he spoke to Blodeuwedd once, and he spoke to her again a second time. But for all this, he could not get from her one word.

"What ails you," said he. "Are you ill?"

"I was thinking," said she, "that I would be sorrowful if you died, if you should go sooner than I."

"Heaven reward your care for me," said he, "but I cannot be easily slain."

"Tell me how you may be slain, for my memory in guarding is better than yours."

"I will tell you," he said. "I cannot easily be slain, except by a wound. And the spear with which I am struck must be a year in the forming. And nothing must be done in making it except during the sacrifice on Sundays. And I cannot be slain within a house nor without. I cannot be slain on horseback nor foot."

"Verily," said she, "in what manner then can you be slain?"

"I will tell you. By making a bath for me by the side of a river, putting a roof over the cauldron, thatching it well and tightly, and bringing a buck, putting it beside the cauldron. Then if I place one foot on the buck's back, and the other on the edge of the cauldron, whosoever strikes me thus will cause my death."

"Well," said she, "I thank Heaven that it will be easy to avoid this."

No sooner had she held this discourse than she sent a message to Gronw Pebyr. Gronw toiled at making the spear, and in time, it was ready, and he informed her of his work.

"Lord," said Blodeuwedd unto Llew, "I have been thinking how it is possible that what you told me can be true; will you show me how you could stand at once upon the edge of a cauldron and upon a buck if I prepare the bath for you?"

"I will show you," he said.

Then she sent another message to Gronw and told him to be in ambush on a nearby hill on the bank of the river. She collected all the goats in the area and had them brought to the other side of the river.

And the next day, she spoke thus. "Lord," said she, "I have caused the roof and the bath to be prepared, and lo! They are ready."

The day after, they came and looked at the bath.

"Will you go into the bath, lord?" said she.

"Willingly will I go in," he answered.

So, into the bath he went, and he anointed himself.

"Lord," said she, "behold the animals you spoke of as being called bucks."

"Well," said he, "cause one of them to be caught and brought here."

And the buck was brought. Then Llew rose out of the bath, put on his trousers, and placed one foot on the edge of the bath and the other on the buck's back. Thereupon, Gronw rose up from the hill and rested on one knee and flung the poisoned dart, striking Llew on the side. Then Llew flew up in the form of an eagle and gave a fearful scream. And thenceforth he was seen no more.

And as soon as Llew departed, Gronw and Blodeuwedd went together to the palace that night. And the next day, Gronw arose and ruled over the land.

Then these tidings reached Math, the son of Mathonwy. And heaviness and grief came upon Math, and much more upon Gwydion than upon him.

"Lord," said Gwydion, "I shall never rest until I have tidings of my nephew."

Then Gwydion set forth. And he came to the house of a vassal, and he alighted at the house, and stayed there that night. The man of the house and his household came in, and last of all came the swineherd.

Said the man of the house to the swineherd, "Well, youth, has your sow come in tonight?'

"She has," said he, "and is this instant returned to the pigs."

"Where does this sow go?" said Gwydion.

"Every day, when the stye is opened, she goes forth, and none can catch sight of her, so it is not known where she goes."

"Will you grant unto me," said Gwydion, "not to open the stye until I am beside it with you?"

"This will I do, right gladly," he answered.

That night, they went to rest. As soon as the swineherd saw the light of day, he awoke Gwydion. And Gwydion arose and went with the swineherd, standing beside the stye. Then the swineherd opened the stye. And as soon as he opened it, the sow leaped forth and set off with great speed. And Gwydion followed her as she went against the course of a river and made for a brook. And there she halted and began feeding.

Gwydion came under the tree and looked at what it might be that the sow was feeding on. And he saw that she was eating putrid flesh and vermin. Then, he looked up to the top of the tree, and as he looked, he beheld on the top of the tree an eagle. When the eagle shook itself, vermin and putrid flesh fell from it, and these the sow devoured. It seemed to him that the eagle was Llew, and he sang an Englyn:

"Oak that grows between the two banks;
Darkened is the sky and hill!
Shall I not tell him by his wounds,
That this is Llew?"

Upon this the eagle came down until he reached the center of the tree. And Gwydion sang another Englyn:

"Oak that grows in upland ground,
Is it not wetted by the rain?
Has it not been drenched
By nine score tempests?
It bears in its branches
Llew Llaw Gyffes!"

Then the eagle came down until he was on the lowest branch of the tree, and thereupon this Englyn did Gwydion sing:

"Oak that grows beneath the steep;
Stately and majestic is its aspect!
Shall I not speak of it
That Llew will come to my lap?"

And the eagle came down upon Gwydion's knee. And Gwydion struck him with his magic wand, so that he returned to his own form. No one ever saw a more piteous sight, for he was nothing but skin and bone. Then Gwydion brought unto him good physicians, and before the end of the year, he was quite healed.

"Lord," said he unto Math, the son of Mathonwy, "it is full time now that I have retribution on him by whom I have suffered all this woe." Then they called together the whole of Gwynedd and set forth. Gwydion went on before, and when Blodeuwedd heard that he was coming, she took her maidens with her and fled to the mountain. They passed through the river and went towards a court that was upon the mountain, and through fear, they could not proceed except with their faces looking backward so that unaware they fell into the lake. And they were all drowned except Blodeuwedd herself, and her Gwydion overtook.

And he said unto her, "I will not slay you, but I will do worse than that. For I will turn you into a bird; and because of the shame you have done unto Llew Llaw Gyffes, you shall never show your face in the light of day henceforth. And you shall not lose your name but shall always be called Blodeuwedd."

For this reason, the owl is hateful unto all birds. And even now, the owl is called Blodeuwedd.

Then Gronw Pebyr withdrew unto Penllyn and dispatched thence an embassy. And the messengers he sent asked Llew Llaw Gyffes if he would take land, domain, gold, or silver for the injury he had received.

"Behold, this is the least that I will accept from him; that he come to the spot where I was when he wounded me with the dart, and that I stand where he did, and with a dart, I take my aim at him. And this is the very least that I will accept."

And this was told unto Gronw Pebyr.

"Verily," said he, "is it needful for me to do thus? My faithful warriors, and my household, and my foster-brothers, is there not one among you who will stand the blow in my stead?"

"There is not," answered they.

"Well," said he, "I will meet it."

The two went forth to the banks of the river, and Gronw stood in the place where Llew Llaw Gyffes was when he struck him, and Llew was in the place where Gronw was. Then said Gronw Pebyr unto Llew, "since it was through the wiles of a woman that I did as I have done, I adjure thee by Heaven to let me place between me and the blow the slab that you see yonder on the river's bank."

"Verily," said Llew, "I will not refuse thee this."

So Gronw took the slab and placed it between him and the blow. Then Llew flung the dart at him, and it pierced the slab and went through the back of Gronw. And thus was Gronw Pebyr slain. A second time did Llew Llaw Gyffes take possession of the land, and prosperously did he govern it. And as the story relates, he was lord after this over Gwynedd.

If we were to interpret this myth in the standard or conventional manner, the Oak King is the Divine Child born in secret at the vernal equinox. The magical nature of Llew's birth and his difficulties in growing to manhood fit the myth. Blodeuwedd is clearly the Goddess of the Land—she is made from the land itself. And presumably, the wounding of Llew Llaw Gyffes takes place on the summer solstice, when the Holly King, represented by Gronw, appears during the Summer King's time of great power and then kills him. Like a shaman, Llew is reborn after skirting the edge of death; presumably, Gwydion finds him on the autumn equinox and he regains his health until he is ready to slay the Holly King at the winter solstice.

If viewed from the perspective of the Clan of Tubal Cain, Llew Llaw Gyffes is clearly a Holly King, youthful, vigorous, and touched with magic. In what seems a rather odd detail, he shoots a bird while disguised as a cordwainer at Arianrhod's castle. But this detail acquires importance because the author specifically states that the bird which is killed is a wren. As we have seen, the wren is associated with the Oak King. I personally doubt that the author chose the wren by coincidence, for Llew's killing of the bird that symbolizes the Oak King announces to us that Llew is destined to slay the King himself. Arianrhod had vowed never to give her child a name, but inadvertently provides him with one when he shoots the wren. Llew marries Blodeuwedd, a suitable Goddess of the Land for she is made from the land itself, and presumably he takes command of his domain at the winter solstice.

The wounding of Llew Llaw Gyffes would therefore take place on the summer solstice, and his healing by Gwydion would be linked with the advent of the autumn, while his killing of Gronw would take place on the winter solstice.

Whether or not kings claiming to be representatives of summer or winter ever fought it out with each other—whether for the Goddess of the Land or just for the sake of a good fight—is questionable. It could have been a new myth born from the fertile imagination of Robert Graves.

Nevertheless, there is a well attested historical example of one ruler killing another for the sake of the Goddess and then reigning in his stead until he himself is killed. We shall meet him in the next chapter.

CHAPTER SIX

THE GODDESSES

THE TRIPLE GODDESS, in her customary manifestation as Maiden, Mother, and Crone, is one of the most deeply held tenets and beloved concepts of contemporary Neopaganism, so it may come as a shock to many that such a goddess—at least in that form—is a relatively modern interpretation of ancient data and may never really have existed at all.

Certainly, there are echoes of a triune goddess concept from ancient times. In Ovid's *Metamorphosis* (7:94–5), the hero Jason pays homage to his witchy paramour Medea as a "threefold goddess." The Neoplatonic philosopher Porphyry describes Hecate as a threefold goddess corresponding to the new, full, and waning moon, and the Orphic cult—always a mysterious and sometimes frustrating presence in ancient Greek theology—may very well have seen the three phases of the moon as a Maiden, Mother, and Crone, though this is the only example in ancient writings that we find the now standard concept. Diana, the Greek Artemis, came to be viewed as a trinity of three goddesses in one, which were viewed as distinct aspects of a single divine being: Diana as huntress, Diana as the moon, Diana of the underworld. But these three aspects of the goddess likewise do not correspond to Maiden, Mother, and Crone.

When we search the annals of Pagan myth for a triple goddess, it is without question that there were in fact three Fates, and that the Fates were known in a number of societies that spoke Indo-European languages: in Greece and in the Baltic States simply as the Fates, and in Scandinavia as the three Norns. It is in the myth of the three Fates that we find the cornerstone for Cochrane's own interpretation of the Triple Goddess.

In Greek myth, the Moirai or Fates are shadowy figures, weavers and spinners of human destiny, and nowhere do we find the well-known triplicity of Maiden, Mother, and Crone. Instead, the Fates are most often perceived as a young girl, Clotho, the Spinner of the thread of life; Lachesis, an older woman who is the Measurer and who establishes our lot in life; and Atropos, an elderly woman, the Cutter, whose name means "that which cannot be turned" and probably refers to death. In Hesiod's *Theogony*, the three Fates are the daughters of the primeval goddess, Nyx (Night), a spirit of primal darkness who also appears in the Orphic Creation Myth, as we have seen in Chapter Three.

The Fates made certain that every mortal and every divine being lived out their destiny in accordance with the laws of the universe. For us mortals, destiny is a thread spun by the Fates. Even the gods feared the Moirai, for even they could not escape Fate. This power is named Ananke (Necessity), who is called the mother of the Moirai in Orphic cosmogony.

The Vikings' Elder or Poetic Edda describes the Norns in this manner:

> *Three wise women*
> *live there,*
> *by that well*
> *under that tree.*
> *Urth is named one,*
> *another is Verthandi,*
> *the third is named Skuld.*
> *They carve men's fates,*
> *they determine destiny's laws,*
> *they choose the lifespan*
> *of every human child,*
> *and how each life will end.*[73]

The three Norns dwell at the base of the World Tree, which stands at the center of the cosmos, drawing water from a sacred well to nourish it as they spin our destinies.

The origin of the word *norn* itself is uncertain, but it may be derived from a word meaning "to weave," which would refer to their twining

---

73 Crawford, Jackson, trans., *The Poetic Edda* (Hackett Publishing Company Inc., 2015) pp. 5–6.

the thread of fate. The name Urðr (the Old English Wyrd) means "fate." The names Urðr and Verðandi are both derived from an Old Norse verb *verða,* which means "to become." Urðr derives from the past tense ("that which has happened"), while Verðandi derives from the present tense ("that which is happening"). *Skuld* is derived from an entirely different verb, *skulu,* which can mean "need," but which also means "ought to be" or "shall be," and therefore "that which should become," or "that which must occur." Thus, it is often said that the three Norns are named Past, Present, and Future. They survived in the northern European imagination for a long time and are the origin of the three witches in Shakespeare's *Macbeth.*[74]

If the Triple Goddess can be found in myth only as the Three Fates and not as Maiden, Mother, and Crone, then where does our cherished archetype of the Triple Goddess come from?

It begins, perhaps, with the scholar Jane Ellen Harrison in the early twentieth century, whose *Prolegomena* to the study of Greek mythology was—and in many ways still is—one of the most influential works on Greek myth ever written.[75] Harrison asserts the existence of female trinities and regards the three Seasons, Fates, and Graces as chronological symbols representing the phases of the moon and the threefold division of the Hellenistic lunar month.

However, Harrison's interpretations of the Triple Goddess were somewhat controversial due to a number of poorly supported ideas in her works. Most notably, Harrison used later historical sources in her argument for the existence of an ancient Triple Moon Goddess and her belief in an ancient matriarchal civilization, which has not stood up to academic scrutiny.

And so, as with the tale of the Oak King and Holly King, we find ourselves once again confronted with the creative but quirky presence of Robert Graves. Graves claimed a historical basis for the Triple Goddess, and though his work is widely discounted by academics as pseudo-history, it continues to have a lasting influence on many areas of Neopaganism.

---

74 Cochrane believed that Shakespeare's grasp of witchcraft is so good that he must have studied the art, and he cites passages from *The Merry Wives of Windsor* to make his point.

75 Harrison, Jane Ellen, *Prolegomena to the Study of Greek Religion* (Princeton University Press, 2021).

Ronald Hutton argues that the concept of the Triple Moon Goddess as Maiden, Mother, and Crone, each facet corresponding to a phase of the moon, is a modern creation of Graves, who drew on Harrison. Graves wrote extensively about the Triple Goddess, whom he saw as the Muse of all true poetry in both ancient and modern literature. He thought that her worship underlays much of classical Greek myth, though reflected in a more or less distorted or incomplete form. Graves regarded "true poetry" as inspired by the Triple Goddess. He asserted that his Triple Goddess is the Great Goddess "in her poetic or incantatory character," and that the goddess in her ancient form took the gods of the waxing and waning year successively as her lovers. Graves believed that the Triple Goddess was an indigenous deity of Britain as well, and that traces of her worship survived in early modern British witchcraft.

While various secondary sources have asserted that Cochrane re-envisioned the Three Fates as a triad comprised of Diana, Hecate, and Persephone, this is simply not true.[76] Cochrane postulated no goddesses whatsoever—at least not as the term is commonly used in Paganism (whether ancient or Neo). While Cochrane sometimes mentions the Norns in his letters, he customarily refers to them in the Anglo-Saxon, rather than the Old Norse, fashion as the Three Wyrd Sisters. Even so, they ought not to be regarded as goddesses. To Cochrane, Fate was a single, unified being. The Mothers may be regarded as representatives of Fate, but within the Northern Tradition (and the Clan of Tubal Cain is fundamentally a Northern Tradition), the Mothers are the female ancestors and hence numerous, a collectivity. They are sometimes perceived as a triad, no doubt due to Classical influences, but they may best be described as primal and ancestral beings, forces of nature.[77]

It is easy to see how such misunderstandings arise. As a goddess of childbirth, Diana makes a rather handy Clotho, while Hecate—who is now often perceived as a goddess of witchcraft but in ancient times was more often regarded as a protectress of households and humanity in general—takes on the role of Lachesis, while Persephone, the Queen of the Dead, may be said to correspond to Atropos, who cuts the thread of life. Myth is fluid; there is no premise, no version of a particular story,

---

76 For example, see Howard, *Children of Cain, op. cit.*
77 Shani Oates, personal communication, September 2024.

which can be nailed down and declared to be the most important or most accurate version. We shall examine these three figures—not because they were important to Cochrane, which they assuredly were not—but because they are often acknowledged in various schools of Traditional Witchcraft and because they illustrate the way in which myths move, metamorphose, transform themselves, and change.

DIANA

Diana's Greek name is Artemis, and the Greek Artemis, like the Latin Diana, has many aspects and incarnations, but she is perhaps best known as a goddess of the hunt and the forest. Virginal and unconcerned with relationships on any level whatsoever, she lives with her troop of maidens in the woods and spends her time hunting. As the goddess of the hunt, she is perhaps best known for the story of Actaeon and his fate.

It is said that Artemis was bathing in the woods when the hunter Actaeon stumbled across her and thus saw her naked. He stopped and stared, amazed at her beauty. Once she realized she had been seen, Artemis became furious and took her revenge on Actaeon. She took away his ability to speak—if he tried to talk, he would be changed into a stag.

Upon hearing the call of his hunting party, Actaeon cried out to them and was immediately transformed into a deer. Terrified, he fled deep into the woods and came upon a pond. Seeing his reflection and realizing what he had become, he groaned. His own hounds then turned upon him and pursued him, not recognizing him. In an endeavor to save himself, he raised his eyes toward Mount Olympus. The gods did not heed his plea, and he was torn to pieces. (If every college student who has inadvertently stumbled upon a female housemate emerging from the shower were to suffer the same fate, the universities would be empty of young men.)

Another aspect of Artemis is her role as the patroness of women in childbirth. Never a mother herself and always a virgin, she is nevertheless the goddess that women in ancient times called upon during the pains of childbirth, and she was regarded as their protector. At her temple in Ephesus, she is depicted with many breasts, as if feeding all the children whose safe delivery into the world she has accomplished.

And of course, there is Diana the Moon Goddess. Here, she is clearly a Roman deity, always called Diana and never Artemis, though she took on some attributes of Artemis after the Romans conquered Greece and the old Roman deities became conflated with the goddesses and gods of Classical Greek literature. And it is as the Moon Goddess that we meet her, centuries later, still in Italy. Folklorist Charles Godfrey Leland published *Aradia, or the Gospel of the Witches* in 1899. This text, which Leland claimed had been given to him by an Italian witch named Maddalena, purports to be the "sacred book" of a witch cult that had survived since Pagan times and still existed in Italy in the late nineteenth century. Though the book has been a source of controversy since its initial publication—even in 1899, scholars were asserting with vehemence that Leland must have been taken in by Maddalena, or that he was purely and simply a liar and Maddalena herself may never have existed—Leland's book has been taken seriously by many Neopagans and is held in high regard. Here, Diana appears as the old Roman Moon Goddess—with Etruscan roots, according to Leland—who mates with Lucifer and gives birth to Aradia, the goddess of the witches. This seems to be the same Diana whose name really does appear in the records of the late medieval witch trials as a leader of the Wild Hunt, a role in which we shall meet her in another chapter. The name "Aradia" would seem to be a dialectical pronunciation of Herodias, the wife of the Biblical King Herod transformed into yet another leader, among many, of the Wild Hunt.

Maddalena, the alleged source of Charles Godfrey Leland's Aradia

In Cochrane's opinion, the entire book of *Aradia* ought to be disposed of by throwing it into the ocean. As we have seen, Cochrane did not believe that witchcraft was the survival of a Pagan nature religion, as *Aradia*'s adherents did, and he may have had a special onus towards Leland's book because it was the source that Gardner used for holding sabbats in the nude.

And yet, there is another Diana who participated in the ritual combat or kingship and sacrifice which is embodied in the Oak King and Holly King myth. This is Diana of Nemi.

Her sanctuary was to be found on the northern shore of Lake Nemi beneath the cliffs of the modern city of Nemi. This lake was referred to by Roman poets as *speculum Dianae*— "Diana's Mirror." The temple of Diana of Nemi was located at a sacred grove where a carved cult image of the goddess stood and was said to be Etruscan in form. The cult image was still there as late as 43 BC.

Diana of Nemi was, herself, a triple goddess. Her cult image has been reconstructed from a sequence of later Roman Republic period coins. In early examples, the three goddesses stand before a forest grove, the central goddess placing her right hand on the shoulder of one goddess and her left on the hip of the other. The three are shown to be one by a horizontal bar behind their necks that connects them. This threefold image of the Latin Diana has sometimes been perceived as a combination of the divine huntress, the Moon Goddess, and the Underworld aspect of Hecate.

The votive offerings, none of which predate the fourth century BC, portray her as a huntress who also grants expectant mothers an easy childbirth and bestows her blessings on men and women who had children. It was said that when Hippolytus, the son of Theseus, was killed, owing to his father's curse, Asclepius raised him from the dead. On returning to the world, he refused to forgive his father; rejecting the prayers of Theseus, Hippolytus went to Italy. There he became a king and devoted a precinct around Lake Nemi to Artemis, where the victor in a rite of single combat became the priest of the goddess. The contest was not open to free men, but only to slaves who had run away from their masters.

In his seminal work *The Golden Bough*, a text well known to Cochrane, James George Frazer argued that the tale of the priesthood of Nemi was an instance of a worldwide myth of a sacred king who must periodically die as part of a regular fertility rite, and it is here that Diana of Nemi connects strongly with the myth of the Oak King and the Holly King, the two monarchs who battle for the changing of the seasons and for the love of the Goddess.

Idealized painting of Lake Nemi by J. W. M. Turner

Legend tells of a tree that stands in the center of the grove and is heavily guarded. No one was to break off its limbs with the exception of runaway slaves, who were allowed to break off one of the boughs. The successful slave was then in turn granted the right to engage in one-on-one mortal combat with the *rex Nemorensis*, the current priest of Diana at the lake. If the slave prevailed, he became the next priest for as long as he could defeat challengers. Always nervously waiting for the next runaway slave to appear and challenge him, the *rex Nemorensis* must have held a very uneasy position indeed.

The somewhat bizarre mode of human sacrifice conducted at Nemi was thought to be highly unusual by the ancients. The geographer Strabo calls it "Scythian," which implies that he found it barbaric. The violence of this institution could barely be justified by reference to its great antiquity and mythological sanctity. Ancient sources appear to concur that an escaped slave who sought refuge in this uneasy office was likely to be a desperate man.

By the time Caligula interfered in the succession of priest-kings, the murder-succession had devolved into gladiatorial combat before an audience. The sources indicate that by the time of the early empire, the custom of succession in the office by combat had become subject to outside control.

HECATE

If there is a goddess who richly deserves a niche in any pantheon of triple goddesses, it is Hecate.

When we first encounter her in one of the earliest epics of ancient Greece (Hesiod's *Theogony* in the eighth century BCE), she is a singular figure, though later on she emerges as a goddess who is more often than not depicted as a triplicity. She is often shown holding a pair of torches, a key, snakes, or accompanied by dogs, and she possesses a wide number of associations: she is a goddess of crossroads, any type of entranceway, night, light, magic (both the practice of and protection from witchcraft), the moon, and knowledge of herbs and plants. She is a goddess of graves, ghosts, and sorcery. When first mentioned by Hesiod, she is said to be a great goddess of considerable honor with domains in sky, Earth, and sea.

Her origins are still debated by scholars. The etymology of the name Hecate (Ἑκάτη, *Hekátē*) and the original country of her worship are both unknown, though several theories have been proposed. She may very well be pre-Greek, a survival from the Neolithic. She had many followers among the witches of Thessaly and an important sanctuary in the Greek province of Caria in Asia Minor. Her oldest known image was found on the island of Sicily.

Here is the first mention of Hecate, in the *Theogony* of Hesiod:

And [Asteria] conceived and bore Hecate whom Zeus the son of Cronos honored above all. He gave her splendid gifts, to have a share of the earth and the unfruitful sea. She received honor also in starry heaven, and is honored exceedingly by the deathless gods. For to this day, whenever any one of men on earth offers rich sacrifices and prays for favor according to custom, he calls upon Hecate. Great honor comes full easily to him

whose prayers the goddess receives favorably, and she bestows wealth upon him; for the power surely is with her. For as many as were born of Earth and Ocean amongst all these she has her due portion. The son of Cronos did her no wrong nor took anything away of all that was her portion among the former Titan gods: but she holds, as the division was at the first from the beginning, privilege both in earth, and in heaven, and in sea.[78]

According to Hesiod, she held sway over many things:

Whom she will she greatly aids and advances: she sits by worshipful kings in judgement, and in the assembly whom she will is distinguished among the people. And when men arm themselves for the battle that destroys men, then the goddess is at hand to give victory and grant glory readily to whom she will. Good is she also when men contend at the games, for there too the goddess is with them and profits them: and he who by might and strength gets the victory wins the rich prize easily with joy, and brings glory to his parents. And she is good to stand by horsemen, whom she will: and to those whose business is in the grey discomfortable sea, and who pray to Hecate and the loud-crashing Earth-Shaker, easily the glorious goddess gives great catch, and easily she takes it away as soon as seen, if so she will. She is good in the byre with Hermes to increase the stock. The droves of kine and wide herds of goats and flocks of fleecy sheep, if she will, she increases from a few, or makes many to be less. So, then, albeit her mother's only child, she is honored amongst all the deathless gods. And the son of Cronos made her a nurse of the young who after that day saw with their eyes the light of all-seeing Dawn. So from the beginning she is a nurse of the young, and these are her honors.[79]

In the *Homeric Hymn to Demeter* (composed c. 600 BCE), Hecate is called "tender-hearted," which, considering her association with witchcraft and poisons, may seem unusual. The epithet may be founded in the assistance she rendered to Demeter during her search for the kidnapped Persephone.

---

78 Hesiod, *Theogony,* trans. Hugh G. Evelyn-White, theoi.com/Text/Hesiod-Theogony.html, retrieved Sept. 30, 2023.

79 *Ibid.*

Later, Hecate became Persephone's companion on her yearly journey to and from the realms of Hades, serving as a psychopomp or "conductor of souls." Because of her association with Demeter and Persephone, Hecate was one of the principal goddesses of the Eleusinian Mysteries, and there was a temple dedicated to her near the main sanctuary at Eleusis.

Hecate was first depicted in triplicate by the sculptor Alcamenes around the late fifth century BCE. Though Alcamenes' original statue has been lost, there are hundreds of copies, and the general motif of a triple Hecate situated around a central pole or column, known as a *hekataion*, was used both at crossroads shrines as well as at the entrances to temples and private homes. These statues depict her holding a variety of items, including torches, keys, serpents, and daggers. Some *hekataia* include additional dancing figures such as the Three Graces (another triplicity) circling Hecate and her central column.

In his third century CE work *On Images*, the Neoplatonic philosopher Porphyry wrote that:

> [T]he moon is Hecate, the symbol of her varying phases and of her power dependent on the phases. Wherefore her power appears in three forms, having as symbol of the new moon the figure in the white robe and golden sandals, and torches lighted: the basket, which she bears when she has mounted high, is the symbol of the cultivation of the crops, which she makes to grow up according to the increase of her light: and again the symbol of the full moon is the goddess of the brazen sandals.[80]

As a triple goddess, Hecate was sometimes linked with the goddesses Luna (moon) in the sky and Diana (hunting) on the earth, while Hecate represents the Underworld. The Greek Magical Papyri and other esoteric texts emphasize a combination of Hecate with Artemis and Persephone, among others. Inasmuch as Persephone is the Queen of the Underworld, and the Triple Goddess of Diana, Hecate, and Persephone seems to have some justification in ancient history, Cochrane's unique understanding of the forms and forces that make up these archaic deific figures differs significantly. Given that his Faith did not incorporate them

---

80 Porphyry, "On Images," trans. Edwin Hamilton Gifford, classics.mit.edu/Porphyry/images.html, retrieved Sept. 30, 2023.

in those forms into the Clan of Tubal Cain's cosmology, his expression of the female dynamic is often challenging.[81]

Hecate was one of several deities worshiped in ancient Athens as a protector of households. This may have something to do with the icons that depict her with a set of keys and might also relate to her appearance with two torches, which, when positioned on either side of a gate or door, illuminated the immediate area and allowed visitors to be identified.

When placed at the doorways to homes, temples, and cities, shrines to Hecate were believed to protect the place from restless spirits of the dead and other unwelcome visitors. Home shrines often took the form of a small *hekataion*, while larger *hekataia* were sometimes placed at public crossroads near places of importance. Food offerings were left at shrines to Hecate at three-way crossroads during the new moon to protect her devotees from malicious spirits.

Drawing of a Hekataion, depicting Hecate as a
triple goddess surrounding a central column.

---

81   For a closer understanding of Cochrane's outlook upon the role of women in his magical philosophy, see the section entitled "Female Mysteries" in Shani Oates, *Tubelo's Green Fire, op. cit.*

Aside from her own temples, Hecate was also worshiped in the sanctuaries of other gods. There was an area sacred to Hecate in the Temple of Artemis at Ephesus. But despite all these shrines, Hecate was most commonly worshiped in the wild, where many natural sacred places served as her power centers. An important sanctuary of this type was a holy cave on the island of Samothrake.[82]

The Athenians honored Hecate during the *deipnon* or evening meal. On the night of the new moon, a meal would be set in a small shrine to Hecate by the front door, with the street in front of the house and the doorway creating a crossroads. The main purpose of the *deipnon* was to honor Hecate and placate unquiet souls. A secondary purpose was to purify the household and atone for any bad deeds a household member may have committed that might offend Hecate and cause her to withdraw her favor from the entire family.

Carrying the symbolism of boundaries to its ultimate conclusion, with realms outside or beyond the world of the living, Hecate appears to have been a "liminal" goddess: one who is able to access the places "between the worlds."

As a goddess who could banish harmful or destructive spirits and protect people as they passed through dangerous liminal places, Hecate became known as a goddess who could also *refuse* to banish the demons, and even make them do harm to others.

Because of her association with boundaries and the spaces between worlds, Hecate is also recognized as a chthonic (Underworld) goddess. As the holder of the keys that can unlock the gates between realms, she can unlock the gates of death. Hecate was equally powerful in both Heaven and Hell. The *Greek Magical Papyri* describe Hecate as the holder of the keys to Tartarus. Like Hermes, Hecate is a guardian—not only of roads but of all journeys, including the journey to the afterlife. She is often shown in the company of Hermes, guiding Persephone back from the Underworld with her torches.

---

82 In ancient times, the island of Samothrake held the unique edifice called "The Temple to All the Gods." In the present, it has become a kind of gathering place for Hellenic Neopagans, some from Greece as well as many expatriates from other nations.

Hecate's Underworld connection led to her transformation into a witch goddess, closely associated with plant lore and the knowledge of both medicines and poisons. She was said to give instruction in these closely related arts. In the *Argonautica,* a third-century BCE Alexandrian poem (much of which is based upon much earlier material), Apollonius of Rhodes writes that the witch Medea was taught by Hecate: "There is a maiden, nurtured in the halls of Aeetes, whom the goddess Hecate taught to handle magic herbs with exceeding skill—all that the land and flowing waters produce."[83] Jason the Argonaut, the hero of the epic, makes his peace with Hecate in a ritual prescribed by Medea. Bathing at midnight in a stream of flowing water and dressed in dark robes, Jason is commanded to dig a round pit and cut the throat of a ewe over it, sacrificing it and then burning it whole on a pyre next to the pit. He is told to sweeten the offering with a libation of honey, then retreat from the site without looking back, even if he hears the sound of footsteps or the barking of dogs. In fragments of Sophocles' lost play *The Root Diggers,* Hecate is described as wearing oak, and a commentary on the *Argonautica* describes her head as surrounded by serpents, twining through branches of oak.

The yew tree was also sacred to Hecate. The yew was associated with death and can be found growing in graveyards all over Europe. Hecate's attendants draped wreaths of yew around the necks of black bulls, which they slaughtered in her honor, and yew boughs were burned on funeral pyres.

Hecate favors offerings of garlic. She is also symbolically linked with the cypress, a tree which, like the yew, represents death and the Underworld and is therefore sacred to a number of chthonic deities.

A number of other plants (often poisonous, medicinal, or psychoactive) were associated with Hecate, including aconite (also called *hecateis*), belladonna, dittany, and mandrake. The use of dogs for digging up mandrake also links this plant with Hecate, since the dog is one of her most important totem animals; as early as the first century CE, there are a number of references to the apparently widespread practice of using dogs to dig up plants associated with magic.

---

83 Apollonius Rhodius, *The Argonautica* (G. P. Putnam's Sons, 1919) trans. R.C. Seaton, p. 231.

More than any other animal, dogs were closely associated with Hecate in the classical world. In art and literature, Hecate is constantly represented as dog-shaped or accompanied by a dog, and her approach was heralded by the howling of a dog. It has been speculated that her association with dogs suggests her connection with birth, for dogs were sacred to birth goddesses. Like Hecate, the dog is a guardian of doors and portals, and thus associated with the liminal space between life and death and the spirits that move across that frontier. The gates of Hades were guarded by the monstrous watchdog Cerberus, who prevented the living from entering the Underworld and the dead from leaving it. In later times, Hecate's dog came to be perceived as a manifestation of the restless spirits who accompanied her, though its docile appearance and its friendship with a Hecate, who frequently has a very gentle appearance in classical art, suggest that such a benign creature is more likely to have arisen from the dog's connection with birth goddesses rather than its Underworld associations.

In her three-headed representations, Hecate often has one or more animal heads, including a cow, dog, boar, serpent, and horse. Lions are associated with Hecate in early artwork, as well as on later coins and in the *Chaldean Oracles*. The frog, which was the symbol of the Egyptian goddess Heqet, has also become sacred to Hecate in modern Pagan literature.

Hecate is an important deity in the post-Christian *Chaldean Oracles* (second or third century CE), where she is associated with a spinning top or wheel used in magic. In these writings she is also said to have rulership over Earth, sea, and sky, as well as a more universal role as Savior (*Soteira*), Mother of Angels, and the Cosmic World Soul.

In the syncretistic blend of religions which took place during the Hellenistic era, Hecate also became closely associated with the Egyptian Isis. In *The Golden Ass* (written in the second century CE and one of Cochrane's favorite books, probably in the 1951 translation by our old friend Robert Graves), the author, Lucius Apuleius, equates Juno, Bellona, Hecate, and Isis with each other, while in the late third and early fourth centuries CE, Hecate was identified with Ereshkigal, the ancient Underworld Goddess of Sumerian and Babylonian mythology. Hecate also appears in a Christian Gnostic text from the third or fourth century CE entitled the *Pistis Sophia*.

It has been claimed that Hecate, syncretized with the figure of Diana, appears in late antiquity and in the early medieval period as part of an "emerging legend complex" known as The Society of Diana, which was associated with gatherings of women, the moon, and witchcraft—a society that eventually became established in northern Italy, southern Germany, and the western Balkans.

Shakespeare mentions Hecate before the end of the sixteenth century in *A Midsummer Night's Dream*, (1594–1596), and shortly afterwards, in *Macbeth* (1605) specifically in Macbeth's "dagger" soliloquy: "Witchcraft celebrates pale Hecate's offerings...."[84] Shakespeare also mentions Hecate in *King Lear*. While disclaiming all his paternal care for Cordelia, Lear says:

> *The mysteries of Hecate and the night,*
> *By all the operations of the orbs*
> *From whom we do exist and cease to be,*
> *Here I disclaim all my paternal care.*[85]

As a "goddess of witchcraft," Hecate has been incorporated into various systems of modern witchcraft, Wicca, and Neopaganism, as well as with the Wild Hunt tradition, which we shall soon examine. In Wicca, Hecate is sometimes identified with the Crone aspect of the Goddess, though in the Clan of Tubal Cain she is eternally youthful.

PERSEPHONE

Persephone may well be one of the oldest deities in the Greek pantheon, and though she plays no role in Cochrane's cosmology, her association or "likening" with the Three Fates mentioned above, her prominence among ancient Mystery Cults (such as Orphism and the Eleusinian mysteries) as seen in the light of Cochrane's assertions that witchcraft

---

84 Shakespeare, William. *Macbeth*, Act II, Scene 1.
85 Shakespeare, William. *King Lear*, Act I, Scene 1.

contained survivals of such cults, and her importance to contemporary Paganism in general merits her some treatment here.

Persephone may have had her origin in an old chthonic or Underworld deity of the Neolithic who received the souls of the dead into the earth and had power over the fertility of the soil. It is possible that the early cults dedicated to Persephone, which in time developed into the Eleusinian Mysteries, had their origin in Minoan Crete. At the Minoan palace of Phaistos on Crete (1900–1730 BCE), there is a plate which depicts a woman with snake lines and dancing girls on either side of her; this may or not be Persephone. One aspect of Persephone which is clearly depicted in Minoan art is the appearance of the goddess from above in the dance. Dance floors have been discovered in Crete, and it is likely that such dances were intended to induce states of ecstasy. Homer tells us of the dance floor which Daedalus built for Ariadne in the remote past. A gold ring from a Minoan tomb depicts four women dancing among flowers, the goddess floating above them. Some religious practices associated with Persephone, especially the Mysteries, may have been transferred from a Cretan priesthood to Eleusis, where Demeter brought the poppy from Crete.

There is evidence of a cult in Eleusis from the Mycenean period, but the cult was clearly private and we have no information about it. Some information can be obtained from the study of the cult of the goddess Eileithyia on Crete.[86] In the cave of Amnisos, Eileithyia is linked with the

---

86 Eileithyia or (in Latin) Ilithyia is a little-known Greek deity of child-birth and midwifery. In the cave of Amnisos (Crete), she was linked with the annual birth of the Divine Child, and her cult was connected with that of *Enesidaon* (the earth shaker), who was the chthonic aspect of the god Poseidon. The earliest form of her name is the Mycenaean Greek Ereutija, written in the Linear B syllabic script. Its etymology is uncertain and may be Pre-Greek. Her name probably links her with the month *Eleusinios* and therefore with Eleusis, which may also be a pre-Greek name. Some scholars believe that Eileithyia shows a clear connection to a pre-existing Minoan goddess, as well as an earlier Neolithic concept. To Homer, she is "the goddess of childbirth." Hesiod (c. 700 BC) describes Eileithyia as a daughter of Hera by Zeus (*Theogony* 921). Also, a poem in the *Greek Anthology*, Book Six, mentions Eileithyia as Hera's daughter. But there are a number of other opinions. In the "Orphic Hymn to Prothyraeia," virginal

annual birth of the Divine Child and connected with the Earth Shaker, the chthonic aspect of the god Poseidon, who appears as a horse. The term *pais* (the Divine Child) also appears in Mycenean inscriptions.

Artemis is given an epithet relating to the goddess of childbirth, making the divine huntress also "she who comes to the aid of women in childbirth":

> *When racked with labour pangs, and sore distressed*
> *the sex invoke thee, as the soul's sure rest;*
> *for thou Eileithyia alone canst give relief to pain,*
> *which art attempts to ease, but tries in vain.*
> *Artemis Eileithyia, venerable power,*
> *who bringest relief in labour's dreadful hour.*

— *Orphic Hymn to Prothyraeia*, translated by Thomas Taylor, 1792

In classical Greek art, Eileithyia is most often depicted assisting childbirth. As the primary goddess of childbirth along with Artemis, Eileithyia had numerous shrines in many locations in Greece dating from Neolithic to Roman times, indicating that she was extremely important to expecting families. People would pray for and leave offerings for fertility, safe childbirth, or to give appreciation for a successful birth. Eileithyia was strongly connected with both Artemis and Hecate, sharing with the latter strong chthonic elements in her cult. Pausanias described two sanctuaries to the goddess in Arcadia, one in the town of Kleitor and the other one in Tegea. In Kleitor, she was worshiped as one of the most important deities, along with Demeter and Asklepios. There were ancient icons of Eileithyia at Athens, one said to have been brought from Crete. Eileithyia, along with Artemis and Persephone, is often shown carrying torches to bring children out of darkness and into light. The Cave of Eileithyia near Amnisos, the harbor of Knossos, mentioned in the *Odyssey* (xix. 189) and was said to be her birthplace. In the river nearby, also named Amnisos, lived nymphs that were sacred to Eileithyia. The goddess is mentioned as Eleuthia in a Linear B fragment from Knossos, where it is stated that her temple is given an amphora of honey. She was mythically related with the annual birth of the Divine Child.

The Rape of Proserpina by Gian Lorenzo Bernini (1621–22) at the Galleria Borghese in Rome.

In Latin, Persephone's name is rendered as *Proserpina*. She was identified by the Romans with the local Italian goddess Libera. The Romans first heard of her from cities in southern Italy, which were known collectively as Magna Graecia because of their large Greek population. In 205 BCE, Rome officially identified Proserpina with Libera, who, along with the wine god Liber, was linked with the Roman grain goddess Ceres (equivalent to the Greek Demeter). The author Gaius Julius Hyginus regarded Proserpina as identical to the Cretan goddess Ariadne, who was the bride of Liber's Greek equivalent, Dionysus. In early Roman religion, Libera was the female aspect of Liber Pater, a protector of plebeian rights and god of wine, male fertility, and liberty. Proserpina was introduced to Rome as the daughter of Ceres in the cult of "Mother and Daughter." The cult's origins lay in southern Italy, which was politically allied to Rome but culturally a part of Magna Graecia. It was based on the women-only Greek ritual of the Thesmophoria, which was partly a public celebration and partly a mystery cult to Demeter and Persephone.

The exclusively female initiates and priestesses of the new Mysteries of Ceres and Proserpina were expected to uphold Rome's traditional social hierarchy and morality. These expectations differed slightly for unmarried women (the chastity of Proserpina in her role as the Maiden) and married women (Ceres, the devoted and fruitful mother). Their rites were held to bring a good harvest and to increase the fertility of those who took part in the Mysteries.

Persephone's abduction, sojourn in the Underworld, and return to the earth embody the eternal cycle of the seasons: the vegetation which disappears into the earth after harvest time, then returns in the spring. Persephone as Kore (the Maiden) was the spring, and in the Eleusinian Mysteries, her return from the Underworld is a promise that we, like the earth itself, can experience immortality.

The essentials of the Abduction Myth are as follows:

Zeus, it is said, permitted Hades, who was in love with the beautiful Persephone, to abduct her despite Demeter's outrage. Persephone was gathering flowers in a field along with the Oceanids, Artemis, and Pallas Athene, when Hades in his chariot came bursting through a fissure in the earth, kidnapped Persephone, and returned to the Underworld with her. When she discovered that her daughter had disappeared, Demeter searched for her all over the world, even at night with light from Hecate's torches.

Helios (the Sun), who sees everything, told Demeter what had happened and where her daughter had been taken. In most versions of the story, Demeter either forbade the earth to produce or else neglected the earth so that nothing grew. Zeus became worried by the cries of hungry mortals and forced Hades to return Persephone.

Although Hades complied with the request, he first tricked Persephone, giving her some pomegranate seeds to eat. Hermes was sent to retrieve her but, because she had tasted the food of the Underworld, she was obligated to spend the winter months there, though she could spend the remaining part of the year on Earth.

Persephone eventually returned from the Underworld and was reunited with her mother near Eleusis. The Mysteries of Demeter were established there. When Demeter and her daughter are reunited, the earth blossoms with vegetation and color, but when Persephone returns to the Underworld, the earth once again becomes a barren realm for some months each year.

In an earlier version of the myth, it was Hecate who rescued Persephone. On an Attic krater from c. 440 BCE, Persephone is rising, as if up a flight of stairs, from a cleft in the earth while Hermes stands aside; Hecate, holding two torches, looks back as she leads Persephone to the enthroned Demeter.

The location of Persephone's abduction differs widely in the various versions of the story. The *Homeric Hymn to Demeter* mentions the "plain of Nysa," a location otherwise unknown and probably mythical, a distant land in the remote past.[87]

In Claudian's Latin version of the myth, the god Dis (a Roman name for Hades) yearns for married love and fatherhood, and threatens to go to war with the other gods if he remains alone in Erebus. The Fates, who determine the destinies of all, prophesy a future marriage for Dis. Jupiter orders Venus to bring love to Dis in fulfillment of the prophecy. Ceres has already sought to conceal the innocent Proserpina by sending her to safety in Sicily, Ceres' earthly home and sanctuary, but Dis comes forth from the volcano at Mount Etna in his chariot, seizes Proserpina at the Pergusa Lake near Enna, and takes her down into the Underworld. The poem ends at this point.[88]

For most Greeks, the marriage of Persephone was a marriage with Death and could not serve as a role for human marriage; however, the people of a town called Locri in Italy regarded her marriage with the Underworld king in a positive light. Persephone accepted her new role as Queen of the Underworld and seems to have chosen not to return above; in the *Georgics*,

---

87 Nagy, Gregory, trans., *Homeric Hymn to Demeter*, uh.edu/~cldue/texts/demeter.html, retrieved Oct 1, 2023.

88 Claudian, *The Complete Works of Claudian*, trans. Neil W. Bernstein, scholar. archive.org/work/nhunstvozncfjnqm37p5cxzo54, retrieved Oct 1, 2023.

Virgil writes that "Proserpina cares not to follow her mother."[89] In Locri, it was Persephone who came to have supreme power over the land of the dead. Persephone's abduction was taken as a model of transition from girlhood to marriage for young women: a terrifying change, but one that provides the bride with status and position in society.[90]

Robert Cochrane asserted that witchcraft was, in some respects, a survival of the ancient Mystery Cults that proliferated in the Mediterranean and Near East, and he saw their perennial wisdom as an allegorical key to unlock the mysteries of the Northern mythic traditions that he loved so dearly. The Orphics revered Dionysus (who had once descended into the Underworld and returned) and Persephone (who did the same thing every year). The central mythos of Orphism was the torment and death of Dionysus at the hands of the Titans. It was said that they had killed, torn apart, and eaten the infant Dionysus. In revenge, Zeus struck the Titans with a thunderbolt and turned them to ashes. From these ashes, humanity was born. Therefore, in Orphic belief humanity has a dual nature: the physical body, inherited from the Titans, and a divine spark or soul (*psyche*), inherited from Dionysus. In order to achieve release from the dreary material world of the Titans, one had to be initiated into the

---

89 Virgil, *The Georgics*, classics.mit.edu/Virgil/georgics.html, retrieved Oct 1, 2023.

90 In the ancient world generally, the transition from maiden to wife was seen as a major passage in the life of a woman. In Babylonia, young women were obligated to spend time giving love services in the temple to weary and wounded warriors before they married, after which they were devoted entirely to their husbands. In ancient Greece, a young woman who was about to be married took all her perfumes, creams, and pretty clothes to the temple of Aphrodite and offered them up on the altar of the Love Goddess, for she would need them no longer. After marriage, she would give all her devotions to Hera, goddess of marriage, rather than to Aphrodite, goddess of love. It may be useful to remember that in ancient Greece, marriage was perceived primarily as a social contract, whereas love, in its aspect of *eros*, is said by Plato in his *Phaedrus* to be the "madness" which comes from Aphrodite and allows those who are seized by it to be drawn up to the world of the gods.

Dionysian Mysteries and experience a ritual purification, as well as a re-enactment of the suffering and death of the god.

The Orphics believed that, after death, they would live eternally alongside Orpheus and other heroes, while the uninitiated would be reincarnated again and again. The Orphics lived a life of asceticism and practiced a vegetarian diet. Orphic views and practices have parallels to elements of Pythagoreanism, and various traditions hold that Pythagoras himself had been initiated into Orphism.

In the mysticism of the Orphic Cult, Kore, the Maiden, is the all-pervading goddess of nature who both produces and destroys everything. In Orphic tradition, Persephone is said to be the daughter of Zeus and his mother Rhea rather than of Demeter. Zeus was filled with desire for his mother. He pursued the unwilling goddess; she turned herself into a serpent. Zeus also turned himself into a serpent, caught Rhea, and made love to her; thus was born Persephone. Afterwards, Rhea became Demeter. Zeus then mated with Persephone, who gave birth to Dionysus. The gods of Olympus were enchanted by Persephone's beauty and desired her. Hermes, Apollo, Ares, and Hephaestus all presented Persephone with a gift to woo her. Demeter was worried that Persephone might end up marrying Hephaestus, the shamanic smith god with an injured leg, so she consulted the astrological deity Astraeus. Astraeus warned her that Persephone would be taken and impregnated by a serpent. Demeter hid Persephone in a cave to protect her from such a fate; but Zeus, in the form of a serpent, entered the cave and made love to Persephone. Persephone became pregnant and gave birth to the god Zagreus. While weaving a dress, Persephone was abducted by Hades. She became the mother of the Furies by him.

Evidence from both the *Orphic Hymns* and the Orphic Gold Leaves demonstrate that Persephone was one of the most important deities worshiped in Orphism. In the Orphic religion, gold leaves with verses were often buried with the dead; they were intended to help the deceased enter into an optimal afterlife. Persephone is mentioned frequently in these tablets. The ideal afterlife destination that the Orphics longed for was sometimes described as the "sacred meadows and groves of Persephone." Other gold leaves describe Persephone's role in receiving and sheltering the dead.

In Orphism, Persephone is believed to be the mother of the first Dionysus. It is said that Zeus came to Persephone in her bedchamber in the Underworld and impregnated her with the child who would become his successor. The infant Dionysus was later dismembered by the Titans, before being reborn as the second Dionysus, who wandered the earth and disseminated his Mystery cult before ascending to Olympus with his second mother, Semele.

The names given to Persephone by the poets reflect her dual role as queen of the Underworld and the dead, and as the force that blossoms in the world and then withdraws into the earth. Her common name as a vegetation goddess is Kore, and in Arcadia she was worshiped as Despoina (the Mistress), a very ancient chthonic deity.[91]

In mythology and literature, she is often called "dreaded Persephone" and Queen of the Underworld, and some cults asserted that it was forbidden to speak her name. This is also true of Despoina, the Mistress, whose real name could not be revealed except to those who were initiated into her Mysteries. As goddess of death, she was also called a daughter of Zeus and Styx, the river that formed the boundary between our world and the Underworld. In Homer's *Iliad* and *Odyssey,* she always appears

---

91 Despoina was the epithet of a goddess worshiped in the Eleusinian Mysteries as the daughter of Demeter and Poseidon. Surviving sources refer to her exclusively under the title Despoina ("the Mistress," cognate of *Despot*) alongside her mother Demeter, as her real name could not be revealed to anyone except those initiated into her mysteries and was consequently lost with the extinction of the Eleusinian Mysteries. The cult of Despoina belonged to an earlier religion in Arcadia. The religious beliefs of the first Greek-speaking people who entered the region were mixed with the beliefs of the Indigenous population. Wanax was her male companion in the Mycenean cult, and this title was often applied to Poseidon as king of the sea. In Arcadia, Poseidon appears as a beast who represents the river spirit of the Underworld. The two great Arcadian goddesses, Demeter and Despoina (later Persephone), were closely related to the springs, animals, and especially the goddess Artemis. Despoina was worshipped in a sanctuary in Lycosura west of the town of Megalopolis. Women who worshiped at the site had to adhere to a dress code that prohibited participants from wearing black or purple, possibly because those colors were worn by priestesses. Later, Despoina was conflated with Kore (Persephone) in a life-death-rebirth cycle. "Despoina" was an epithet for several goddesses, especially Aphrodite, Demeter, Persephone, and Hecate.

together with Hades, and she seems to have shared control over the dead in the Underworld with Hades. In Homer's *Odyssey*, Odysseus encounters this "dreaded Persephone" when he visits his dead mother. Odysseus sacrifices a ram to her and the ghosts of the dead. The Underworld was sometimes called "The House of Persephone."

The Return of Persephone by Frederic Leighton (1891)

The myth of Persephone's abduction and return served as the basis for the secret rites at Eleusis. To the initiates, she was the terrible Queen of the Dead, whose name was not safe to speak aloud, and who was euphemistically called simply Kore or "the Maiden."

The *Orphic Hymn to Persephone* identifies Praxidike, "the Subterranean Queen," as an epithet of Persephone (despite the fact that it will sound to many like the title of a Bob Dylan song):

> *Jupiter's daughter, divine Persephone,*
> *Come to us, beloved queen,*
> *Bend down to these, our rites.*
> *You are the only-begotten,*
> *Pluto's honored bride.*
> *You are the venerated Goddess,*
> *You are the source of life.*
> *It is your path to dwell deep inside the earth,*
> *At the gates of Hell, so wide and grim,*
> *You are Jupiter's sacred child,*
> *And beautiful,*
> *An avenger,*
> *And the Subterranean Queen.*[92]

Persephone figures in a number of myths about visitors to the Underworld. Adonis was a beautiful mortal man; after he was born, Aphrodite entrusted him to Persephone to raise. But when Persephone experienced his beauty—finding him as attractive as Aphrodite did—she refused to give him back. The matter was brought to Zeus, who decreed that Adonis would spend one third of the year with each goddess and have the last third for himself. Adonis chose to spend his own portion of the year with Aphrodite. In another version of the story, Persephone met Adonis only after he had been slain by a boar. Aphrodite descended into the Underworld to take him back, but Persephone, smitten with him, would not let him go until they agreed that Adonis would divide his time between the Earth and the Underworld.

Another visitor to Persephone's realm was the musician Orpheus, who descended into the Underworld seeking to reclaim his wife Eurydice, who had died of a snakebite. So beautiful was the music he played on his lyre that it charmed Persephone—and even Hades. Persephone allowed Orpheus into the Underworld without losing his life; enchanted by his

---

92 Johnson, Kenneth, trans. "Hymn to Proserpine," *Orphic Hymns XIX*. I have no idea why the hymn uses both her Latin and her Greek name.

music, she allowed him to take his wife back to the land of the living, with the proviso that he must not look back during his journey of return. But Orpheus couldn't resist one backward glance, and thus Eurydice was lost to him forever.

When Dionysus, the god of wine, descended into the Underworld with Demeter to retrieve his dead mother Semele and bring her back to the land of the living, he is said to have offered a myrtle plant to Persephone in exchange for Semele.

The rites of Orpheus were not the only Mystery Cult that involved Persephone. Both Persephone and Demeter were intimately connected with a festival called the Thesmophoria, a group of secret rituals for women only—men were forbidden to see or hear about these rites which celebrated marriage and fertility, as well as the abduction and return of Persephone. The festival was held annually, around the time that seeds were sown in late autumn. It was held in several different regions throughout the ancient world, each one having different customs and rituals from the others.

Kore, daughter of Demeter, celebrated with
her mother at the Thesmophoria.

The Athenian Thesmophoria was regarded as the most beautiful, featuring flowers, music, and peaceful celebration. The Sicilian festival was perhaps the deepest from a spiritual point of view, and it is worth noting that one of the sacred places that was venerated as the site of Persephone's abduction was in Sicily, and that the Orphic Cult which honored the Goddess of the Underworld was also centered in southern Italy and Sicily.

In Athens, the Thesmophoria took place over three days in the month of Pyanepsion, which corresponds to our late October. In other places the festival lasted longer—in Syracuse, Sicily, the Thesmophoria was a ten-day event.

The first day of the Thesmophoria at Athens was called *anodos* (ascent), when the women celebrating the festival ascended to the shrine called the Thesmophorion. The term *anodos* may, however, relate to the "ascent" of Persephone from the Underworld, which was celebrated at the festival. Preparations for the rest of the festival were made on this day. Women set up tents; they would spend the rest of the festival there.

The second day of the festival was called the *nesteia*. This was a day of fasting and represented Demeter's mourning for the loss of her daughter, while the third day was *kalligeneia*, or "beautiful birth." On this day, women called upon the goddess Kalligeneia, praying for their own fertility.

But despite the importance of the Thesmophoria, it is the Mysteries of Eleusis which have captured the attention of poets, scholars, and mystics throughout history, and which are without doubt the most important of all the ancient Greek Mystery Cults.

The Eleusinian Mysteries were held every year and may have been derived from spiritual practices of the Mycenean period. The Mysteries dealt with the myth of the abduction and return of Persephone in a cycle with three phases: the *descent,* the *search,* and the *ascent,* with the main theme being the *ascent* of Persephone and her reunion with her mother. These phases of Persephone's cycle are important in the sense that Cochrane's analogous forays into Greek and other cultural mythologies may be understood as a search for the wisdom of such cyclic phases and how they were disseminated, understood, practiced, remembered, honored, and celebrated.[93]

---

93   Shani Oates, personal communication, January 2024.

A votive plaque known as the Ninnion Tablet depicting elements of the Eleusinian Mysteries, discovered in the sanctuary at Eleusis (mid-fourth century BC)

The rites, ceremonies, and beliefs of the Eleusinian Mysteries were kept secret throughout antiquity. For the initiated, the rebirth of Persephone symbolized the energy of life itself, and the initiates believed that they would have a blessed afterlife. The Mysteries were intended to bring mortals into consciousness of the divine.

The name of the town Eleusis seems to be pre-Greek and is probably linguistically connected with the beautiful afterlife in the mythic land of Elysium.

There is much about the Eleusinian Mysteries that still remains secret. We know that only initiates were aware of what the *kiste,* a sacred chest, and the *calathus,* a lidded basket, contained. Hippolytus of Rome, one of the Church Fathers writing in the early third century CE, asserts in his *Refutation of All Heresies* that "...the Athenians, while initiating people into the Eleusinian rites, likewise display to those who are being admitted to the highest grade at these mysteries, the mighty, and marvelous, and most perfect secret suitable for one initiated into the highest mystic truths: [I allude to] an ear of corn in silence reaped."[94] But Hippolytus must be regarded as a hostile witness.

The Greater Mysteries took place in Boedromion—the third month of the Attic calendar, falling around September or October—and lasted ten days.

The first phase was bringing sacred objects from Eleusis to a temple at the base of the Acropolis of Athens. On the fifteenth of Boedromion, a day called the Gathering, the priests (*hierophantes*) declared the formal beginning of the Mysteries and carried out the sacrifices.

On the sixteenth of Boedromion, the prospective initiates washed themselves in the sea at Phaleron. On the seventeenth, a festival called the *Epidauria* was held to celebrate the arrival of Asklepios and his daughter Hygeia at Athens.

On the eighteenth, the people walked to Eleusis along the Sacred Way, swinging branches called *bacchoi.* Along the way, they shouted obscenities to commemorate an old woman called Baubo, whose dirty jokes had made Demeter smile even as she mourned the loss of her daughter.

Upon reaching Eleusis, there was an all-night vigil. At some point, initiates had a special drink (*kykeon*) of barley and pennyroyal, which may have had psychotropic effects from ergot (a fungus containing psychedelic alkaloids similar to LSD that grows on barley). It has been argued that the discovery of fragments of ergot in a temple dedicated to the two Eleusinian goddesses in Spain suggests that the psychoactive properties of *kykeon* may have been for real. Ergot fragments were also found inside a vase and within the dental calculus of a twenty-five-year-old man, which demonstrates that he ingested it.

94　Hippolytus Romanus, *The Refutation of All Heresies,* trans. J. H. MacMahon, retrieved Oct 3, 2023.

On the nineteenth of Boedromion, initiates entered a great hall called the Telesterion; in the center stood a palace built of ruins dating back to the Mycenaean Age, which only hierophants could enter. Before initiates could enter the Telesterion, they had to repeat, "I have fasted, I have drunk the *kykeon*, I have taken from the *kiste* [box] and, after working it, I have put it back in the *calathus* [open basket]."

Initiation to Eleusinian Mysteries. c. 100–50 BCE; relief, Louvre Museum (Paris, France)

Following the rites in the Telesterion was an all-night feast accompanied by dancing and merriment. This portion of the festivities was open to the public. The dances took place in the Rharian Field, said to be the first spot where grain grew. A bull sacrifice also took place late that night or early the next morning. On the twenty-second of Boedromion, the initiates honored the dead by pouring libations to them.

On the twenty-third of Boedromion, the Mysteries ended and everyone went home.

As Christianity gained in popularity in the fourth and fifth centuries, Eleusis's prestige began to fade. The last Pagan emperor of Rome, Julian, reigned from 361 to 363 CE, after about fifty years of exclusively Christian emperors. Julian attempted to restore the Eleusinian Mysteries and was the last emperor to be initiated into them. The Eleusinian Mysteries were permanently closed down in 392 CE by the emperor Theodosius I.

"The Myth of Er," part of Plato's *Republic,* is thought by some to be based upon the teachings of the Eleusinian Mysteries. Er, after being killed in battle and brought to the Underworld, is reincarnated without drinking from the River Lethe. He retains his memories and tells the living about his experience in the Underworld, no longer afraid of death.

Initiates into the Eleusinian Mysteries included Plato, the emperor Augustus, Plutarch, the emperors Hadrian, Julian, and Marcus Aurelius, and Aurelius' son Commodus (the villain of the film *The Gladiator*).

THE WOMEN OF THE TRIBE OF CAIN

NA'AMAH

While one might expect a strong showing from Jubal, the first musician and the archetypal forefather of all those who play upon "the harp and the organ," instead it is Na'amah—mentioned only once in Genesis 4 and simply named as the sister of Tubal Cain—who has gained a reputation in Traditional Witchcraft.

Na'amah means "charmer" or "seductress" in Hebrew; Andrew Chumbley, a well-known figure in Traditional Witchcraft, casts her in such a role. She is also regarded as something of a witch: a maker of spells. In the Talmud, she is described as a cymbal player and a singer whose enchanting voice could charm the worshipers of Yahweh away from their faith and return them to the ancient Pagan gods. Some say that she invented music altogether, though she seems to have given her attention to laments, dirges, and torrid love songs. Ian Chambers draws attention to lines in Aramaic translations of the Hebrew Bible (spanning the second Temple Period to the Middle Ages), which inform us that: "...the sister of Tubal-Cain was Na'amah, the inventor of dirges and songs." As Chambers also points out: "Like the sirens of Greek myth, she resides in the sea and makes music that lures men."[95]

Na'amah is also said to have invented weaving and spinning, which links her with the three goddesses of Fate. Na'amah is said to have had love affairs with Azazel, a goat god and leader of the fallen angels, as well as with King Solomon and the dark angel Samael, sometimes alleged to be the father of her ancestor Cain. In this respect, Na'amah can be included among the Daughters of Men with whom the fallen angels had intercourse after being seduced by her beauty and song. As a succubus, Na'amah comes in the night to fill the hearts of the Sons of Men with—as Chambers puts it— "fire and passion, with their song enticing the soul with the sacred alchemy of the *unio mystica* to awaken it from slumber and bring forth a divine child that they will steal away and raise as a demon."[96]

Often identified with Adam's legendary and rebellious first wife Lilith or represented as one of her daughters, Na'amah is said to have given birth to entire races of beings, such as elves, goblins, and faeries. She is also said to have been the mother of the demon Asmodeus.

Despite Na'amah's somewhat promiscuous reputation, Ian Chambers finds a mystical meaning in her singing, and in the songs of all other mythic sirens. While the songs of Na'amah or the sirens may well be a lament, the customary theme is love or desire. Chambers goes on to speculate that all love songs contain within them the threat of heartbreak, just as life brings with it the promise of death.

The pain of love is the pain of separation: the soul's lamentation at being separated from its source, the *anima mundi*. The soul longs for a reunion with that source, for though the flesh may perish, the soul may awaken and unite with the *anima mundi* in a *hieros gamos* or mystical marriage. And while Chambers asserts that the call of the siren calls us home, not to a worldly home but to "the sacred isle to which Morgan le Fey and her company of songstresses escorted the wounded Arthur,"[97] the Clan of Tubal Cain sees such laments as the transformation of death into a lover.[98]

---

95 Chambers, Ian, "Siren Song—*quid Sirenes cantare sint solitae?*" clanoftubal-cain.org.uk/sirensong.html, retrieved Oct 4, 2023.

96 *Ibid.*

97 Chambers, "Siren Song," *op. cit.*

98 Shani Oates, personal communication, January 2024.

LILITH

Lilith (Hebrew: לִילִית) was said in Near Eastern legend and lore to be the rebellious first wife of Adam, created before Eve. We have already encountered her in the mythology of the Horseman's Word, where she offers to teach Tubal Cain the lore of horses and women but is washed away by a river with only half the knowledge of horses and none of the knowledge of women conveyed to Tubal Cain. But just because she is washed away doesn't mean she was killed. Lilith is one of the immortals.

We would expect to find her here, in the myths and ceremonies of Traditional Witchcraft, where we find so many other ambivalent figures from Biblical lore re-envisioned and re-interpreted. Cochrane did not make use of her, nor does the current Clan of Tubal Cain, but she has gained a strong presence in the myths of later practitioners of Traditional Witchcraft for whom Cochrane's work was an inspiration, and thus she has a place in the canon.

It is said that Lilith was created after God's words in Genesis 2:18: "It is not good for man to be alone." God forms Lilith out of the clay from which he made Adam, but she and Adam simply don't get along. Lilith claims that since both of them were created in the same way, they are equals and Adam is not her master.

She said, "I will not lie below you," and he said, "I will not lie beneath you, but only on top. For you are fit only to be in the bottom position, while I am to be the superior one." Lilith responded, "We are equal to each other inasmuch as we were both created from the earth." But they would not listen to one another. When Lilith realized this, she flew away.

Adam said to God, "[t]he woman you gave me has run away." God sent three angels to bring her back, and told Adam, "[i]f she agrees to return, what was made is good. If she doesn't, she must permit one hundred of her children to die every day." The angels left God and pursued Lilith, whom they overtook in the midst of the Red Sea. They told her God's word, but she rejected it.

The angels said, "we shall drown you in the sea."

"Leave me alone!" she said. "I was created to cause sickness to infants. If the infant is male, I have rulership over him for eight days after his birth, and if female, for twenty days."

When the angels heard Lilith's words, they insisted she go back. But she swore to them by God's name: "Whenever I see you or your names or your forms in an amulet, I will have no power over that infant." She also agreed to have one hundred of her children die every day. Every day, one hundred demons perish. The names of the angels were written on amulets to protect young children.

In time, Lilith did return to Adam and bore children to him. But before doing so, she became the lover of Cain and bore him numerous spirits and demons.

The Kabbalistic *Zohar* has even more to say about Lilith:

> *She roams at night, and goes all about the world and makes sport with men and causes them to emit seed. In every place where a man sleeps alone in a house, she visits him and grabs him and attaches herself to him and has her desire from him, and bears from him. And she also afflicts him with sickness, and he knows it not, and all this takes place when the moon is on the wane.*[99]

The *Zohar* brings us back to the lore of Tubal Cain by informing us that there are two female spirits, Lilith and Na'amah, who desired Adam and seduced him. The children of these unions were demons and spirits who plagued humankind.

The word *lilit* (or *lilith*) appears only once in the Hebrew Bible, in a prophecy regarding the fate of Edom. Isaiah 34 reads:

> *(12) Her nobles shall be no more, nor shall kings be proclaimed there; all her princes are gone.*

> *(13) Her castles shall be overgrown with thorns, her fortresses with thistles and briars. She shall become an abode for jackals and a haunt for ostriches.*

> *(14) Wildcats shall meet with desert beasts, satyrs shall call to one another; There shall the Lilith repose, and find for herself a place to rest.*

---

99 *Sefer ha Zohar*, quoted in Patai, Raphael, "Lilith" in *The Hebrew Goddess*, Third Enlarged Edition (Wayne State University Press, 1990) pp. 221–251.

(15) There the hoot owl shall nest and lay eggs, hatch them out and gather them in her shadow; there shall the kites assemble, none shall be missing its mate.

(16) Look in the book of the Lord and read: No one of these shall be lacking, For the mouth of the Lord has ordered it, and His spirit shall gather them there.

(17) It is He who casts the lot for them, and with His hands He marks off their shares of her; They shall possess her forever, and dwell there from generation to generation.

The fifth-century Vulgate translated the same word as *lamia*, while in the King James Version, Isaiah 34:14 reads: "The wild beasts of the desert shall also meet with the wild beasts of the island, and the satyr shall cry to his fellow; the screech owl also shall rest there, and find for herself a place of rest."

The Dead Sea Scrolls contain one clear reference to Lilith in *Songs of the Sage* (4Q510–511), fragment 1:

And I, the Instructor, proclaim His glorious splendor so as to frighten and to te[rrify] all the spirits of the destroying angels, spirits of the bastards, demons, Lilith, howlers, and [desert dwellers]…and those which fall upon men without warning to lead them astray from a spirit of understanding and to make their heart and their … desolate during the present dominion of wickedness and predetermined time of humiliations for the sons of lig[ht], by the guilt of the ages of [those] smitten by iniquity—not for eternal destruction, [bu]t for an era of humiliation for transgression.

Lilith is much older than the Bible. Her name is derived from the Akkadian word *lilu*, which is related to the Hebrew word *lilit* in Isaiah 34:14 and is believed by some scholars to be a night bird. In Hebrew-language texts, the term *lilith* or *lilit* is variously translated as "night creatures," "night monster," "night hag," or "screech owl."

Lilith features prominently in protective spells on Jewish occult incantation bowls from the Sassanid Empire in Babylon (fourth to sixth century CE). These bowls were buried upside down below the structure of houses or on the land of the house to trap demons. Almost every house had such protective bowls.

Incantation bowl with an Aramaic inscription around a demon,
from Nippur, Mesopotamia, sixth or seventh century

Medieval Hebrew amulet intended to protect a mother and her child from Lilith

The incantation bowls are inscribed in various languages, notably Hebrew, Babylonian, Aramaic, Syriac, Mandaic, Middle Persian, and Arabic. A correctly worded incantation bowl was capable of keeping

 110

Lilith away from the household. Lilith could transform herself into a semblance of any woman she pleased, seduce her husband, and conceive a child. However, Lilith would then become hateful toward such children and the man's wife and seek to kill them.

It is as the lover and mother of demons that Lilith is best known, especially in Traditional Witchcraft. It is said that she had no interest in returning to the Garden of Eden after she had made love with the archangel Samael. Another version that was also present among Kabbalistic circles in the Middle Ages names Lilith as the first of Samael's four wives, which included our familiar friend Na'amah. As personifications of lust gone wild, they are the mothers of demons and have their own hosts of evil spirits.

In the early Middle Ages, Lilith became identified as the bride of Asmodeus, King of Demons. Asmodeus was already well known by this time due to the legends about him in the Talmud. Asmodeus and Lilith were said to constantly give birth to demons and create chaos everywhere.

Lilith has been perceived in legend as the incarnation of lust, causing men to be led astray, and as a child-killing witch who strangles helpless neonates.[100] But during the Romantic movement of the nineteenth century,

---

100 It is not my intention to discourage readers from working with some of the darker and more difficult deities. After all, those who never do shadow work never experience the fullness of life. I do, however, advise those who choose to work with challenging archetypes such as Lilith to exercise caution and ensure their own protection. I am acquainted with a relatively well-known writer on the subject of feminist mythology who worked extensively with Lilith and even wrote a book about her. She was at a conference and feeling quite delighted because her first granddaughter had been born about a week earlier. During her lecture at the conference, she read some poetry that she had written in honor of Lilith. As soon as her speech was done, she was taken in hand by some of the conference facilitators and led to the telephone (this was before the days of cell phones). On the other end of the line was her son-in-law, openly weeping. He gave her the terrible news that her granddaughter had just died unexpectedly. When she began to gain control of her mind and emotions, she asked for a precise time of death. Her granddaughter had passed away at the exact moment that she had been reading her poetry to Lilith during her lecture. She never worked with Lilith again. Be cautious when approaching the darker deities.

Lilith begins to get some good press. Perhaps it begins with the first part of Goethe's *Faust* in 1808:

Faust:	*Lilith? Who is that?*
Mephistopheles:	*Adam's wife, his first. Beware of her.*
	Her beauty's one boast is her dangerous hair.
	When Lilith winds it tight around young men
	She doesn't soon let go of them again.[101]

Lady Lilith by Dante Gabriel Rossetti (1866–1868, 1872–1873)

The Pre-Raphaelite Brotherhood, which flourished in the midnineteenth century, was greatly influenced by Goethe's work on the theme of Lilith, as were the Victorian writers who followed them. Dante

---

101 Goethe, Johann Wolfgang von, *Faust: A Tragedy* (Yale University Press, 2014) trans. Martin Greenberg, Part 1, lines 4206–11.

Gabriel Rosetti wrote a sonnet in her honor, and the Victorian poet Robert Browning penned an even longer work. Rosetti, who was also an artist, dedicated one of his finest paintings to her. Both Rosetti and Browning seem to have had a fascination with the eroticism of her long, seductive hair.

A fair number of Traditional Witchcraft groups inspired by Cochrane have venerated Lilith and Na'amah. Victor Anderson (1917–2001), the founder of the modern Feri tradition, asserted that "[the] worship of the Goddess was the very heart of our religion and magic. Lilith was one of the names used in our ritual worship of the Lady."[102] The primary goddess form in Feri is Mother Nox (Night), who can be identified with Lilith (and who is also the Orphic creatrix in Cochrane's personal creation myth).

One modern practitioner of Traditional Witchcraft, Andrew D. Chumbley, leader of the Cultus Sabbati or Sabbatic Cult, speaks of a "gnostic faith in the Divine Serpent of Light, the Host of the Grigori [Watchers], the children of Earth sired by the Watchers [the Nephilim], in the lineage of descent via Lilith, Mahazael, Cain, Tubal Cain, Naamah and the Clans of the Wanderers…onward to the present day initiates of the Arte."[103]

"Witch blood," "elven blood," or "faery blood" does not imply a transmission of powers and knowledge through hereditary families but refers instead to the various Children of Cain. In the Cultus Sabbati, Cain and Lilith are regarded as the founders of the tradition and the Bearers of Light from the Ancient Serpent, Lucifer.

In Traditional Witchcraft, Lilith has borne a number of names and titles: she is the Dark of the Moon when it cannot be seen in the sky. This time of darkness is dedicated to Lilith and auspicious for scrying; it is a time when some female witches feel that they can work their most powerful magic. Lilith is sometimes the Lady of the Evening Star (Venus or the Babylonian Ishtar as Love Goddess rather than Battle Goddess; the full moon is sometimes known as "Lilith's Lantern"). Mary Magdalene has been called an avatar of Lilith, though her devotees also accept the Gnostic doctrine that she was the wife of Jesus. Lilith is also identified with the Biblical Queen of Sheba, and among some traditional witches, the seven-pointed star is her symbol.

---

102 Quoted in Howard, *Children of Cain, op. cit.*, p. 176.
103 Quoted in Howard, *Children of Cain, op. cit.*, p. 209.

Truth

As discussed at the beginning of this chapter, Cochrane rejected the common perception of the Triple Goddess as Maiden, Mother, and Crone, preferring to designate the triplicity as the Three Fates. Yet, instead of relying upon Greek myth for the Classical Fates—Clotho, Lachesis, and Atropos—or invoking the Norns of Viking myth, I believe his vision of the Fates could be "likened to" the well-known goddesses Diana, Hecate, and Persephone. Cochrane regarded many deities as merely "close approximations" of the Virtue those names and titles represent. To him, they personified the mystery we all perceive, albeit hampered by cultural restraints. Furthermore, all these figures are merely agents of Fate.[104]

But beyond the Goddess and the God, Cochrane postulated one Divine Power in the universe. As in most other spiritual paths, this Divine Power was said to be unknowable and without attributes, a oneness which could not be described.

And yet, with his usual gift for turning things round and round about, Cochrane asserted that this Oneness, this Divine Essence which lay behind all things, was feminine.

He also claimed to have seen her.

According to Cochrane, he was in bed, whether dreaming or in a mystical state of consciousness, when the One Essence came to him, as if riding out of the woods on a horse.

And she had long hair, and she was naked.

And the vision of her, of this One Essence, overwhelmed him.

And even though the Divine Essence was said to be without attributes but was capable of manifesting in the form of a woman, this allegorical figure exampled by the Lady Godiva, according to Cochrane, also had a name.

And her name was Truth.

---

104 Shani Oates, personal communication, September 2024. The word "Virtue" in this context should be understood as it is in magical thought—the indwelling quality or essence of a deity, archetype, and so on. It has nothing to do with the common understanding of "virtue" as obedience to prurient Christian behavioral restrictions.

CHAPTER SEVEN

THE WILD HUNT

ROBERT COCHRANE HAD A PASSION for what his ancestors knew as the Wild Hunt. The spirit leaders of his rituals, who mediate the tutelary spirit of Tubal Cain, possessed many different names—Arthur, Gwyn ap Nudd, and Herne the Hunter among them—but all these names can be found in folklore as leaders of the Wild Hunt, which was the hosting of the spirits, the faery folk.

To travel with the faery folk was no mere romp in the garden. One roamed the sky upon animals, accompanied by a host of spectral beings. The sight of this great gathering of spirits was a terrifying thing for many Europeans, and thus they called it the Wild Hunt.[105]

The concept of the Wild Hunt was first defined by the German folklorist Jacob Grimm in his *Deutsche Mythologie* in 1835. Grimm asserted that the Wild Hunt, like other themes from folklore, was a survival of Pagan belief. Grimm identified the male figure who often appeared as the leader of the Wild Hunt as the god Odin. Often, the leader of the Hunt is a woman, whom Grimm referred to as Holda or Berchta. Grimm believed that in pre-Christian Europe, the hunt, led by a god and a goddess, visited "the land at some holy tide, bringing welfare and blessing, accepting gifts and offerings of the people" or sometimes floated "unseen through the air, perceptible in cloudy shapes, in the roar and howl of

---

105 And not only in Europe. The story of the Wild Hunt was apparently brought to the United States, even as far as the Western frontier. The song "Ghost Riders in the Sky" seems to be based on the legend of the Wild Hunt.

the winds, carrying on *war, hunting* or the game of *ninepins,* the chief employments of ancient heroes: an array which, less tied down to a definite time, explains more the natural phenomenon."[106]

Asgardsreien [The Wild Hunt of Odin] by Peter Nicolai Arbo (1872)

Though Grimm's theories were not enunciated until the nineteenth century, many examples of the presence of the Wild Hunt can be found in medieval sources. The *Ecclesiastical History of Orderic Vitalis* records an event which allegedly took place in 1091.[107] A priest was strolling along a path one night when he heard a clamor that sounded like an army on the march. He then beheld an enormous being with a club and knew himself to be in the presence of the terrible Herlechin, one of various and sundry characters who were known as the leader of the Wild Hunt in one region or another. This creature was followed by a crowd of people, some on foot and others on horseback, but all tormented by demons. These were the souls of those who had died in a state of sin, and they complained of their sorry fate.

---

106 Grimm, Jacob, *Teutonic Mythology: Volume III* (Dover, 2004) trans. James Steven Stallybrass, p. 947.

107 Johnson, *Witchcraft and the Shamanic Journey, op. cit.,* p. 70.

 116

Another early account comes from England in 1127. In the *Peterborough Chronicle,* Henry d'Angely writes that many men, including monks, both saw and heard tribes of coal-black horsemen with packs of black dogs in the deer park of the town of Peterborough and the surrounding woods.

The spectral legions who made up the Wild Hunt were comprised of those who had passed from this mortal world and been carried away to the shadowy realms. Sometimes, however, the doors between the worlds are open. The earliest records from the witch trials specify Thursdays (sacred to the god Thor or Jupiter), as well as the Ember Days between Christmas and Epiphany. When the doors between this world and the next stand open, the spirits come pouring through, led by their king, or, just as often, their queen. In Scotland, the sixteenth-century *Ballad of Tam Lin* portrays the Queen of the Fairies (who lives in a "green hill" or barrow mound, which is what the very talkative Scottish witch Isobel Gowdie claimed) leading her cohorts on a fearsome "riding" on Halloween night.[108]

As we shall see, the Goddess as leader of the Wild Hunt may have played a very special role in Cochrane's personal mythos.

But the Fairy Queen must have a Fairy King—a figure whom Cochrane characteristically envisioned as the Horned God, who held many names but was ultimately perceived as yet another transmutation of Tubal Cain. The leader of the Wild Hunt may be Herne the Hunter, Odin, or, in the tale told by Orderic Vitalicus, Herlechin (hence the name Harlequin, a nature spirit disguised as a Renaissance comedian).

The Underworld Lord is a deity of Earth and sea. His names are legion, for, like all good shamans, he dies and is reborn again and again, even as the fruits of the earth die and are reborn with the seasons. Because he rules over the abundance of the wild earth, he is a god of the forests and the woods, and thus he may appear as the Green Man, as in the tale of *Sir Gawain and the Green Knight.* Because animals dwell in those woods, and because the animal kingdom is part of the world of vast Nature, he is a Lord of the Animals as well.

This, then, is the god who rode forth to lead the Wild Hunt. In the Otherworld, the dead (or at least the male dead) spent their time in hunting as well as feasting. On nights when the dead rode forth, led by

---

108 The folk-rock version of "Tam Lin" on the classic *Liege and Lief* album by Fairport Convention, sung by Sandy Denny at the peak of her career, is highly recommended.

their king and queen, most medieval peasants stayed safely indoors, for fear of meeting them—except, of course, for the witches, who happily joined them in their travels.

To meet up with the Lord of the Wild Hunt was not necessarily an inauspicious thing, for the Underworld Lord was not evil, but such a meeting might constitute a rather harrowing encounter with the unknown. In time, however, the ecclesiastical doctrine that identified the Underworld Lord with the Christian Devil took its toll, and the Lord of the Wild Hunt came more and more to be feared.

As a Master of Animals, the Underworld Lord occasionally wore horns, and it is these horns, more than any other physical feature, that have had the greatest impact on our picture of the Devil. The original Lucifer or Satan of the Near East had no such headgear—the horns are linked clearly and incontestably with old European deities of the woods and animals. Thus, modern Neopagans have made much of the old Celtic deity Cernunnos, the Horned One, though it must be admitted that Cernunnos himself never actually appears by name in the records of the witch trials. Nevertheless, he is a typical incarnation of the Otherworld Lord.

Robert Cochrane's rituals always included an individual who, though he might hold many names, was always the "Horned One." It is he who typically led the sabbats of the original Clan of Tubal Cain—sabbats which strongly resembled the Wild Hunt itself.

The leader of the Wild Hunt bore many names, some of which reveal his true identity: Odin was a shamanic god of the dead, and Arthur, who was carried off to the Land of Youth by that enchantress whom the anonymous Gawain poet called "Morgan the Goddess," is returning from that Otherworld Avalon when he appears as leader of the Wild Hunt. This is particularly true in Cochrane's theology.

It is clear that the Otherworld Lord has a great deal in common with the Devil of the witch trials. He is a "wild man," associated with the wilderness. He may appear as a large dark-skinned man, or in animal form, as the leader of a pack of animals, or, very often, with antlers.

Throughout the Middle Ages, peasants continued to celebrate their folk festivals, set tables for the dead, and journey with the Wild Hunt. Though the Church disapproved of such customs, it never persecuted the peasantry. Then, in the late 1300s and early 1400s, the Church decided that a whole new sect of heretics had arisen, and that these heretical "witches" constituted a grave threat to the spiritual security of Christendom. And so the witch trials began.

And what do the dead do when they enter our world? They look for food and drink. After all, feasting is the principal mode of activity in the Otherworld. The Valkyries carried warriors off to an eternal feast in Valhalla, and the fairies were feasting in a barrow mound when Isobel Gowdie went to visit them. Their food itself is magical, for it is well-known in Irish and Scottish lore that those who wander into the barrow mounds and feast with the fairies will probably return only hundreds of years later, if at all (and even if they return promptly, they will never be the same again). The spirits of the dead can be treacherous; they are sometimes well disposed toward us and sometimes hostile.

Therefore, it is the better part of wisdom to set a table for them in your home, in case they choose to pass through. They like good food and wine, and a clean, well-swept house. William of Auvergne wrote in the thirteenth century that the "ladies of the night," led by Domina Abundia or Satia, fly through the air and invade people's cellars, where they eat and drink the provisions set out for them and, in return, bring prosperity upon the house. If there is nothing for them to eat, they withhold their blessings. (They may do worse than that—some European peasants claimed that they would defecate in your wine barrels if they were angry.)

It was night when Isobel Gowdie flew away from her body to travel in the spirit. In the Land of Faerie, however, it was day. Herein lies a fact of great importance: the Otherworld is a mirror image of our own. Everything is the same but seen as through a mirror, in reverse. The dead come forth to ride on the Wild Hunt when our world is cloaked in darkness; in their world, however, it is day, and hence time for riding. Though the hunger of the dead may call forth images of the hungry, chittering ghosts in the gray Asphodel Fields, and though the feasts set forth for them may remind us of the ancient Greeks pouring blood onto the earth so that the dead might drink and henceforth speak, there is another idea at work here as well—in their own world, the dead are eternally at feast, while in our world they are eternally hungry. The image in the mirror is reversed.

The Wild Hunt, led by the Witch God or Goddess, was as much a procession of animals as of the dead, for after all, these deities are also the Lord and Lady of the Animals. Their human followers who joined the furious journey frequently rode mounted upon animals.

Almost any animal would do. The Goddess herself seems to have ridden horseback more often than not, for the regions of Western Europe wherein we find the tradition of the Wild Hunt are also the regions where ancient Celts worshiped a goddess on horseback: Gallic Epona, Welsh Rhiannon, the Fairy Queen who figures in the ballads of *Tam Lin* and *Thomas the Rhymer*, and even (in folklore) Lady Godiva.

On certain nights, medieval peasants laid out a feast for the spirits of the dead, fell into a trance, and either rode upon—or were transformed into—animals as they journeyed in spirit to join the Wild Hunt, the procession of departed spirits led by the old Pagan Lord and Lady of the Otherworld.

When Italian countryfolk left their bodies at night in a dream or trance state and rode forth to wage nocturnal battles against evil spirits who might attempt to blight their crops, they were mounted upon a veritable menagerie of livestock: boars, dogs, hares, pigs, and roosters. In Sicily and southern Italy, sheep were preferred. The Sicilian women who followed the "ladies from outside" rode mounted upon castrated rams.

Dogs play the most important role among the animals. When Robert Cochrane drew the magic circle for his ceremonies, he invoked the hounds of the Wild Hunt to come and surround his circle, guarding it against the intrusion of any unwelcome spirits. There is an old legend from Cornwall about a fellow named Dando whose dogs were stolen by the leader of the Wild Hunt—as was Dando himself. They became known as "Dando and his Dogs," or sometimes as "the Devil and his Dandy Dogs." It is quite likely that it was these dogs in particular that Cochrane had in mind when he summoned the dogs of the Wild Hunt as his guardians.

Regarding the importance of animals in the witchcraft trials generally, and the transformation of witches into animals during their shamanic journeys, the Italian historian Carlo Ginzburg remarks: "Metamorphoses, cavalcades, ecstasies, followed by the egress of the soul in the shape of an animal—these are different paths to a single goal. Between animals and souls, animals and the dead, animals and the beyond, there exists a profound connection."[109]

It is time now to summarize what we have learned about the Wild Hunt.

Sometimes the doorways between our world and the Otherworld stand open. In medieval times, such interfaces were attributed to Thursdays, the Ember Days between Christmas and Epiphany, and, at least in Celtic countries, to Samhain or Halloween. The spirits of the dead or the "fairy folk" rode forth as a Wild Hunt, sometimes led by the Goddess herself, and at other times by her mate, who was called by many names, and most of them were used by Cochrane at one time or another: Gwyn ap Nudd, Herne the Hunter, Odin, or King Arthur. (Of course, Cochrane considered all of them to be aspects of Tubal Cain in one way or another.)

Mounted on various wild animals, the spirit members of the Wild Hunt raced through the night and entered the houses of the living. What they sought was meat and drink, for the dead, who feast eternally in the Otherworld, have insatiable appetites. Medieval people believed that if the riders of the Wild Hunt remained unsatisfied, they could be treacherous and even cause property damage. Thus, it was best to honor them by referring to them as "the good people" or "the good neighbors," whose leader was the "good mistress"; one should set a table for them and keep the room clean and well-swept.

Setting forth food and drink for the dead was a practice that the Church condemned and tried to eradicate, but worse still was the ability of some peasants, especially women, to actually join in the Wild Hunt. These individuals would enter a shamanic trance and travel forth "in spirit," leaving their bodies behind and passing through locked doorways in the process. They would fly through the air with the hosts of the dead, perhaps to accompany them in their quest for food and drink, dance with them beneath a Fairy Tree, or to join with their ancestors in taking up arms against the wrathful dead who might seek to harm their village communities.

---

109 Ginzburg, Carlo, *Ecstasies: Deciphering the Witches' Sabbath* (Pantheon, 1991) p. 263.

Those who possessed magical abilities acquired knowledge of their talents through an initiatory experience. A man you had known all your life might come to your house beating on a spirit drum or approach you on a dark country road. You might hear and see spirits calling you to a mystical vocation. The goal of the initiatory process was to acquire the ability to undertake the trance journey common to all shamans, and hence to interface with the Otherworld, the original source of wisdom and abundance. Those who possessed such shamanic abilities, and who continued to revere the Lord and Lady of the old Pagan Otherworld, were often accused of witchcraft.

Shamanism is remarkably persistent. It has its roots in the religious experiences of prehistoric humanity. These religious experiences were carried from its original home (which was possibly, but not certainly, in Siberia) to Europe, Asia, the Americas, and even the islands of the Pacific. Different mythologies came and went throughout the course of human history, but shamanism remained essentially the same. Capable of endless adaptation and variation, its core experience was easily assimilated into any number of religions.

In Europe, the earth-centered ancestral cult of the Neolithic was replaced by the sky-centered mythologies of the Indo-European peoples, which were in turn replaced by Christianity. Shamanism survived them all and was still alive and well during the witch trials of the Renaissance and Reformation. Those who affirm that the Diana of the witch trials is, in fact, an ancient goddess are clearly correct; under other names, she was Queen of the Otherworld and Lady of Abundance.

Though most people were content simply to take part in the festivals and perhaps set a table for the dead, there were others who acted as community shamans, though the word itself would have been foreign to them. When the doors between the worlds opened, these individuals went into a trance and left their bodies. They rode with the fairies and traveled with the Wild Hunt.

Some who possessed great natural talent simply fell into a trance, while others probably used fly agaric mushrooms or belladonna to assist them in their journeys. In vision, they rode a broomstick or spirit horse to the Otherworld. Some of them took the shapes of animals, and indeed, many such individuals kept household pets of various types, their "familiars" who assisted them in their journeys.

The Wild Hunt itself was not unlike a folk festival. There was dancing and feasting aplenty on those astral journeys, and witches often went with the dead to visit houses throughout the village, taking part with the good folk in their spirit feasts. And when they returned to their bodies, they brought back a special kind of knowledge—the same knowledge sought by shamans everywhere, in all cultures.

They learned about the fate of the dead, and thus were able to comfort relations still living, letting them know their departed loved ones were happy in the Otherworld, or, if the need arose, instructing them as to how they might serve their dead and better their condition. Even during times when the doors to the Otherworld were not fully open, the village shaman or witch could "scry" into that world by gazing into a bowl of water, imitating the Norns who peered eternally into the Well of Memory. By so doing, they could keep informed about events in the Otherworld and thus serve the community as a whole.

To serve the dead was to serve the living. Medieval Europeans believed in a symbiosis between this world and the Otherworld that necessitated caring for both worlds at once. The harvest upon which all villagers depended was itself dependent upon activities in the Otherworld, where the Master and Mistress of Earth and Animals had their dwelling. The witches served the living directly, too, for useful knowledge such as herblore was given to them during their astral journeys.

What heals may, of course, also harm. Shamanic talent does not necessarily imply goodness or wholeness of heart, and some individuals almost certainly used their knowledge and abilities to inflict illness, blight an enemy's crops, and so on. But there were groups, like the Italian *benandanti* or "good walkers" who traveled the astral worlds at night and protected their villages from malign influences, to help one deal with such problems.

And so it went for centuries. This syncretistic blend of Christianity and Pagan shamanism persisted from the beginnings of Christian missionary work in Europe (c. 400 CE) until the close of the Middle Ages (c. 1400). As Europe became more densely settled and urbanized, the old shamanic practices lost their hold on many people, especially those who lived in cities. The old ways survived most powerfully in the isolated parts of Europe: the wild mountain reaches of the Alps and the Pyrenees.

The Church looked the other way; it could easily dismiss astral participation in the Wild Hunt as a collective dream or fantasy, a mere hallucination, and though there were a few isolated trials for *maleficium* or sorcery, there were very few instances in which the old folk beliefs were persecuted until after 1400.

The witches revered a figure whom the judges identified as the Devil, but who bears many of the symbolic attributes of the Underworld Lord. He frequently appeared in animal disguise and had blazing eyes, and his sabbats bore a strong resemblance to the hunting festivals and folk rituals celebrated in honor of the Otherworld Lord and Animal Master.

Robert Cochrane recognized a number of individuals in European folklore who, at one time and place or another, were regarded as leaders of the Wild Hunt. Though all of them, at a certain level, were incarnations of Tubal Cain, they all had their special myths and stories.

CHAPTER EIGHT

THE WILD HUNTERS

THERE ARE MANY FIGURES, mythic and magical, who were regarded as leaders of the Wild Hunt. In England, King Arthur was popular, as he was in the French province of Brittany, which had always had strong Celtic links with Britain.

Odin seems to have been a common figure all over northern Europe, especially in Scandinavia. Germany also acknowledged a number of goddess figures, including Mother Holda and Perchta or Bertha, while England was rich in the variety of its Wild Hunt leaders. Not only was King Arthur common there, but a figure known as Herne the Hunter, the Welsh Underworld Lord Gwyn ap Nudd, and a Saxon rebel called Wild Edric also were. Even Lady Godiva found her place in British folklore as a goddess who led the Wild Hunt. On the island of Guernsey, the Biblical Herodias, the wife of the evil King Herod, transformed into a witch goddess who led the Wild Hunt. (Her name is probably rendered in Italian dialect as Aradia.) Diana was popular in Italy as well.

True to his eclectic vision—which has been criticized for its inconsistencies by some, while acclaimed for its creativity by others—Cochrane made use of many of these traditional leaders of the Wild Hunt. But he also chose some of his own candidates for the leadership of the Wild Hunt, as we shall see.

 125

TRADITIONAL FIGURES

Odin

Odin was often named as the leader of the Wild Hunt. He was a special favorite of Robert Cochrane, who called himself "Od's man" or "Odin's man," and who felt a powerful affinity with the old Norse deity who hung, like a shaman, on the World Tree for nine days and nights to gain esoteric knowledge of the runes.

Odin's shamanic quest to gain the knowledge of the runes is described in the poem entitled "Havamal," which is included in the collection commonly known as the *Elder Edda* or *Poetic Edda*:

> *I know that I hung on a wind-battered tree*
> *nine long nights,*
> *pierced by a spear*
> *and given to Odin,*
> *myself to myself,*
> *on that tree*
> *whose roots grow in a place*
> *no one has ever seen.*
> *No one gave me food,*
> *no one gave me drink.*
> *At the end I peered down,*
> *I took the runes—*
> *screaming, I took them—*
> *and then I fell.*[110]

We have already encountered Odin (in Chapter Three) as one of the figures associated with the Castle of the North. We have spoken of this complex deity in his role of the eternal wanderer with his long white beard, one-eyed and dressed in a cloak of gray and carrying a staff. Where he wanders, magic happens. Having crossed the threshold of sacred knowledge, he can travel through all the worlds: the heavenly world of Asgard, where he lived among the gods, the human world of Middle Earth, and the dark Underworld ruled by the goddess Hel.

---

110 Crawford, trans., *The Poetic Edda, op. cit.,* pp. 42–3.

 126

In all the king of the Norse god's manifestations, we see Odin the Master of Wisdom, a god of knowledge, sorcery, poetry, and healing.

Worshiped in many northern lands, Odin was known in Old English as *Wōden*, Old Saxon as *Uuôden*, Old Dutch as *Wuodan*, Old Frisian as *Wêda*, Old High German as *Wuotan*, and Low German as *Wodan* (Richard Wagner renamed him *Wotan* for his *Ring of the Nibelungs* operas). All of these names are derived from a proto-Germanic word, *Wōðanaz*, which means "lord of frenzy" or "leader of the possessed." (The Viking warriors who were called "berserkers" and possessed by an insane frenzy during battle, which made their fighting so intense that few could stand against them, regarded Odin as their sacred patron.)

It is in this manifestation—his darker side as a god of death, war, and frenzy—that he acts as the leader of the Wild Hunt. His sacred residence in Asgard, the world of the gods, is Valhalla, where he receives half of all the warriors who die in battle (while sending the other half to the love goddess Freya). He is the lord of the Valkyries, the maidens who fly down to the bloody fields of battle on their magic horses to gather up the dead bodies of the slain—and the Valkyries are sometimes mentioned as riders in the Wild Hunt.

In Scandinavia, the Wild Hunt was known as *Oskoreia*, which appears to mean "the Asgard ride," for Asgard is the name of the world of the gods in Norse mythology. Those who ride in the Wild Hunt were known as *Oensjægeren* (Odin's Hunters). Odin's hunt was heard but rarely seen, and when it was heard, it portended either changing weather or war and unrest. The barking of dogs was frequently heard when the Wild Hunt passed by.

GWYN AP NUDD

Gwyn ap Nudd is a Welsh mythological figure, the king of the "fair folk" and ruler of the Welsh Otherworld, Annwn. His name means "Gwyn, son of Nudd." Gwyn is intimately associated with the Otherworld in medieval Welsh literature, as well as with the tradition of the Wild Hunt.

The Wild Hunt is led by Gwyn ap Nudd in the region around Glastonbury, once regarded as the most magical and sacred place in all of England (although now best known as the site of a relatively rowdy rock festival). He was known as the king of the "fair folk" and ruler of the Welsh Otherworld, Annwn, as he placed over the brood of devils in Annwn, lest they should destroy the present race. Gwyn is closely associated with the tradition of the Wild Hunt.

Gwyn ap Nudd may also lay claim to a place in the Oak King and Holly King mythos. In *Culhwch and Olwen*, a tale which was included in the Welsh mythological epic known as *The Mabinogion* by one of its first translators, Lady Charlotte Guest—and has remained in the collection of stories ever since—Gwyn is the lover of Creiddylad, the daughter of Lludd (and Goddess of the Land, in terms of the Oak King and Holly King myth).

Gwyn abducts Creiddylad from her betrothed, Gwythyr ap Greidawl (the Oak King). In retaliation, Gwythyr raises a great host against Gwyn, leading to a fierce battle between the two. Gwyn is victorious (the Holly King wins) and, following the conflict, captures a number of Gwythyr's noblemen, including Nwython and his son Cyledr. Gwyn later murders Nwython and forces Cyledr to eat his father's heart. As a result of his torture at Gwyn's hands, Cyledr goes mad.

After the intervention of Arthur, Gwyn and Gwythr agree to fight for Creiddylad every May Day until Judgment Day. The warrior who is victorious on this final day will at last take the maiden. According to *Culhwch and Olwen*, Gwyn became the ruler of the Otherworld.

Gwyn ap Nudd is a psychopomp, a conductor of souls from one world to another (in this case, the Otherworld). In later tradition, he is one of the best-known leaders of the Wild Hunt, in which he leads a pack of supernatural hounds known as the *Cŵn Annwn* to harvest human souls. In Welsh folklore, to hear the baying of Gwyn's hounds was a portent of imminent death in the family.

Over time, Gwyn's role would diminish, and, in later folklore, he was regarded as the king of the fairies of Welsh lore. According to the *Speculum Christiani*, a fourteenth-century manuscript against divination, Welsh soothsayers would invoke Gwyn's name before entering woodlands, proclaiming: "To the king of Spirits, and to his queen—Gwyn ap Nudd, you who are yonder in the forest, for love of your mate, permit us to enter your dwelling."[111] He appears in the medieval *Life of Saint Collen*,

---

111 Guest, Charlotte, trans., *The Mabinogion* (Global Grey, 2018) pp. 107–38.

in which he and his retinue are banished from Glastonbury Tor with the use of holy water.

Those who still reverence Glastonbury as a place of High Magick are unconvinced that Gwyn's alleged banishment was effective, and it is said that he and his hunters are still there.

ARTHUR

Whether or not the legendary monarch ever existed in reality has been debated for centuries. If there ever was such an individual, he was most likely a Romano-Celtic war leader who turned back the invading Anglo-Saxon tide at the Battle of Badon Hill somewhere around 500 or 550 CE.

But there are problems with the notion of a historical Arthur. Gildas's sixth-century work (*On the Ruin and Conquest of Britain*), written within living memory of Badon, mentions the battle but does not mention Arthur. Arthur is not mentioned in any surviving manuscript written between 400 and 820. It is in the *Historia Brittonum*, a ninth-century Latin work sometimes attributed to a Welsh cleric called Nennius, where we first find the name of King Arthur; here, he is credited with victory at the Battle of Badon Hill.

The other text that seems to support the case for Arthur's historical existence is the tenth-century *Annales Cambriae*, which also links Arthur with the Battle of Badon. The *Annales* dates this battle to 516–518, and also mentions the Battle of Camlann, in which Arthur and Medraut (Mordred) were both killed, dated to 537–539.

But the Arthur so beloved to the world of myth, legend, and fairytale to children and adults alike is another Arthur entirely. This Arthur first appears in Geoffrey of Monmouth's *History of the Kings of Britain,* completed c. 1138, which contains the first detailed narrative account of Arthur's life. Geoffrey introduces Arthur's father Uther Pendragon and his magician advisor Merlin. Arthur and his warriors (not yet a Round Table) conquer much of Europe before hearing word that Arthur's nephew Modredus (Mordred)—whom he had left in charge of Britain—has married his wife Guenhumara (Guinevere) and seized the throne. Arthur returns to Britain and defeats and kills Modredus on the river Camblan in Cornwall, but he is mortally wounded. He hands the crown to his kinsman Constantine and is taken to the isle of Avalon to be healed of his wounds, never to be seen again.

The popularity of Geoffrey's *History* gave rise to a significant number of new Arthurian works in continental Europe during the twelfth and thirteenth centuries, though much of this twelfth-century and later Arthurian literature centers less on Arthur than on other characters who have also become part of medieval myth—Lancelot and Guinevere, Galahad, Percival, Tristan, and Iseult among them.

Arthur's role in these works is the Arthur so beloved in our folklore—a wise, dignified, even-tempered monarch. It was the work of a French poet, Chrétien de Troyes, that had the greatest influence with regard to the development of Arthur's character and legend. Chrétien wrote five Arthurian romances between c.1170 and 1190. *Erec and Enide* and *Cligès* are tales of courtly love with Arthur's court as their backdrop, while *Yvain, the Knight of the Lion* features Yvain and Gawain in a supernatural adventure. However, the most significant works for the development of the Arthurian legend are *Lancelot, the Knight of the Cart*, which introduces Lancelot and his adulterous relationship with Guinevere, and *Perceval, the Story of the Grail*, which introduces the Holy Grail and the Fisher King.

Much of what came after Chrétien, in terms of the portrayal of Arthur and his world, was built upon the foundations he had laid. By introducing the theme of the Quest for the Holy Grail, Chretien created the story which Carl Jung regarded as the most significant mythic creation of the medieval era. Lancelot and his cuckolding of Arthur with Guinevere also became one of the classic motifs of the Arthurian legend.

The development of the medieval Arthurian cycle and the character of the "Arthur of romance" culminated in *Le Morte d'Arthur*, Thomas Malory's retelling of the entire legend in a single work in English in the late fifteenth century. Malory based his book on the various prior romance versions and appears to have aimed at creating a comprehensive and authoritative collection of Arthurian stories. Perhaps as a result of this, and the fact that *Le Morte d'Arthur* was one of the earliest printed books in England, published by William Caxton in 1485, most later Arthurian works are based upon Malory's.

And yet there was another Arthur altogether: the Arthur who appears in early Welsh poems which are only marginally Christianized, and which appear to have been of paramount importance to Cochrane's vision of Arthur.

Several poems attributed to Taliesin, a poet said to have lived in the sixth century (although the poems as we have them now probably date from between the eighth and twelfth centuries), also refer to Arthur. For our purposes, the most important of the Taliesin poems is *Preiddeu Annwn* (*The Spoils of Annwn*), which recounts an expedition of Arthur to the Otherworld. This poem was studied by Cochrane in great detail and appears to have been the source of some of his ideas; we, too, shall examine this work in detail later on. The Welsh prose tale *Culhwch and Olwen* (c. 1100) tells of Arthur helping his kinsman Culhwch win the hand of Olwen, daughter of Ysbaddaden Chief-Giant, by completing a series of apparently impossible tasks, including the hunt for the great semi-divine boar Twrch Trwyth. Finally, Arthur is mentioned numerous times in the Welsh Triads, a collection of short summaries of Welsh tradition and legend. The earliest versions of these stories are usually agreed to refer to ancient Welsh traditions.

While the Welsh material introduces us to an older and clearly more Pagan Arthur, it still does not tell us why the lord of chivalrous, idyllic Camelot is accounted as a leader of the furious and chaotic Wild Hunt. But Arthur is not altogether of this world; rather, he is a Walker Between the Worlds who has just as much stake in the world of the dead as in the world of the living; a common mythological motif claims that Arthur lives on in an Otherworld to which he was transported by Morgan le Fay and will someday return to the people of Britain. The possibility of Arthur's return is first mentioned by William of Malmesbury in 1125, who writes that Arthur's grave is nowhere to be seen and that legend claims that he will return. This belief in Arthur's eventual return was a powerful aspect of the Arthurian legend through the medieval period and beyond.

A number of locations were suggested for Arthur's actual return. The earliest-recorded suggestion was Avalon, which is associated with

Glastonbury.[112] Geoffrey of Monmouth asserted that Arthur "was mortally wounded" at Camlann but was then carried "to the Isle of Avalon to be cured of his wounds." The assertion that he would at some point be cured and return from Avalon was made explicit in Geoffrey's later *Life of Merlin*. Another tradition held that Arthur was awaiting

---

112 Glastonbury is considered the most sacred place in England. The legend that Joseph of Arimathea brought certain holy relics to Glastonbury was introduced by the French poet Robert de Boron in his thirteenth-century version of the Grail story. De Boron's account relates how Joseph captured Jesus's blood in a cup (the "Holy Grail") and took it with him when he sailed to Britain. On disembarking, he stuck his staff into the ground, and it flowered miraculously into the Glastonbury Thorn (also called Holy Thorn). The original Holy Thorn was a center of pilgrimage in the Middle Ages, but was chopped down during the English Civil War. A replacement thorn was planted in the twentieth century on Wearyall Hill. The Wearyall Hill Holy Thorn was vandalized in 2010 and all its branches were chopped off. It now appears to be dead, and a new sapling has been planted nearby. Today, Glastonbury Abbey presents itself as "traditionally the oldest above-ground Christian church in the world," which, according to the legend, was built at Joseph's behest to house the Holy Grail. The legend also says that Jesus, as a child, had visited Glastonbury with Joseph of Arimathea. This was the subject of William Blake's famous hymn, "Jerusalem":

> *And did those feet in ancient time*
> *Walk upon Englands mountains green:*
> *And was the holy Lamb of God,*
> *On Englands pleasant pastures seen!*
> *And did the Countenance Divine,*
> *Shine forth upon our clouded hills?*
> *And was Jerusalem builded here,*
> *Among these dark Satanic Mills?*
>
> *Bring me my Bow of burning gold:*
> *Bring me my arrows of desire:*
> *Bring me my Spear: O clouds unfold!*
> *Bring me my Chariot of fire!*

his return beneath some mountain or hill. Arthur is just as much a part of the Otherworld as he is of this one, and as such, he merits a claim to be the leader of the ancestral spirits and their Wild Hunt. As the leader of the Wild Hunt, Arthur was associated with the constellation called the Great Bear (the Big Dipper). This circumpolar star group was sometimes called "Arthur's Wagon" and regarded as the vehicle that enabled him to circle the pole star.

An alternative theory, which has gained only limited acceptance among scholars, derives the name Arthur from Arcturus, the brightest star in the constellation Boötes, near Ursa Major or the Great Bear.

I will not cease from Mental Fight,
Nor shall my sword sleep in my hand:
Till we have built Jerusalem,
In Englands green & pleasant Land.

In 1934, artist Katherine Maltwood suggested a landscape zodiac, a map of the stars on a gigantic scale, formed by features in the landscape such as roads, streams and field boundaries, could be found situated around Glastonbury. Glastonbury is also said to be the center of several ley lines.

In the summer of 1973, a friend and I paid a visit to an elderly woman whose name I shall not mention. She lived in a house which was actually on Glastonbury Tor, near the bottom of the hill. During the Second World War, she had worked as personal secretary to the well-known occultist Dion Fortune. During high tea, she told my friend and I a fair number of Glastonbury stories, including some that dealt with long ago days when Glastonbury had been an island. "Do you see that road down there?" she asked us. "That was once a river that was part of the watery surroundings of the island. At the right time and under the right circumstances, some can see it still." My friend and I were sitting side by side drinking tea. Our hostess stepped up behind us, firmly placing one hand upon my right shoulder and the other on my friend's left shoulder. As we gazed down at the road, our vision began to blur and fade. The landscape altered and changed before our very eyes. We agreed, later on, that both of us could see the exact same thing—the road replaced by a lake surrounding the Tor. When the lady removed her hands from our shoulders, the vision faded. We both agreed at that she had done it on purpose.

We have already encountered this constellation in Chapter Four as a celestial counterpart of Cain himself. Those who support the idea that Arthur is linked with Boötes point out that Latin *Arcturus* would have become *Art(h)ur* in Welsh.

At Cadbury Castle in Somerset, an old lane near the castle was called King Arthur's Lane and, even in the nineteenth century, the idea survived that on wild winter nights, the king and his hounds could be heard rushing along with it. And though we most naturally associate King Arthur with Britain, his legends were known throughout Europe, and he is shown as the leader of the Wild Hunt mounted on a ram in the cathedral of Otranto in Sicily.

HERNE THE HUNTER

Herne the Hunter has the distinction of making his first appearance in a Shakespearean play: in this case, a seemingly harmless comedy romp entitled *The Merry Wives of Windsor*. Herne shows up thusly:

> *There is an old tale goes, that Herne the Hunter*
> *(sometime a keeper here in Windsor Forest)*
> *Doth all the winter-time, at still midnight*
> *Walk round about an oak, with great ragg'd horns;*
> *And there he blasts the tree, and takes the cattle,*
> *And makes milch-kine yield blood, and shakes a chain*
> *In a most hideous and dreadful manner.*
> *You have heard of such a spirit, and well you know*
> *The superstitious idle-headed eld*
> *Receiv'd, and did deliver to our age*
> *This tale of Herne the Hunter for a truth.*[113]

Whether Shakespeare made it all up or he was repeating a legend already old and well-known is not clear. Jacob Grimm, master of Germanic folklore, was the first to suggest that Herne had once been thought of as the leader of the Wild Hunt. If, however, Herne was ever known as a leader of the Hunt, his range appears to have been very limited, since he

---

113 Shakespeare, William, *The Merry Wives of Windsor*, Act IV Scene 4.

is associated only with the Great Park in the British county of Berkshire and Windsor Forest, which is where Shakespeare places him.

We have met few leaders of the Wild Hunt who sprout a rack of antlers, and we shall not meet any more. The antlers are comparatively rare in the literature of the Wild Hunt, and it has even been suggested by skeptics that Shakespeare was appealing to the bawdy sense of humor common with Elizabethan audiences by giving his ghost the horns of a cuckold. In any case, tormenting cattle and rattling chains is also otherwise unknown among leaders of the Wild Hunt.

Cochrane, however, often seems to have called upon Herne and apparently agreed with Jacob Grimm. Other scholars have suggested that Herne, as well as other Wild Hunters, may be aspects of the Celtic god Cernunnos, whom we have met earlier in these pages. This idea is based largely on the possibility that Herne might be a linguistic cognate of *Cerne,* much as the English word "horn" is a linguistic cognate of the Latin *cornu.* The always-influential Margaret Murray also suggested that Herne and Cernunnos are one and the same. One problem with this interpretation is that the name Cernunnos is found only on the European continent, never in Britain, and in Britain Herne's activities are strictly limited to Berkshire and Windsor Forest.

Nevertheless, in the twentieth century, a number of sightings of Herne were reported in Windsor Forest and those who encountered him reported hearing the barking of hounds and the sound of a horn, as would be consistent with a leader of the Wild Hunt.

COCHRANE'S COHORTS

While Cochrane made abundant use of well-known and traditional leaders of the Wild Hunt in his rituals as mentioned above, he also exercised his usual talent for inventiveness and originality, naming a number of figures as leaders of the Wild Hunt who, outside of Cochrane's personal vision, do not seem to have played that role in folklore.

Brân

Brân, a mythological king of Britain and a truly gigantic individual, is usually known as Brân the Blessed, though his full Welsh name, Bendigeidfran, literally means "blessed crow." He appears in several of the *Welsh Triads,* but the most detailed account of his life brings us back to the *Mabinogion* (clearly one of Cochrane's favorite texts), this time to the Second Branch, entitled *Branwen ferch Llŷr* (*Branwen Daughter of Llyr*).

The Irish king Matholwch sailed to Britain to speak with Brân the Blessed and ask for the hand of his sister Branwen in marriage, thus forging an alliance between the two islands. Brân agreed to Matholwch's request, but the marriage celebrations were cut short when Efnysien, a half-brother of Brân and Branwen, brutally mutilated Matholwch's horses, angry that his permission was not sought in regard to the marriage.

Matholwch's courtiers advised him to see this as a calculated insult from the Welsh and was persuaded to head back home in anger. The two kings met again, but during the meeting Matholwch expressed his feeling that Brân's compensation was too small. Brân could not stand for that, so he offered Matholwch a magic black cauldron that could bring the dead back to life, although they could not speak. Matholwch was astounded by this great gift and forgot all the unpleasantries that had come before. Matholwch and Branwen sailed back to Ireland to reign.

At first sight, the Irish loved their new queen, and in due time Branwen bore a son named Gwern and the realm rejoiced. A few years passed, and the counselors once more began to reflect on the maiming of the horses. They believed that Matholwch had not acted like a man and probed him to take out this injustice on his wife Branwen. The council made him expel her from his court and forced her to work in the kitchen. In the kitchen, she faced being bullied by the cook and stared at by the kitchen boys, who boxed her ears. This situation continued for three years; in that time, Branwen had been taming a starling to help take her mind off things. One day, she fastened a letter to the starling and sent it to her brother Brân, pleading for help. The bird succeeded in reaching Wales, and Brân felt despair, then fury from what he read. He declared war on the Irish to take revenge for the mistreatment of his sister.

Brân waded across the Irish Sea to rescue her, for he was so gigantic that no mere boat could hold him. Following him in ships were his brother Manawydan and a huge host of warriors. Matholwch's men told the Welsh invaders that they would atone for the injustice done to Branwen by declaring her son Gwern the heir to the throne. That alone did not satisfy Brân, so they offered to build him a house that would accommodate his massive body. But the house the Irish built was a trick.

They hid one hundred soldiers inside bags throughout the home and instructed them to jump out at the feast and kill the nearest Welshman. But along came Efnysien, who expected foul play.

He went around and crushed the skull of every man hidden inside a bag. Soon after, the great feast took place. Efnysien complained that Gwern had not greeted him. Then he grabbed the boy by his heels and cast him headfirst into the huge fire. Branwen, in a fit of madness, tried to leap into the fire, but Brân stopped her.

The Welsh had the advantage until the Irish brought out their secret weapon: the black cauldron that Brân had given them, which could bring the dead back to life. Efnysien, seeing the great trouble he had caused, decided upon one last act of valor. He hid himself among the bodies of the fallen Irish. When the cauldron attendants came along and threw him in, he spread his body out in all directions, shattering the cauldron but sacrificing himself in the process.

During the great fight, Brân took a fatal blow to the foot. Only seven men survived the conflict, among them Brân's brother Manawydan and the legendary bard Taliesin. As Brân lay on his deathbed, he told his men: "Cut my head off and take it to London. Eventually, you must bury it on the White Hill of London, turning my head towards France." Ceremonially, they cut off Brân's head and left Ireland. When Branwen returned to Wales, she died on the spot of a broken heart.

For seven years, the seven survivors stayed in Harlech, where they were entertained by Brân's head, which continued to speak. They later moved on to Gwales, where they lived for eighty years without perceiving the passing of time. Eventually, a warrior named Heilyn fab Gwyn opened the door of the hall facing Cornwall, and the sorrow of what had befallen them returned. They took the now silent head to the "White Hill" (thought to be the location where the Tower of London now stands), where they buried it facing France to ward off any invasion. There have been attempts in modern times to link the still-current practice of keeping ravens at the Tower of London under the care of a Yeoman Warder Ravenmaster with this story of Brân. As noted earlier, among Celtic languages, in Welsh *brân* means crow, and *bran* is the raven in both Cornish and Irish.

Several scholars have noted similarities between Brân the Blessed and the Fisher King, the keeper of the Holy Grail. The Fisher King has been dealt a mortal wound in the leg (Brân's wound was in his foot) but stays alive in his mystical castle due to the effects of the Grail, waiting to be healed. A later author who took up the story, Robert de Boron, wrote that the first Fisher King was a man called "Bron." The Welsh story *Peredur son of Efrawg* speaks of the hero visiting a mysterious castle. Although he does not find the Grail there, he finds a severed human head. Additionally, some works attribute to the Grail the power to restore the fallen, making it somewhat similar to Brân's cauldron.

THE GODDESS

In the records of the witch trials, many names of the Goddess appear as the leader of the Wild Hunt. In southern Germany, the goddess of the Wild Hunt was called Perchta, Bertha, or Berta, also known as "the bright one"; she was a huntress, an Animal Mother. According to Tyrolese poet Hans Vintler writing in c. 1410, she had "an iron nose," and in central Germany, her name was Holt, Holle, or Hulda ("the friendly one," who survived in the stories of the Brothers Grimm).[114] In those parts, she was essentially an agricultural goddess, and we may tentatively link her name with Hel, goddess of the Viking Underworld.

In France, she is Abundia (the Habonde or Habondia of Jean de Meung) or Satia, both of which mean "abundance"; in northern Italy, we meet her under the name of Richella, which means precisely the same thing. Christian preachers with a Latin education tended to identify her with Diana.

The Goddess and her consort reigned over the interior of the earth and the spirits of the dead. Their Otherworld realm was entered through particular mountains, like the Venusberg which figures so strongly in Wagner's opera *Tannhauser*, or through old Stone Age barrow mounds in the British Isles.

The spirits of the Otherworld—who are variously identified as elves, fairies, or simply as "the dead"—spent their time feasting eternally. They were fed from a cauldron or cup of abundance which was—and still is—the symbol of the Goddess.

The Goddess beneath the earth ruled all things associated with the earth. Many traditional peoples still regard the world as receiving its sustenance from a primordial force arising from beneath the surface

---

114 Johnson, *Witchcraft and the Shamanic Journey, op. cit.* p. 70.

of the earth. This power is the source of the crops, which is the single most important form of "abundance" for agricultural peoples. So the Goddess is responsible for both the growth of the crops and for worldly abundance—hence she was called Abundia or Richella. She is also responsible for the health and welfare of the animals, which, for meat-eating societies, constituted yet another form of abundance. One of her ancient titles was the Animal Mother or Mistress of the Animals.

As we have seen in Chapter Six, Cochrane himself claimed to have received a vision of the Divine Power, whom he perceived as a goddess called Truth, though the form in which she appeared—a naked woman with long shining hair who rode on horseback—more closely resembles the folkloric Lady Godiva.

PART III

RITUALS

CHAPTER NINE

THE POWER OF CEREMONY

Every ritual is a new beginning. It returns us to a time and place that is neither time nor place. Each time we draw the circle, a new world is made. Each word spoken is a poem, a song of joy, or a primal scream to the universe. Each participant is in communion with our essence, as we are in communion with theirs. Ritual is an essential component of all magic.

As anthropologist Victor Turner defined it, rituals bring to us an experience of transition. He called this transition "liminality." To participate in a liminal experience such as a ritual is to undergo a process of moving between two states; it is the time spent in that transitional zone when one is neither one nor the other but in the process of becoming. Liminality is the journey of transformation.

Carl Jung used the word "liminal" to describe that time in the process of individuation where you know you cannot go back to who you were but don't yet know what you are becoming. The first or pre-liminal stage is the stage in which we separate ourselves from ordinary reality. The second or middle stage is the liminal stage, the ritual, and the stage of transition; the third or post-liminal stage is one of re-integration into the community, but the reality to which we return is not reality as we knew it previously.

The liminal experience brings about a state which Turner calls *communitas*. Turner defines it as a relatively structureless society based on relations of equality and solidarity and thus opposed to the normative social structure. This is the social transformation which brings the participants in magical ritual into a special relationship with each other—a society, a coven, or a clan.

 143

THE SABBATS

We do have a few descriptions of Cochrane's sabbats. We know that he preferred to work outdoors, in nature, and that the members of the clan wore long black robes. It is also clear that Cochrane improvised many facets of his rituals, in contrast to the carefully outlined rituals in Gardner's *Book of Shadows* or the elaborate ceremonies of the Golden Dawn.

It is also clear that Cochrane possessed a magical personality, seemed full of occult energy, and was sometimes even a little bit scary. We have heard Marian Green, editor of *Quest Magazine,* assert that Cochrane's rituals were noisier, wilder, and more primitive than anything she had previously experienced. She described his energy as "raw and ancient," and claimed that he evoked visions of "things halfseen [sic] by firelight" as well as the presence of "elemental forces and the wild beings of the land, both visible and invisible,"[115] while occultist Bill Gray believed Cochrane had "real power" and appeared to be "transfigured" at times.[116]

The most detailed description of one of his sabbats, however, comes from the well-known writer and important figure in the twentieth-century revival of witchcraft, Doreen Valiente.[117]

Valiente writes of a Samhain sabbat held on the Sussex Downs. There was a fairly large crowd of people, though not all of them were regular coven members. Cochrane enjoyed inviting sympathetic people to attend the sabbats. He said that it was part of the old tradition to invite guests. A location had been chosen on the Downs where the clan thought they could celebrate safely.

They had all assembled at Doreen Valiente's flat in Brighton; most of them bedded down near there in sleeping bags, rather uncomfortably, when the sabbat was over. The clan went by car to the ritual site and parked their vehicles in a place they had previously scouted off the main road. Carrying lanterns and torches, they set off up a wooded hill to the higher part of the Downs. It was a long climb and a dark night, but they made it without trouble and set down their gear at the top of the hill—Cochrane always preferred to perform ceremonies on a hilltop. They wore their traditional black-hooded cloaks, and had brought their

---

115 Marian Green, quoted in Howard, *The Children of Cain, op. cit.,* p. 83.
116 Howard, *The Children of Cain, op. cit.*
117 Valiente, *The Rebirth of Witchcraft, op. cit.,* pp. 125–8.

ritual tools and a small cauldron. They had food, wine, and the materials to build a bonfire.

They lit incense in a censer and wafted it around the circle, which had to be of a wide circumference in order to accommodate the dance that had been planned. The circle was outlined with a ring of fine ash, which Cochrane had brought with him in a bag. Ash and soot were traditional materials to outline a witches' circle but could be supplemented with brushwood, as their only real purpose was to delineate the bounds of the circle. It was not the circle itself but its ritual consecration which gave the circle its power.

The four quarters of the circle were marked by candles, protected from the wind by their placement in lanterns. The scent of incense mingled with woodsmoke from the fire and the aroma of fallen leaves and the earth that the celebrants danced upon. Above, the stars shone intermittently through the clouds and the wind blew gently. Winter was already in the air. The witches were in a hollow to screen the fire from any watchful eyes; they could see no lights in the surrounding countryside. Valiente says that the modern world seemed to have faded away and left them in a sort of timelessness—a liminal state.

Cochrane's coven used ritual tools. These consisted mainly of a knife, a staff (or stang), a cord, a cup (preferably made of horn), and a stone. The stang had a forked top which represented the horns of the Horned God. The other end of it was pointed so that it could be stuck upright in the ground when a ritual was held outdoors. They raised the stang and placed the cauldron beside it to symbolize the Goddess. The cup was used at the full moon esbat to drink a ritual toast to the old Gods.

It was an important part of this ritual that the full moon should be reflected in the wine with which the cup was filled before the toast was drunk. To do this, the priestess held up a small mirror to reflect the moon's light into the cup while the coven paced nine times sunwise around her. Then, the priest stepped forward, with a lighted lantern in his left hand and the ritual knife in his right. He spoke ritualistic words to the priestess, to which she replied. Then he ritually sharpened the knife upon the stone, plunged it into the cup, and stirred the wine around three times with the blade. He took the knife out of the wine and splashed the drops to the four quarters. He kissed the priestess, drank from the cup, and then passed it sunwise round the circle to the rest of the coven. Another woman handed round the cakes on a platter.

Into the cauldron, they poured water and mingled it with wine and some scented herbs. Then, they put the cauldron by the fire to heat and steam. Valiente writes that the cauldron is a fitting emblem of the great mother of nature because, being a hollow vessel, it represents the womb, and it involves the four elements of life because it needs fire to heat it, water to fill it, and the products of earth (such as green herbs) to put in it, while its steam rises into the air.[118] It fulfilled a practical purpose as well—at the end of the rite, the fire could be ceremonially quenched with the contents of the cauldron.

They danced sunwise around the bonfire, slowly and purposefully, chanting as they went—slowly at first, for they all meant to conserve their strength and keep up the dance as long as they could. The dance they danced that Samhain night was called "The Mill" because it resembled the continuous grinding of an old millstone or the steady turning of the sails of a windmill, round and round until the corn was ground. They wanted the Old Religion to live and grow again, so they danced and ground out their magical intention as a mill grinds corn. But eventually, as excitement arose, they danced faster with loud shrieks and yells.

They did not feel alone upon those wild hills. Ancestral spirits from the past were with them, invisible but there. A kind of green fire seemed to be spreading and sparkling over the ground. Doreen Valiente remarks that she saw this phenomenon quite distinctly, whatever may have been the cause of it. Later, she recalled an account of the witches of Forfar, Scotland, in 1661, one of whom confessed that she had taken part in a witch-meeting in the old churchyard of Forfar at midnight, when, "[t]hey daunced togither, and the ground under them was all fyre flauchter."[119]

Eventually, they all fell exhausted to the ground and lay there, getting their collective breath back. There was nothing but the night and the silence, broken only by the soughing of the wind and crackling of the bonfire. They had raised power and they knew it. Satisfied, they distributed the food and drink they had brought with them. It was bread and cheese, cold meat, bottles of wine, apples, and small loaves with butter. It seemed to them a true feast, eaten round the bonfire under the stars. As the night wore on, it was time to go.

They ceremonially closed the circle and said farewell to the Old Gods. They gathered up their possessions, carefully extinguished the fire, and

---

118 Valiente, *The Rebirth of Witchcraft, op. cit.,* pp. 125–8.
119 *Ibid.*

made their way down the hill and through the dark woods. Before they reached the cars they removed their black hooded cloaks, hoping to look like star gazers or a group of nature observers by night. They returned to Valiente's home to sleep for what was left of the night and have a good breakfast before going their separate ways.

THE PRIESTLY MYSTERIES

During Cochrane's lifetime, the Clan of Tubal Cain practiced three major rituals in addition to the seasonal sabbats. These were the Cave and Cauldron, the Rose Beyond the Grave (also known as the Chapel of the Grave), and the Stone Stile, which was a prelude to a fourth ritual, the Castle of the Four Winds or Castle Perilous. Although Cochrane had composed the ritual of the Castle, he died before he had the opportunity to perform it; it was enacted only later. These four rituals, known collectively as the Priestly Mysteries, are performed separately from seasonal rituals and only by experienced members of the Clan.[120]

Cochrane, as we have seen, ardently believed that witchcraft contained a great deal of the knowledge of the ancient Mystery Schools. He divided the Mysteries into three categories: Men's Mysteries, Women's Mysteries, and Priestly Mysteries. His interpretation of those Mysteries was at least partly drawn from a Neolithic menhir in Brittany, upon which someone had carved images and magical sigils perhaps a few hundred years ago. The four rituals exemplify the wisdom of the Priestly Mysteries, and, at least in my own opinion, represent one of the most mystical, as well as one of the most universal, of all spiritual concepts: the cycle of death and rebirth.

It is here, in his final opus, that I personally feel the deepest and most powerful statement of Cochrane's world view and spiritual outlook is to be found. The imagery—the Three Fates and their cauldron, a single rose in an open grave, a skull decorated with roses, and a castle surrounded by beautiful flowers yet still containing a hint of danger—shows Cochrane at his most poetic. In the ritual cycle called "The Priestly Mysteries," Cochrane is at the height of his powers.[121]

---

120 Shani Oates, personal communication, April 2024.

121 The account of the four rituals given here can be found in Jones and Oates, *The Star Crossed Serpent I: Origins, op. cit.*

THE RITE OF THE CAVE AND CAULDRON

The symbolism of the Cave and Cauldron rite is a mixture of Celtic, Anglo-Saxon, and Norse mythology. This blend of ideas from different cultural heritage traditions was typical of Cochrane's thinking.[122]

The rite of the Cave and the Cauldron is founded in the mythos of the Three Fates, also known as the Three Norns (Old Norse) or the Three Sisters of Wyrd (Anglo-Saxon), emphasizing the prophetic role of women. The divinations in the ritual may be regarded as harbingers of the year ahead. The only male participant in the ritual is the Magister of the Clan, though male members may be present simply as the "congregation."

This ritual is optimally performed in an actual cave—Cochrane was an avid spelunker. The significance of caves as Otherworld gateways is encountered all over the world and in many different mythologies. For example, in India, caves are regarded as the birth canal of the goddess Kali. This well-known goddess has a less familiar ancestress from the *Rig Veda,* the earliest scripture in Sanskrit, and she is called Niritta. In the constellational calendar of the *nakshatras* or lunar mansions, Niritta occupies the Great Rift of the Milky Way, which is also the galactic center. Thus, a "cave" in the sky is yet another birth canal of the Goddess—as above, so below.

In this ritual, a central fire is inappropriate because it smokes up the cave (and therefore the participants), as well as harms the underground environment; hence, candles are used.

The perimeter of a circle is marked with ten to fifteen small stones which are either naturally white or have been whitened. The size of the circle is not important as long as the three women who represent the Sisters of Wyrd have room to move around the cauldron easily. Outside the inner circle, there is sufficient space for others within the gathering to pace the dance called the Mill.

---

122 Shani Oates, personal communication, September 2024. Though Cochrane's personal outlook may be described as a "Northern" path, in literal and historical terms there are no such things as cultural, racial, or ethnic purity. In reality, everything is a glorious mix, a layering over time of influences drawn from various things. Only fantasy constructs attempt to keep pure (and therefore false) lines of histories and ideals for themselves. Their perceptions are colored by desire or ignorance and are utterly removed from fact or reality.

Lots are drawn between all female members, including the Maid of the Clan, to portray the Sisters. After they are chosen and all the other members are standing outside the circle, the three Sisters of Wyrd will enter it. The first Sister carries the Sword; the second carries the Cup and a small cauldron or bowl, which she places in the center next to the cup. The third priestess carries a large flagon of spring water to pour into the cauldron, and a ladle which is placed beside it on the opposite side from the cup.

The Magister makes his address and challenge to the Sisters, asking them: "Who art thou? Who do you stand for?" and "By what right are you here?" The First Sister replies: "We three represent the daughters of the Goddess Night, born of the sacred union of the Sun King and Moon Queen, mated in the deepest of silence according to the Testament of the Old Covenant."

The Magister challenges them: "Name the three daughters of the Goddess Night whom you claim to represent." The Sisters answer, one by one, that their names are Wyrd, Weorthend, and Skuld, the three sisters who keep the cauldron.[123] They then declare, in unison: "In the name of the Goddess Night and her three daughters, we claim the right to serve the cauldron: one to stir, one to see, and one to tend it, as the Fates decree." The Magister recognizes their right to be present and to do their magical working.

Wyrd, the first sister, steps close to the cauldron and uses the sword's point to stir the water while declaring that, by joining the sword and the water, she re-enacts the union between the Sun King and Moon Queen, which gave birth to all events and things that have been, all that are of the present, and all that have yet to come. She speaks of the eternal movement of the Cauldron which births all creation; were it to cease, it would mean the death and the end to all things. In its swirlings, primal Chaos charges the water with the very spirit and essence of life.

Removing the sword from the cauldron, she hallows the cardinal points by flicking the few drops of water from the sword point, first while facing north, then east, then south and west. When she is finished, she moves silently aside to allow the second priestess to approach the cauldron.

Kneeling down, the second sister Weorthend, acting as Seeress, focuses the whole of her attention on the water in the cauldron until her instinct

---

123 These are the Anglo-Saxon names of the Three Norns; Cochrane preferred the native British terms when dealing with Northern traditions. The Old Norse names of the Sisters, as per the *Elder Edda*, are Urth, Verthandi, and Skuld.

tells her that the time has come for her sisters to begin a slow rhythmic chant, an incantation that carries the Seeress into a trance state. Meanwhile, the Magister silently leads the gathering in a slow, widdershins Mill; the only thing heard apart from the chant is the sound of feet. The participants keep pacing until the Seeress gets to her feet, no matter how long it takes for her to catch something of their *wyrd* or Fate from within the Cauldron.

When the Seeress is finished with her trance and the vision within the cauldron becomes clouded, she rises to her feet. The participants cease to dance the Mill. In silence, the Seeress takes up the cup, which serves as a signal for the third sister to approach the Cauldron and take up the ladle.

The third sister takes the cup, fills her ladle with water, and pours it into the cup. She replaces the ladle in the cauldron and turns to face the entrance of the cave. Holding the cup in both hands, she raises it above her head and invokes a blessing, beseeching wisdom to all true seekers within the covenant.

Lowering her cup, she takes a sip before offering it first to her two sisters, then to the Magister, and finally to all present. If the cup is emptied before everyone has tasted from it, she refills it without ceremony. If there is any water left over, it is returned to the Cauldron.

With this, the ritual of the Cave and the Cauldron is finished. A final blessing is given by the Maid of the Clan, whichever sister she has been fated to portray for this rite.

The gathering then leaves the cave, with the Seeress carrying the cauldron and being very careful not to spill any water, which must be poured into a bottle once outside the cave, as the water is now magically charged water and can be used in other rituals.

Finally, all the participants gather in a quiet place for a feast, even if it is a token one. This is done as close as possible to the ritual site and outside rather than in.

The Rose Beyond the Grave

This ritual focuses primarily upon preparation for the afterlife, leading to a rebirth among like souls, an important mythic theme in the Clan of Tubal Cain. The rose as a symbol of occult secrecy may be traced to Pagan Roman times. Today, in law as well as in politics, proceedings that are *sub rosa,* or "under the rose," are those held behind closed doors for the select few.

In the Clan of Tubal Cain, the rose is also associated with the grave. They picture a rose lying at the bottom of an open grave, a symbol of the belief that there is something yet to be revealed in the experiences that take place when we cross from life to death.

Cochrane asserted that there are as many Otherworlds as there are religions, each created by the collective consciousness of one's beliefs. The following meditation, as written by the Clan's former (late) Magister Evan John Jones, is helpful in understanding the symbolism of the Rose Beyond the Grave.

After the ferryman has brought you across the river at the edge of the Otherworld and has left you out standing on its further bank you see in front of you stretches a desolate plain covered by gnarled and stunted bushes. A Castle stands in the distance, perched on a rocky outcrop. As you begin to walk along the path threading its way across this barren landscape, the thorny bushes on either side of the path start to burst into life, first budding, then flowering. With gathering speed, more and more bushes burst into life as you walk along. By the end of your walk, the whole landscape is abloom—a rich carpet of blood-red flowers that encircle the Castle which rises imposingly above them.[124]

The rose at the bottom of the grave has been transformed into beautiful blooming bushes. This is the rose that blooms beyond the grave. The soul which has reached the end of its present mortal journey will then discover what the Clan of Tubal Cain believes to be hidden within the Spiral Castle of the Pale-Faced Goddess. The Castle surrounded by roses shows the wandering soul that there are secrets to be discovered here in the home of the Divine Creatrix. Though some of these secrets may first be revealed through shamanic trance rituals, there are new discoveries that occur only after death.

Another symbol which is relevant to the ritual is a chalice decorated with skulls and roses. The chalice represents the feminine side of the Old Faith, symbolized by the cup of wine carried by the Maid inside the ritual circle. When the Magister lowers the point of the knife into the horn cup or chalice, he is re-creating a sexual union. Transformed, the wine becomes the very essence of life itself. The Maid then offers every participant a sip

---

124 Jones and Oates, *The Star Crossed Serpent I: Origins, op. cit.*

of the wine, symbolically from the original Cauldron of Creation found within the Castle, where souls await rebirth.

The Maid with the cup represents the Goddess giving life to the body, but She who gives life also gives death. The skull on the cup is a symbol of this inescapable truth. In death, one may realize the promise represented by the rose as reincarnation blossoms for us once again.

The rose-skull chalice is often called the Poisoned Chalice. The same concept can be found in alchemy, where it is said that the poison of the primal dragon or basilisk contains the essence of the Philosopher's Stone, the bringer of eternal life. Links between the Craft and shamanism have existed since the earliest times. Both witches and shamans possess knowledge of herbs and plants, and shamans develop relationships with certain plants that induce non-ordinary levels of reality. Within European traditions, *Amanita muscaria* mushrooms, mandrake, and other psychotropic substances can be dangerous.

The Rose Beyond the Grave is an attempt to understand and somewhat experience the mysteries of the afterlife. Cochrane asserted that there are as many Otherworlds as there are religions, each created by the collective consciousness of one's beliefs. Thus, witches create their own personal versions of the Otherworld, for after passing from this life they journey to a place formed by the collective belief and faith of the ancestors of their clan.[125] They cross a moat which leads to an island whereupon stands Caer Sidi, also known as the four-square Castle of the Rose, the underworld home of the Goddess.

The Poisoned Chalice is an entirely separate rite, though it can and has been used as a prelude to The Rose Beyond the Grave Rite and is connected with a practice known as the Perilous Seat. Those who experience this test choose a high and lonely place. They take their seat when the first evening stars begin to appear during the dark of the moon.

---

125 Although this may seem like a somewhat unusual idea to many, support for a variety of culturally defined Otherworlds can be found in many studies of near-death experiences. When Tibetan Buddhists take the road to the Otherworld, they experience visions of bodhisattvas and dakinis. In medieval Christian manuals for the dying, the road is inhabited by angels, demons, and so on, and similar visionary phenomena is still alive and well in the near-death experiences of those whose ancestors dwelt in medieval Europe. Cochrane appears to have been correct.

They are given a chalice containing a mixture of wine and a potentially poisonous entheogen which they must swallow in a single gulp.

The participant is left alone all night, then their comrades come at dawn to retrieve them. It is said that a person having undertaken it becomes either dead, mad, or inspired, and as Evan John Jones remarks, "[t]hat just about sums it up."[126]

The rite of the Poisoned Chalice encourages one to challenge the Fates in pursuit of knowledge. One's very soul is laid bare as the body attempts to deal with the effects of the toxin. Physical suffering in a ritual setting can gift the practitioner with knowledge, wisdom and, as the Clan of Tubal Cain believes, the gift of seeing beyond this world and into the next.

When Robert Cochrane designed this ritual, he was focused on death as the final transformation. While many (including the Hindu scriptures) will claim that one is reborn in accordance with one's conduct in previous lives, the Clan of Tubal Cain finds this teaching too simplistic, for it doesn't answer the question: "Why?" But if the soul evolves from unknowing to knowing, it accumulates gnosis through many lives until it unites with the Divine Intelligence. Thus, the journey ends where it began.

Those who have taken part in the ritual and lain in the cold damp earth of an open grave assert that the experience does not induce a state of spiritual perfection in which reincarnation becomes unnecessary. Instead, it creates a meaningful illusion of the experience that all of us shall face one day.

A site representing the "chapel," often simply an abandoned building, is chosen. The grave should be dug at the north end of an east-west line drawn through the center of the building. There should be enough room between the north wall and the grave for people to walk up to it and then step over it, and the grave need not be more than a foot to eighteen inches deep. If you are unable to find a ruined building, the ritual can be held in an open space with the walls symbolically marked.

The grave is oriented to an east-west axis, for only the living greet the rising Sun, while the souls of the dead go to the west. The western direction is connected with death in many traditions, from Hellenistic and Hindu astrology as well as among the Maya of Central America, for west is where the sun, symbolic of life itself, dips beneath the horizon and darkness takes over.

The participants build a small fire to the south of the grave, so that everyone must step over the grave when moving from the north to reach

---

126 Jones and Oates, *The Star Crossed Serpent I: Origins, op. cit.*

the fire and the ritual area. When they do so, they ritually leave all the trials and tribulations of mortal life behind them. They leave the northern quarter, ruled by the Old Hag, and enter the quarter of the Mother in the south, she who protects lost souls in search of peace and comfort.

The ritual officers are chosen by lot. The selection of officers is thus placed in the hands of Blind Fate; she takes those to whom she wishes to reveal her Mysteries. The drawing of the lots should be held a few days before the ritual so that the three assistants will have time to prepare certain items.

One assistant prepares a brush which is used to sprinkle the magically charged water that has been saved from the ritual of the Cave and the Cauldron. They collect a bundle of twigs and tie them at one end with natural hemp twine to form a handle, then trim the unbound ends to make them all one length. Ideally, the brush should be comprised of willow for mourning, birch for rebirth, and ash for the Horned God. If willow, birch, and ash don't grow naturally in your region, use whatever grows locally.

The servitors and officers should bring to the ritual site the lustration brush, a small glass or metal bowl, one red rose, a bottle of magically charged water saved from the Cave and Cauldron rite, a bottle of red wine, a chalice, enough bread for everyone to have a token piece, a small bag of salt wrapped up in a twist of paper, and wood for a small fire.

It is appropriate to begin the ritual just before midnight, when the tides of time and life are at their lowest ebb. The assistants would arrive about 11:30 p.m. or earlier. First, they build the fire and light it, then fill and set out the bowl of water. The brush, salt, and rose are placed near the fire, and the participants assemble on the northern side of the grave. The assistants walk around the east end of the grave to the fire, where the water, lustration brush, salt, and rose have been placed. One assistant takes the bowl of water while another takes the rose, while the third takes up the lustration brush. All three of them move to the near edge of the grave. The assistant carrying the bowl offers it to the one with the lustration brush, going down on one knee. That holder of the brush dips it into the water to hallow the grave and the northern quarter by sprinkling water and reciting an invocation composed of a few simple but succinct lines of inspirational poetry to sanctify the space in and around the grave. For example:

> *"With water from the Cauldron, I sanctify this grave and in doing*
> *so, though it stands empty, it is now symbolic of the Royal Cairn, the*

 154

empty mausoleum, and the symbolic dividing line between the world of the flesh and that of the spirit."

The assistant with the rose also bends a knee and presents it to the officiating officer as before, who then drops it in the open grave with the flower head pointing to the east, the "head" of the grave. Another simple invocation is spoken, describing the journey which the participants are about to experience, the hopes for its journeymen, and the needs for discretion concerning what they may witness there. Here is another example:

"By placing the rose in the grave, we express the mystery that is death as well as the secret of the grave and what lies beyond it in the final transformation. When each of you have crossed this grave, you have placed yourself under the rose, the symbol of secrecy. By doing this, you have pledged never to reveal what has been experienced to anyone not of this gathering. Anyone not willing to abide by this rule should leave now and go in peace. For those who stay and then break the pledge of the rose shall be cast out body and soul from this communion of the faithful. Should any participant not want to continue, he or she should leave now, before the rest of the group swear their assent by saying: This we know and this we accept. In the name of the rose, so be it sworn."

One by one, each person steps over the open grave to become part of the circle forming around the fire. When everyone has crossed over, the officiating officer hallows the three remaining directions. Cochrane did this in silence, but if anyone who wishes to perform this rite for themselves feels the need for words to be spoken aloud, create an appropriate invocation for each direction. For example, the officiating officer, accompanied by the assistants and moving to the east, which is dedicated to the Young Horn King, the Lord of the Fiery Dawn and son of the Morning Star, sprinkles a few drops of magically charged water and might say, silently or aloud:

"With this water, I hallow the East and the Young Horn King."

This process is repeated at the southern and western quarters, accordingly, making the following substitutions.

The south is dedicated to the Goddess of the Grain. Hers is the spirit which, in former times, was chased around the fields by the reapers until she was trapped in the last sheaf to be cut. She is the New that is birthed from the Old, and her quarter is hallowed with a few more drops of water sprinkled from the brush with the prayer of:

"With this water, I hallow South and the spirit of the Corn Goddess."

West is the quarter of the Old Lord of the Mound as Gwynn ap Nudd, Prince of the Welsh Underworld. It is through his realm that the timeless river of Lethe flows. The officer sprinkles more water and makes an invocation (this time preferably silently, as befits the Underworld Lord):

"With this water, I hallow West and the Old Lord of the Mound."

Finally, they bless the participants with a few more drops of water together with a benediction which should be expressed aloud:

"May She who stands before all things indescribable and incomprehensible through Her Grace and Charity fill us with the knowledge of Her ways and to fear not the life we have in this world, thus living it to the full. For what we do now will shape our coming lives. In the name of the Mother of all Creation, I give this blessing."

The actual experiences that form the purpose of this rite are strictly *sub rosa* (under the rose and secret). Cochrane's vision of the Goddess as Truth (in Chapter Six) has been seen by others who practiced this ritual. May you see Her too. Returning to your body after such a visionary experience, you will realize that the other members of the convocation are still trodding the widdershins Mill and that no one has stopped doing it. This dance will wind down of its own accord, typically leaving everyone quite drained.

The ceremony ends with the consecration of the bread and wine or "houzle," which is done with everyone facing the west. We dedicate this bread and wine to the spirit of the Castle, the home of all those souls who have departed within the Faith, awaiting rebirth. If the rite is led by a man and if the assistants are male, then the priest must choose a woman to help him consecrate the bread and wine. If one of the assistants is female, she should be the one chosen. If the officer is female, she must choose a male helper from the gathering—only a man and woman working together can consecrate the bread and wine. This may take the following form, by way of yet another example: the participants gather in a half-circle around the eastern side of the fire, facing west. The officer and the Maid stand west of the fire, also facing west. The Maid holds the bread on a platter while the priest sprinkles it with a bit of salt, saying:

"With this salt which symbolizes man's labor, I dedicate this food to the grace of our Lady who is before all things, the eternal and everlasting Goddess. May she fill us from within, increasing the knowledge of Her and Her wisdom as we partake of this food in Her presence."

Putting the platter to one side, the Maid holds out the cup for the priest to fill. When he has done this, she elevates the cup while he says:

"I dedicate this cup to our Lady and invoke the blessing of Her spirit and grace to flow into this wine and thus to all who partake of Her cup, imbibed with Her serene mystery."

The two of them stand close together while the Maid raises the cup again, high enough to allow the priest to pass his arms around the outside of hers. Then, grasping the hilt of the knife with both hands, he lowers its point into the wine. Taking up the platter of bread, he offers a piece to each person, saying:

"In the name of our Lady, eat and share Her bounty."

The Maid follows him with the cup until each person has eaten a piece of the bread, then offers them a sip of wine, saying:

"Partake of our Lady's grace, supped here in Her presence."

After all have been served, the officiants serve each other with the last of the bread and wine. Finally, the cup is refilled. The Maid stands facing west with the fire at her back and pours a final libation to the Lady of the Castle, declaring:

"To you, Lady, as Suzerain of the Castle wherein one day our souls will find rest, we pour this final libation. We pour it for the shades of those

of the Shadow Company.¹²⁷ May they be reborn once again into the Faith, as may we all. Lady, by your grace and charity, may it be so."

The wine is poured onto the ground very slowly, then the cup is turned over. If the Maid is one of the servitors or a member of the gathering, she must place the cup by the fire to indicate that she now reverts to her former status. If she is the presiding officer, she formally closes the ritual with another invocation:

"The rite is finished, the libation poured; time calls us to leave this sacred place, but not before I call down a final benediction upon you all. May our Lady and the Old Horned One serve and keep you. So Mote Ye."

In order to leave the circle, everyone must re-cross the grave in the north. The servitors stay behind and gather all the ritual implements, as well as douse the fire. Traditionally, the feast which follows this rite is held a short distance away from the site, around a second fire which has been lit for the occasion.

To anyone reading this rite, please change the wording to work it in a way that feels right for you. It is the pattern of the ritual that is important, not the precise words that are said.

THE STONE STILE

The ritual of the Stone Stile deals with the relationship between the practitioner and the energies within the earth itself, including the spirit paths we now know as ley lines which are centered around "prehistoric trackways, hilltops, streams and rivers, crossroads and ancient sites of ancestor worship."¹²⁸ The energetic fields within a landscape also include the spirits, faerie folk, and people who live there. The concept of ley lines was first enunciated by Alfred Watkins in his book *The Old Straight Track,* a favorite of Cochrane's.

---

127 The Shadow Company is one of many names for those who have passed over into the Otherworld but whose spirits remain close to us as guides, helpers, and advisors.

128 Jones and Oates, *Star Crossed Serpent I: Origins, op. cit.*

Cochrane asserted that all the old "clans" were comprised of three groups, each of which served as guardians of a specific sacred site. Cochrane wanted to restore the whole system in order to access the earth mysteries of ancient times. In the early 1960s, he was in search of a cave in which to conduct the rite of the Cave and the Cauldron, and needed to find an abandoned barn or other deserted structure while within a reasonable distance that could be worked on to resemble a ruined chapel with an open grave. The third site he sought consisted of a mound topped by a plateau upon which to establish the Castle and its rings.

Apart from the symbolism of caves as womb openings of the Great Earth Mother, there is also the Anglo-Saxon tradition of the three Wyrd Sisters, who make their home within a cave around their cauldron and spin the thread of a person's fate.[129] They end it by cutting the thread. The cauldron may be understood as a magical one where past, present, and future are one, always in movement and changing, the symbolic resting place of souls awaiting rebirth. When Fate wills it, such souls leave the cauldron and the Sisters once again weave the thread of that person's life, and once again they will cut it, and the souls return to their place of rest. If the Sisters could no longer perform their task, the sacred World Tree that unites the Underworld, Middle Earth, and Heaven would die. The movement of the Cauldron would cease, as would past, present, and future. Even the Gods would perish.

As the following ritual will demonstrate, when taking something from the cauldron after the rite, you can, in your mind's eye, link the action to the Mythos behind and central to it.

For twenty years after Robert Cochrane's death, Evan John Jones and Bill Gray climbed Newtimber Hill every summer to an oak tree where they had first cast a circle to commemorate his passing. Upon reaching the site, they added two fist-sized stones to a pile of stones. Their intention was to create a miniature royal cairn as a memorial to Cochrane, with a stone threshold that had to be crossed to enter it. After crossing the "stile," which was a small stone set in the ground to symbolically represent a full stile, they then returned to the oak tree and lit a candle and poured a

---

129 The Anglo-Saxon myth thus differs somewhat from the more familiar Norse tradition of the Three Norns whose home is at the base of the World Tree, Yggdrasil. The symbolism of caves as openings to the birth channel of the Divine Mother is, however, universal. In India, caves are regarded as entrances to the womb of the goddess Kali.

libation to "times past and absent friends." They then visited a small clump of holly; Bill Gray left a small token tied to a branch in remembrance of Cochrane.[130] Their last stop was the stump of an old oak, and there they held their token meal, finishing what was left of the wine after pouring a libation to the elemental spirits of the place.

Just as temples, megalithic circles, and other ancient holy places sanctified the earth energies upon which they were built, so one may follow another ancient tradition in which a place associated with a certain person can become a site of worship, a shrine to someone's memory.

The Castle of The Four Winds (Castle Perilous)

The Ritual of the Castle leads us to "the four-square castle of the winds" and its four elemental gates. As Cochrane wrote to Bill Gray:

> "This is purely a religious exercise, based upon an exceedingly ancient myth. It has to do with the structure and creation of the Ring. Like all witch religion, magic comes into it very strongly and it can be adapted for all purposes. With a slight alteration, it can become a purely magical symbol. Altered again, and it is the Gateway or Malkuth to the Mysteries of the Craft."[131]

Cochrane provides an illustration comprised of three concentric circles, optimally constructed as follows:

> "The River: (1) Water and wine, vinegar and salt.
>
> Death: (2) Willow for mourning. Birch for birth. From the end to the beginning, back to the end. The ash from these woods is usually used.
>
> Life: (3) Man's labour and his work.

---

130 This is yet another custom which may be called universal. The author used to visit an unexcavated Anasazi ruin in Bandelier National Monument, accessible only by an all-day hike. Members of some Native American tribes were accustomed to making pilgrimages to the ruins, where they hung offerings of sage, tobacco, and other items to the spirits of the ancestors.

131 Jones and Oates, *Star Crossed Serpent I: Origins, op. cit.*

The center is Avalon or to use the popular concept, Arianrhod's Castle. The centre is the Inner Plane of Qabbalism and the ring is altered to the purpose of the ritual so that it adapts to whatever form the energy invoked takes, but still remains within the Castle. It is basically four-sided, representing the elements in their original form of the winds. Again it becomes eight-aspected in the symbol of the white horse. Now around the Castle winds the River or Time. It is this that distinguishes us [witches] from the 'quick and the dead.' I suppose this is classically the river 'Lethe.' It is also the beginning of power and the distinguishing mark between a witch and a pagan, since a witch crosses the river and a pagan remains with the quick."[132]

The ash ring symbolizes death and sacrifice, which all of us must experience in order to cross the river. It is comprised of the ash of two woods. Salt is the ring of life and fire. It symbolizes the illusion of the flesh and the bitterness of life, as well as its necessity.

"That comprises the basic format of the ring. Like all witch symbols it leads to many other things. I leave these answers to your intuition. In the ring the witch paces widdershins, never deosil. This is in honour of the triple Hecate, the Goddess of Life, Death and Wisdom who is Queen of the Castle. It is also correct psychically.

Now for the implements. You will need:

KNIFE.
This is the masculine tree. It represents intellect, Will, and represents the actual search for wisdom, experience and knowledge. It is also Choice, Love physical and generosity, Victory and conflict. Also Courage. To that we add that the knife physically expresses the owner's soul, because at its dedication, part of the owner's personality and identity is instilled into the blade at the same time that it is magically charged. So when Cochrane ascribed these various qualities to the knife, they must also concern the soul and all the things we search for in this life.

---

132 Jones and Oates, *Star Crossed Serpent I: Origins, op. cit.*

The Noose.

This is the feminine tree and should have five and three knots with a noose at one end. Traditionally, it should also be comprised of many materials, but hemp will do. The five knots are the round of life. The three knots are the moon triad. It represents the feminine aspects of the knife, among other things. In terms of the Mythos, the five knots represent the "round of life" or the five points of the pentagram, here symbolizing five stages of development of a person's life. Those are birth, youth, maturity, old age, and finally death, which eventually leads to rebirth. The noose is the traditional sign of subjugation to Hekate as the End and Beginning of life, umbilical and a hangman's noose in one. It has many magical uses, most of which will come with intuition. One part of its use is to create induce intuition by hanging: obvious reason, to overcome the flesh à la Tantrics. This mystical experience was also induced by its use for self-flagellation by some of the more mystical witches.

Staff or Stang: The Horse.

It is the supreme implement. It represents the middle pillar Yggdrasill, the Ash at one end, the Rowan at the other. Its roots are Malkuth or the Gateway, that is physical experience, and at its top is the highest mystical experience. It should be forked at the top and bound at its base with iron. It is called the Gateway because it is phallic and presents Hermes the Guide, the Moon because it is the path to the mysteries, the foundation of wisdom and spiritual experience. It is Love because it is Beauty, the child of Wisdom (Horn Child). It is Death, the final transformation. In other words it is the single path of enlightenment. The Stang in our tradition equates with the 'World Tree' of archaic shamanism exampled around the world, as well as the Middle Pillar of the Qabbalists. It spans the range of spiritual existence from the Underworld to that of our own ('Middle Earth'), and beyond to the world of 'enlightened souls,' which is in fact the symbolic 'Castle' of the all-embracing primal spirit. Associations include the Greek god Hermes, who as guide between the worlds was manifest within the erect phallus and in the 'herm' posts strewn along the trackways, marking boundaries for travellers and pilgrims. The horns of the Stang signify the thighs of the 'Mother' ripe with Child; thus the stave itself becomes the umbilical cord linking the Earth Mother and the Old Horned God through Her son, the Young Horn King. Thus it is love, the union between male and female, attraction and counter-attraction that together generate beauty, the child of wisdom. To love is to find beauty, the art of giving, the joy of taking and above all, the pleasure of sharing. In an esoteric sense, the Stang also represents the Moon, symbol of the lunar mysteries, because by knowing, loving, and worshiping the Goddess as the foundation of all spiritual experience and wisdom, you can find the path of soul self-enlightenment that reaches far beyond the materialism of this world.

Finally, the Stang is death, the ultimate transformation, where the questions posed by all religions find at last their answers. Although many are convinced of the soul's survival, most traditional witches subscribe to the concept of reincarnation and probe deep into our innermost being to discover traces of our past lives. Having said this, remember that we must all face death alone, whether it leads to nothing or to a spiritual existence beyond the grave. We of Tubal Cain believe the oft-reincarnated soul will return eventually to the Source of all being.

The Cloak.

The Cloak represents the concealment of the mystery and Night the hider of Light. Also Humility and Charity which equals magical power. The cloak conceals us both literally and mystically. Worn in the circle it hides outward signs of rank and status. As all cats look the same in the dark, so should witches in the circle, so that to the outsider, all will look the same. There are no crowns in the Clan; only when the rite begins will the functions of the Maid, the Magister and other Officers be revealed. Thus the cloak also stands for humility.

In its mystic attributes the cloak represents the Goddess Night who cloaks the heavens with darkness, leaving only the tiny light from the witches' fire to show where Her Mysteries are being worked. Through working the Castle and kindred rites, we learn Her secrets under the cloak of darkness. It is not the Clan's way to advertise ourselves with outward signs, with visible ornamentation, for we know that we stand before the gods who see beneath the cloak."

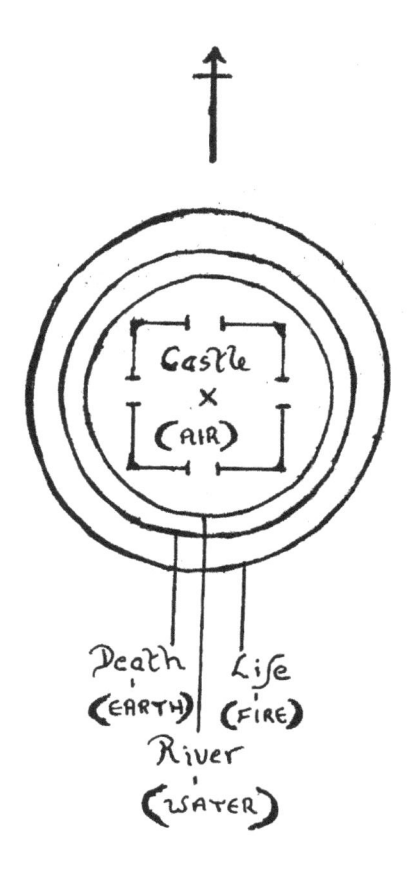

Illustration by Evan John Jones, in Star Crossed Serpent I: Origins

In the Ritual of the Castle and its mythos, a path to the Castle is described. Because the rite has to do with altering one's consciousness, it uses a spiral rather than a linear path, re-creating the spiral journey within.

The circle's outermost ring or moat, which represents human labour, is formed with salt, which symbolizes life and work.

By making the outer circle of salt, the ritual becomes consecrated to the Pale Faced Underworld Goddess.

The second circle is formed by the ashes of two woods, traditionally birch and willow. Willow is symbolically linked with sorrow and mourning, while birch, as one of the earliest trees to blossom in the year, represents rebirth. Together, they stand for death and rebirth. Though we can leave an imprint on this cycle which lives on in human memory, worldly power and glory are temporary at best. Only the immortal soul knows the reality of existence before and after the grave.

Greek mythology asserts that after death, we must cross Lethe, the river of forgetfulness, symbolized in the ritual by a mixture of water, wine, vinegar, and salt. All our memories of earthly life are washed away here. The wine represents the good things of life, all of our joys. The vinegar represents life's sorrows, bitterness, and disappointments. The salt is a symbol of our life's work, while the water cleanses and heals the soul that passes through it.

Cochrane believed it was important to choose the spiral path and prepare oneself for the afterlife while still inhabiting this physical body. Cochrane also taught that, in time, the soul will reach a state of spiritual awareness which makes it unnecessary to continue incarnating in a physical body and possible to return to the Source from whence it came.

Each individual soul acquires a little more spiritual awareness, understanding, and knowledge with each rebirth. Thus, at some point, certain souls will find themselves standing at the metaphoric crossroads.

The Ritual of the Castle focuses upon self-discovery rather than group consciousness. Those who undertake it open themselves to the forces commonly known as The Old Ones. The witch works alone, though as many as four may participate if the bond between them is strong and intimate.

This rite is best when performed outdoors. If this isn't possible, adaptations and allowances can be made for working indoors. One must bring some salt, a small bag of ashes from the burning of willow and birch twigs, plus a small plastic bottle filled with a fifty-fifty mixture of water, wine, vinegar, and salt. A cloak, knife, magnetic compass, and personal stang or staff will also be needed. Light can be provided by four candles in wind-proof jars or candle lanterns.

In the Ritual of the Castle, the compass is not laid out. Instead, each ring or moat is laid from inside its boundary. The candles are placed at the four cardinal points and lit last of all. Those who undertake this journey will walk the spiral path through life into death, and then beyond as they cross the River Lethe to the Spinning Castle of the Pale-Faced Goddess. When the witch leaves the Castle, the path of return re-establishes the power of the conscious mind within the earthly plane, hopefully the richer for it.

The ritual is very easy to perform. Each person begins by placing their stang/staff in the center of the circle. Either the Magister or one person only is elected to lay out the rings while the others follow, making the transition between the realms as they step through each ring towards the center, beginning at the outermost circle of salt, life and manifestation. When the rings are laid out, the words spoken can be very simple:

"With this salt, which represents my life, its labors and the work, I set the ring of life to the plane of earth."

Beginning at the northern marker, lay out a full circle of salt from the container, and be sure to stay inside it. This is the circle of life. Everyone steps back from it.

The next ring to be set is the circle of death, which is typically about ten to twelve inches in from the salt circle.

"With the ashes of willow and birch, signifying the mourning of death and rebirth from it, I separate myself from the circle of life, just as death severs life itself. Thus from the end to the beginning and back to the end shall time and experience run their course. Here I set the ring of death to the plane of the heavens."

Starting again in the north, lay out the circle of ash. Once again, everyone steps back.

Move towards the center, about ten to twelve inches once again, to set forth the final ring, representing the Lethe itself. Pour the wine and vinegar mix, full circle:

"Thus, the river has separated me from the plane of death and death itself, for I have advanced beyond the place of the quick to stand upon the threshold of the Void. I have trodden the path in spirit before, now purposefully, I do so in the flesh. Finally, I set the ring of time within the eternal Cosmos."

Now you may light your four candles, starting in the north and placing one at each compass point in the following order: north, south, east, and west, thus marking the four cardinal gateways of the compass. You can place white-painted stones or poles at each cardinal point to establish the image of the four-square castle. If more than one person is participating in the rite, all now gather around the central Stang, which symbolizes the *axis mundi*, which is linked to the Source from which all power originates.

In a sense, the stang has now become a horse upon which we may travel through the realms of the Unmanifest to the ultimate Source.

The Magister activates the compass by summoning the Four Winds at each cardinal point. The participants must now seek for their own connection with the Winds.

The method of working with the magical tools (the Knife, Noose, Stang, and Cloak) is an individual choice for each participant. Some people seek silent contemplation; others may prefer a chant. It is essential for each tool to be recognized as a major "key" before undertaking this ritual, a process which may require both study and meditation. A set of invocations could begin like this:

"I call on the Knife, the male in essence, intellect, will, and the search for wisdom, experience and knowledge."

It is good for the mind to become blank so that one may access the unconscious and clearly understand the meaning of the knife and symbolism: intellect, will, wisdom, and knowledge.

Treat the Noose in the same way, paying special attention to the meanings of the five and three knots, the round of life. Move on to the Stang and the Cloak. Pause and contemplate the essential purpose of this rite.

When all meditations are finished, dowse the candles and gather up everything, remaining in silence, then move toward the south (life) and directly across all three rings. Cross the Lethe once again and return through death to the circle of life and the world that was symbolically left behind when the ritual began.

The Ritual of the Castle of the Four Winds induces a profound and transformative experience for each individual, illuminating the path to the Spinning Castle. [133]

---

133 Excerpts concerning these four rituals reprinted with permission from Shani Oates.

CHAPTER TEN

DREAMS

Some readers, especially those who live in large cities, may be able to find a Traditional Witchcraft coven or association near you—other individuals with whom you can share the craft. But there will be many—those who live in small towns, rural regions, or simply in areas where such occult pastimes are neither practiced nor respected—who may find that they must make their own single and solitary journey down the crooked path.

For those who must practice alone, there are several guidelines:

Cochrane wrote that there were a number of stages by which one attained the true status of a traditional witch. The first such phase on his list was "Poetic Vision," which made use of the symbols and images that appear in our dreams. Next came "The Vision of Memory," in which the aspirant achieved memory of past lives.

Cochrane's next phase was only vaguely described as "Magical Vision," by which the student reached "certain levels." Then Cochrane steps clearly onto the path of mystical Gnosticism with "Religious Vision," in which the student experiences oneness with God, followed by "Mystical Vision," in which the union with God became deeper and more permanent.

Cochrane also worked with sigils, especially the Viking runes used as sigils, and he placed strong emphasis on the study of magical texts such as the Old Welsh poem *Preiddeu Annwn,* which is concerned with King Arthur's journey to the Otherworld and was allegedly written by the master bard Taliesin, and *The Song of Amergin,* a poem from the Irish mythological cycle which celebrates Amergin's shamanic experiences.

We have seen that Cochrane preferred to perform his magical workings in nature. The woods and the wilderness are an important factor in Traditional Witchcraft, and Cochrane was an early student of ley lines and power centers, which are now a common passion in many forms of occult study.

We shall begin our survey of exercises for solitary practitioners with the study of dreams.

REMEMBERING YOUR DREAMS

Some people say they never dream. This is not true. Everyone dreams, though some people lack recollection of their dreams so thoroughly that they believe they don't dream. But more commonly, I hear people say, "I know I have dreams every night, but I never remember anything about them."

For those who have trouble remembering their dreams, there are several things you can do. First of all, be sure to keep something to record your dreams right next to your bed. In the old days, this would have been a notebook and a pen or pencil, but at the present time, most people prefer to type the dream on a cell phone or speak into a digital voice recorder. It doesn't really matter what medium you use (although writing it down with pen and paper clearly has a stronger emotional impact).

In magic, words of power are commonly used, and you can create words of power here too, affirming and asserting that you will remember your dreams. Speak your words like a mantra while drifting off to sleep, but be very clear in stating your intention because magic words need to be perfectly constructed. Don't say, "I will remember my dreams," because the word "will" places the event in the future tense, and in the future is where it is likely to stay.

A better phrase for your magical intention would be, "tonight, I remember my dreams." You may have to repeat such a phrase for quite some time—maybe even months—as you fall asleep, but in time, your magical affirmation will reach your unconscious and the memories will come. When you awake from the dream, turn to your recording device (whether notebook, cell phone, or digital voice recorder) and make a record of the dream immediately.

When you have remembered and recorded an important dream, you will want to interpret it and understand its meaning. Here we must distinguish between two very different approaches to dreaming; I leave it to the reader to decide which outlook suits you best.

SHAMANIC DREAMING

The idea that a particular aspect of the human soul may depart from the body temporarily and go wandering in dreams is known throughout the world and extends deep into antiquity. In some Western occult traditions, this part of the soul is called the "subtle body" or "astral double," but here we shall call it "the dreaming soul." It may detach itself from the physical body and travel on its own. This is what shamans do when they undertake their spiritual journeys to the Otherworld. When the shaman's subtle body or "dreaming soul" departs from his physical body and "takes flight" to the spirit realm, it often takes on the nature of an animal, typically a bird, for birds are capable of flight.

In ancient India, the *Brhadaranyaka Upanishad* (c. 500 BCE) tells us that in sleep, the subtle body—in which the *atman* or permanent Self resides—detaches itself from the physical shell and wanders at will, flying like a spirit bird through a medial world between this one and the next. When finished, the bird returns to its nest, enfolds its wings, and slips into a dreamless sleep.[134]

The same concept can be found two thousand years later in a remote mountain region of Italy. During the sixteenth and seventeenth centuries, individuals who called themselves *benandanti* or "good walkers" make frequent appearances in the court records of the European witch trials. The *benandanti* claimed to travel out of their bodies while asleep, often taking the form of small animals such as mice, cats, rabbits, or butterflies.

During their dream journeys, their spirits rode into the sky upon various animals and traveled around the countryside, where they took part in battles with malevolent witches who threatened both their crops and their communities. Sometimes they also traveled to great feasts presided

---

134 *Brhadaranyaka Upanishad*, IV, iii, in Radhakrishnan, S., ed. and trans., *The Principal Upaniṣads*. (Humanity Books, 1992) pp. 257–61.

over by a woman called "the abbess," who sat on the edge of a well. They danced, ate, and drank with a procession of other spirits and animals.[135]

The beliefs of the Italian *benandanti* were part of a shamanic worldview which was once shared by many of our European ancestors. Because of its geographical isolation and Siberian-based language, Finland sustained this world view longer and to a greater degree than most other European countries, and, as we will see, their world view is an almost precise match for Mayan cosmovision in the Western hemisphere. The pre-Christian Finns recognized two separate souls: the body soul, called *löyly,* and the free soul, called *itse,* meaning "the self."

The body-soul or *löyly* was believed to be inextricably linked to the physical body; it came to us with the first breath of life, and after death it disappeared. In many of the Finno-Ugric languages, the body soul is related to words for "breathing," and is thus affiliated with the physical body. If the body soul left the body, the man died. The free soul, by contrast, could leave the body and return to it. This was believed to happen when a person was sleeping. It was important not to awaken a sleeping person suddenly; one had to be careful so that the free soul could return to the body in the right way. A shaman had the ability to leave the body at any chosen moment, using their free soul as their vehicle to make journeys to the upper or lower world.

The dreaming soul is still an important part of contemporary Mayan spirituality, and according to the Tzotzil Maya of San Lorenzo Zinacantán in Chiapas, to dream is to "see [in or with] one's soul." In the Tzotzil language, the soul is called the *ch'ulel,* and some say it is lodged in the back of the head, while others claim that it is in the heart. Though the *ch'ulel* is immortal, it can be shaken from the body by fear, sex, or magic. Some even say that if a person is awakened from sleep while the soul is still wandering, they may become nervous or "crazy" and must pay a visit to a shaman who will perform a ceremony to bring the soul back into the body.

Generally, however, it is part of the soul's natural activity to leave the body during sleep and "go for a walk." The dreaming soul, emerging from the body, may sit on the tip of its owner's nose and study the world all around it. Some say the soul is strongest when the body is strongest, around

---

135 Ginzburg, Carlo, *The Night Battles: Witchcraft and Agrarian Cults in the Sixteenth and Seventeenth Centuries* (Johns Hopkins Press, 1983).

the age of forty, though others believe that the soul grows in strength and majesty as we grow older and become elders, sages, and mentors.

The Kaqchikel Maya around Lake Atitlán agree with the Tzotzil that the soul is located either in the heart or the head, perhaps by your temples or in the back of the head. It is said that the dreaming soul departs from the body through the ears or the nose, and then flies away "like a dove." There are some who can hear the soul leave the body as they drift off to sleep; they can hear it returning as they wake. To many, it sounds like a gust of wind or a buzzing in one's ear. If you experience this phenomenon, you should cup your hand, blow into it, and place your hand beside your ear four times.

The K'iche' Maya of Momostenango, Guatemala, with whom I have studied for many years now, believe that a human being is born with two souls. One of these souls is known as the *uxlab*, though the Spanish word *anima* is often used to describe this aspect, since it is believed to be identical to what Catholic Christians perceive as the soul. It is vested in the body and in breathing. It remains within the body until the moment of death.

The second aspect of the soul, the dreaming soul, is called *uwach uq'ij*, which literally means "the face of their day." In Momostenango, the term *uwach uq'ij* refers to the energy template or imprint of the Mayan Calendar day upon which we are born. My *uwach uk'ij* is Imox: I have an Imox soul because I was born upon the day called Imox, and I share a common bond with all others born upon Imox. As with the word *uxlab*, the term *uwach uq'ij* is seldom heard in ordinary conversation. The K'iche' typically use the word *nawal* to describe this aspect of the soul. The term is borrowed from the word *nagual* in the central Mexican Nahuatl language. This is a word which may be familiar to many, largely through the writings of Carlos Castaneda, though the way it is used by the K'iche' is quite different.

Our *nawal* is our "day-sign soul," our spiritual essence, and our archetypal imprint. Here, as in the material from India and Finland, the dreaming soul is not merely a detached adjunct of the soul; it is the essence of the soul itself. This is the soul which dreams. The *anima* may be vested within the human body, but the *nawal* is not. It can roam freely through the astral world while we are asleep. It can travel to different places, towns, and sometimes even different worlds. In its travels, it may meet and interact with the wandering *nawales* of others, whether humans, animals, plants, or even minerals. From such interactions are our dreams fashioned and created.

For many people, the familiar landscapes of our daily lives may also become the scenes of our dreams. In the Western view of dreaming, these landscapes are fashioned from the mind's image-making faculties, but in the shamanic view of dreaming, we are actually visiting these familiar places—our dreaming souls can stroll down the streets of our hometown or take a jaunt through the countryside. The Italian *benandanti* roamed the fields surrounding their villages, searching for sorcerers who might attempt to blight the crops.

Even ordinary landscapes can be infused with magical qualities when they appear in dreams. Sacred places, filled with energy and power, are often discovered through dreams. Rigoberto Itzep Chanchavac, one of my Momostecan sources, says:

There is a process whereby people dream of a place and then go to the places they found in a dream. A person dreams of the place; they are feeling an attraction to the place, and they are drawn to that place. They go there to do ceremony. When the person arrives at such a place to do ceremony, they are confirming with firmness and resolution that there is power and wisdom there. All our current sacred sites were discovered in this same way.[136]

Spirits may use dreams to guide us to real, physical locations in our environment where healing plants or stones may be found. In Yucatán, healers are often taught by spirits who appear to them in dreams, telling them where to find specific healing herbs. The Yucatec healers assert with great certainty that the right herbs are to be found growing in the exact locations indicated by their dream teachers.

Of course, we all know that dreams often take place in imaginal landscapes rather than recognizable physical locations. According to the *Brhadaranyaka Upanishad,* it is the dreaming soul itself which creates these landscapes—or, more precisely, dreamscapes, acting as a creative artist in the dream world, fashioning people and places according to its own desire. But to the Maya, such locations are still quite real in their

---

136 Johnson, Kenneth and Anita Garr, *Jaguar Medicine: An Introduction to Mayan Healing Traditions* (Mystical Jaguar Productions, 2013) p. 108.

own way, though not to be found in any worldly landscape or upon any map. We do not create them. They simply exist in a different dimension, which in many ways is equivalent to what Western occultists describe as "the astral plane." The K'iche' still speak of visiting "other realms" associated with the ancestors, the spirits, or perhaps the ruling deities of the Calendar Day signs.

As with dreamscapes, so it is with the people we meet in our dreams. These are the dreaming souls of others. If you encounter a friend or neighbor in your dreams, you are in fact encountering the essential soul of that person. This is especially true if the individual in question appears in your dream with all semblance of reality, vivid, tangible, and clear.[137]

When you begin to remember and record your dreams, it is likely that the ones you recall first will be those which come in the earliest hours of the morning, just before you awaken for the day. These should be recorded in the greatest possible detail you remember, for our ancestors in Greece and Rome, as well as contemporary Indigenous societies, all agree that these dreams which occur just before the dawning are the most significant. During my own studies with Maya day keepers and shamans in Momostenango, Guatemala, this same point was repeated to me over and over again.

---

137 In former days, people seldom traveled beyond the region of their birth; if they were asleep, it was likely that their friends and neighbors were also asleep and their dreaming souls were wandering. The Italian *benandanti* vividly remembered meeting specific people from their own village on specific nights. But in our modern world, inhabited by digital nomads and other people who travel widely, what should an Englishman make, while dreaming at night, of meeting someone from Australia, where everyone should be awake? I posed this question to some of my Maya teachers in Momostenango and they had to ponder it a bit, for they, like the Italian *benandanti* some six hundred years earlier, seldom traveled widely or en-countered the dreaming souls of those who lived in different time zones. They all agreed, however, that we must surely be meeting the *nawales,* or dreaming souls of friends and acquaintances whom we encountered in dreams, and the most common point of agreement is that the linear time in which we live, here in this world, does not exist in the astral worlds of dreaming. Thus, it is possible for two people to meet with each other even though their physical bodies are asleep at different times.

MODERN PSYCHOLOGY

The modern psychological outlook on dreaming is quite different from the ancient shamanic approach. In the contemporary psychological approach, all the characters who inhabit our dreams are parts of our own self—some of whom remain largely unfamiliar to us, while others we know quite well. First of all, there is *you*, the person having the dream, the principal actor upon the stage: the dreamer.

Carl Jung believed that every human being was comprised of a polarity—a masculine and feminine side, much like the Chinese yin-yang. In this way of envisioning and interpreting our dreams, a woman who plays a powerful role in a man's dream is symbolic of his feminine side, what Jung would have called his *anima*. In the same way, a man who plays a powerful role in a woman's dream is symbolic of her masculine side, her *animus*.

One of the most potent archetypes in our dreams is the Shadow, who has recently become popular in New Age thinking as well as psychology. The Shadow is almost always the same gender as the dreamer and shows us our dark side. The behavior of the Shadow—which is usually atrocious—shows us the unknown darkness within us. When the gentle, bearded fellow who works at the health food store and is an expert in negotiating with other employees goes to sleep at night and dreams of himself in jack boots and armed with a machine gun, he is experiencing his Shadow, which carries within it all the anger, desire for power, and hatred for those he considers inferior—thoughts that he would never allow to enter his conscious mind during the day.

Learning to become friends with the Shadow is some of the most valuable dreamwork we can do, for we cannot fully know ourselves as long as we are ignorant of our darker side. And learning where the darkness comes from, how it was born, and how we drove it away from our conscious mind is the first step towards transforming the Shadow from an unacknowledged figure of darkness into a helper and perhaps even a friend.

When you have recorded a dream as a story, write down the images that occurred in the dream, one by one. Here is an example of the images that appeared in someone's dream: filming a Western movie, two teenaged Japanese girls (one of them about fourteen years of age and the other about sixteen), and a movie gunfight.

When listing the images associated with a dream, there are several important points to remember:

Record *all* the images, even if they don't seem important at the time. An important dream may include as many as fifteen or twenty images. I have chosen a very simple dream here, because this is only an example. Many of your dreams will include more than just a few images.

Write down your personal relationships to the images: for example, when the dreamer wrote "filming a Western movie," the associations were listed as follows: Hollywood (his hometown), Sam Peckinpah (his favorite Western director), family history (his mother's family was part of the Frontier West), and conflict (because the director was filming a gunfight).

There is an interesting question raised by the dream: what are two teenaged Japanese girls doing at the filming of a Western movie?

The associations you make with the images will give you the answers to all these questions.

Be careful to keep the associations personal because it's your dream, which, in this example, means keeping them close to the original image of a Western movie. In the past (though not so often anymore), psychotherapists used what we call "free association," which might run like this: filming a Western movie (the dreamer had always wanted to work in the film industry), his mother (who sometimes worked as an equestrian double for Western movies back in the 1940s), fear (because she was a harsh mother and often frightened him), and rage (because her anger caused him to rage against the world for some years).

See how far we have departed from the essential image? All the way from filming a Western to rage against the world. This is why you must keep the associations close to the image and not let them wander astray.

When you have collected all the images, you will find yourself confronted with a number of potential meanings: again, for "filming a Western movie," the dreamer ended up with Hollywood, Sam Peckinpah, family history, and conflict. Don't just leap on the simplest and most obvious possible meaning for an image. Reflect. Let the images linger in your mind, playing themselves out in your imagination over and over again. Sooner or later, something will "click" and you will experience a "eureka" moment. For the dreamer, the most powerful association with "filming a Western movie" turned out to be his mother's family history.

When you have examined all the images in your dream and each one of them has received the all-important "click" telling you that you have found the right meaning, you are ready to write down all the meanings of the dream images and move on to the next step: asking yourself where all these factors are active in your life right now and why. After answering this question successfully, you will be ready to continue to the important phase of interpretation.

In this case, the dreamer was undertaking a Master of Arts degree in Eastern Studies (which explained the presence of the two teenaged Japanese girls) because he was fascinated with meditation, Taoism, Zen, and so on. And yet, his own spiritual practice had always been linked with Pagan paths from the Western world, so he wondered whether there was some "conflict" (the gunfight) between his ancestral path and Eastern spiritual practices.

At times we may dream of archetypal figures—the Wise Old Man or Wisdom Crone, the hero, a monster, and so on. It can be valuable to explore these archetypes through the study of myth and folklore, but only up to a certain point. Archetypes are vast and stretch across history, appearing in many different world cultures, and traveling deep into the archetypal world can lead us far away from the personal element needed to interpret a dream with accuracy.

In this case, the dreamer recognized the Old West as an archetypal image of the United States—a cultural and historical archetype, if you will. But he held it close to himself personally by remembering that his own family had participated in that archetypal historical period, and it was close to him in a personal way just as his own studies of Celtic and Germanic myth had been—the powerful call of his own DNA.

The gunfight being filmed brought forth a "click" on the topic of "conflict," but he quickly realized that a movie conflict wasn't real—it was just an act, part of a fictional drama. The conflict he perceived between his Pagan world view and the very different world view of Eastern spirituality wasn't real.

There was nothing wrong with the Japanese girls—anima figures who symbolized his emotional attraction to Eastern spirituality—joining him to watch the filming of the movie. Any conflict between his enjoyment of Western and Eastern spiritual practices was only apparent. It wasn't real. He decided to continue with his investigations into both kinds of spirituality.

But it is not enough to simply *understand* a dream. Honoring the dream means transforming it from mere intellectual understanding into a personal ritual. It is said that when clients came to the office of Carl Jung's colleague Toni Wolff and announced with pride that they had successfully interpreted a dream, she told them to go away and not come back until they had done something about it.[138]

In this case, the dreamer lived in a village near Santa Fe, New Mexico, a region renowned for its fruit trees. It was spring and the cherry trees were blossoming. Cherry trees reminded him of Japan, so he gathered up a whole bag of cherry tree blossoms, borrowed a horse from a neighbor, and went riding on a remote trail which still resembled the Old West. As he rode down the trail, he scattered beautiful cherry blossoms everywhere. That was his own personal ritual to honor the dream.

---

138 Johnson, Robert, *Inner Work: Using Dreams and Active Imagination for Personal Growth* (HarperCollins, 1986) p. 100.

CHAPTER ELEVEN

PAST LIFE MEMORIES

ROBERT COCHRANE WENT SO FAR as to claim that no one could be a serious practitioner of the Craft unless they were in fact able to remember past lives, so this was clearly an important facet of the early Clan of Tubal Cain.

But what precisely did Cochrane believe was an accurate way to access information about past lives?

Today, regression hypnosis is one of the most popular ways for people to seek information about past lives. Cochrane would have been familiar with *The Search for Bridey Murphy,* a best-selling book in 1956. However, Cochrane's *Pentagram* article, which lists knowledge of previous incarnations as a necessity for the practitioner of Traditional Witchcraft, seems clear on the fact that this is something that aspirants must do for themselves, not something that is accomplished with the aid of a hypnotist.

At the present time, there are many who devote themselves to Tibetan Buddhist practices for remembering past lives. But Cochrane showed no interest in Tibet and never mentions it in his letters to Bill Gray or Joe Wilson.

Edgar Cayce first mentioned reincarnation in 1923 and had passed away in 1945, so it is possible that Cochrane was thinking that the gnosis-seeking individual must develop the ability to enter a trance state, as Cayce did, though certainly any such effort must include a helpful friend (for Edgar Cayce remembered nothing of his trance experiences after he awoke).

Reincarnation and the quest for knowledge of past lives had been around for quite some time in the Spiritualist community in Cochrane's day; his aunt remarked that she had once taken him to attend a meeting of the Society for Psychical Research. The methods used by Spiritualists are still being used today and are practiced by the seekers themselves.

First of all, there are dreams, the topic of the previous chapter in this book and a source that Cochrane lists as essential for the seeker of Traditional Witchcraft's gnosis. One ought to keep a dream journal to watch for patterns, for it is possible that we may experience past life memories while dreaming. Writing down your dreams can help you recognize recurring themes or dreams that feel more "real" to you. And though the term *déjà vu* may seem terribly hackneyed in the present moment, it is still important for those who seek memories of past lives to pay attention to the feeling that you've done something or been somewhere before.

Déjà vu happens because you're remembering something from your past, including memories that are buried quite deeply. Some of these memories may come from past lives. When you have experiences of *déjà vu,* document it and look at it now and again as you continue your search for past life memories. Maybe you're on vacation and feel like a certain location is extremely familiar, as if you've been there before.

People can be the same as locations—many of us have met someone who feels thoroughly familiar to us in quite an uncanny way, and this inexplicable sense of knowing and recognition may come from a past life.

Explore memories that simply don't fit in with your present life. Memories of previous incarnations may simply burst forth without our realizing what they are. When this happens, write down everything you remember so you can examine it in detail now and then. You could remember a gathering that never happened, or working at a job which you know perfectly well that you have never undertaken. Your fears can also constitute important memories. Are you afraid to swim or get in the water? Perhaps you drowned in an earlier lifetime. Your greatest fears and phobias are important guidelines to past incarnations.

Examine your passions or overwhelming interests in other cultures. Some people who have lingering memories from past lives have a deep interest in places where they used to live or things that they used to do. Sometimes you might even feel like you're meant to do something or you belong somewhere else. I once wrote a book about the spiritual practices of the Indigenous Maya in Central America. I did not make any strong past life connections with the book at that time because at that time I was in the habit of writing a book every year about the legend and lore of one culture or another. But the book about the Maya had an unexpected success and led to my being invited by Maya teachers to study with them in Guatemala. While my friend Anna and I were out on a walk with a well-known spiritual teacher in the K'iche' highlands, he turned to us and said, "in these times, the ancestors often return to us in different bodies, not in Mayan bodies—like you two."

It is also possible for experiences you had in a past life to cause difficulties or obstacles in the present. Your current struggles may have their source in a problem you had in a past life. Perhaps you struggle in relationships if you suffered from painful relationships in a prior lifetime. Maybe your leg hurts because you injured it in a previous life. Do you have a tendency to hoard food? Maybe you experienced starvation in a past life.

Sometimes it is possible to find independent verification of your past life. Research your memories. Check them against historical and genealogical records. Read books about the time period of historical figures who recur without any apparent reason in your memories. Try to verify names, dates, and locations if you can. Talk to people who know about the people and places you remember. If your prior lifetime was recent, you may be able to find people who knew you. You might be able to connect with people who are from the region or culture where you lived in the past. Historians and teachers may be able to help if you remember a past life that occurred a long time ago.

Visit the places that keep recurring in your past life memories. This can help you to verify what you remember. Often, visiting such a place will bring back more memories. While you're there, consult historical documents to see if you can back up your memories.

Beginning with the Spiritualist movement in the nineteenth century and continuing through current proponents of the New Age, a number of techniques have evolved that aim at past life recall. What follows is a mix of some of the most common practices.

Begin with meditation. Close your eyes and focus on your breathing. Try to clear your mind and imagination by regarding your thoughts as clouds floating across the sky. Watch them float out of sight until your mind is clear and you are focused on your breathing. You can also use a mantra to help you clear your mind.

When all is calm, mentally call out to those spiritual entities that surround you. You may know some of them already, even by name. In the New Age community, such entities are often called "spirit guides." Ask them to open up the doorway to the knowledge of all your previous lives. In Tibetan Buddhism, this storehouse of universal wisdom is called *alaya vijñana*, while in Hinduism, the repository of all the experiences of your past lives and the karma associated with them is called your *samhita karma*. In New Age thinking, the most common name for this treasure trove of all life experience is called the "Akashic Records," a term popularized by Edgar Cayce.

Ask permission from the guiding spirits to enter this storehouse, and when you feel that such permission has been granted, visualize a door in front of you. Open the door. More often than not, you will find yourself in a vast library with the shelves packed to overflowing with books, manuscripts, and so on. The treasure house of all your life experiences—all your *samhita karma*—resides on a plane of existence very different than our own, and it is not unusual for us to perceive it in individualistic ways, though the library seems to be the most common.

Begin with a question. You could simply ask, "who was I in my life previous to this one?" or, if you have reason to be focused on a particular incarnation in a particular time and place, you can ask about it specifically, as I might ask, "who was I and what did I do when I lived a life among the Maya?" You can also ask what lessons you are meant to learn in this life, or who you know presently whom you also knew in a past life. The possibilities are endless, but take care: your own imagination and ego can easily interfere with the answers you receive, giving you a series of mistaken information and false premises.

This is why one must be very rigorous in clearing the mind before you begin this exercise. Stay close to your feelings. If your ego is interfering with the knowledge you receive in the Akashic Records, you can sense it. True information is likely to feel airy and light, like a freshening breeze, while false information may very well feel heavy, cloying, and a bit uncomfortable. If you happen to be researching a lifetime for which you have already done historical research or visited some of the relevant locations, all the better.

When you have received the information you asked for, visualize yourself turning around, leaving the room, and closing the door.

After finishing this meditation, write down the results.

 182

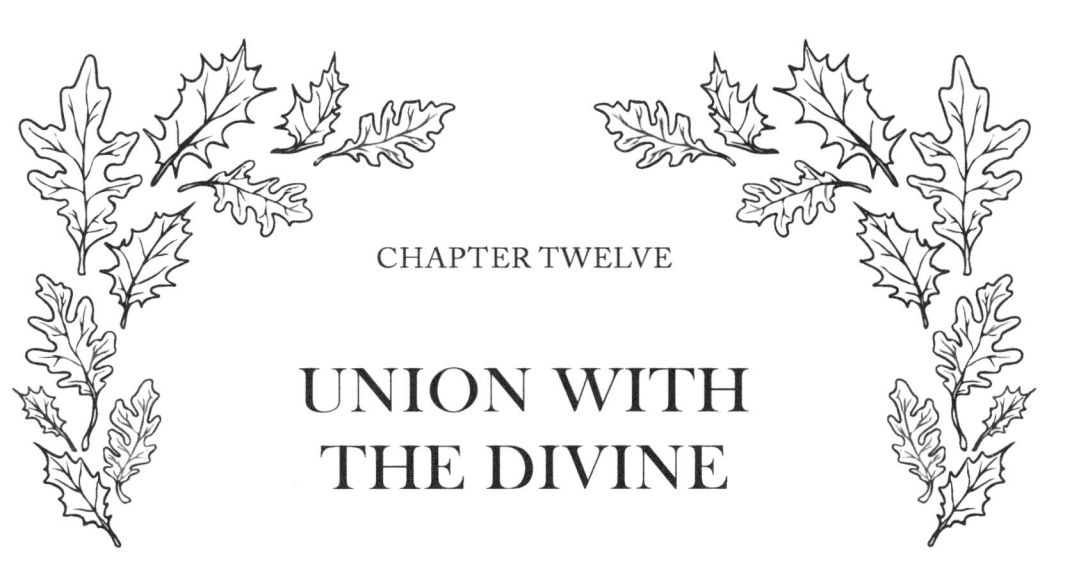

CHAPTER TWELVE

UNION WITH THE DIVINE

In his article "The Faith of the Wise," Cochrane named five stages of consciousness through which an aspirant must pass in order to attain the gnosis of Traditional Witchcraft. We have already discussed the first two stages. The first phase was "Poetic Vision," which made use of the symbols and images that appear in dreams. Then came "The Vision of Memory," in which the aspirant achieved memory of past lives.

The next three phases are only vaguely described, but they all seem to be bound together in the quest for union with the Divine. The first of the three was "Magical Vision," by which the student reached "certain levels"—though, unfortunately, Cochrane does not describe what these "levels" are. The next phase was "Religious Vision," in which the aspirant experiences oneness with God, followed by "Mystical Vision," in which the union with God becomes deeper and more permanent.

Some may be surprised that Cochrane used the word "God" to describe the Divine Intelligence at the heart of the universe. But let us remember that Cochrane always insisted it was entirely possible to be a traditional witch and a Christian at the same time, though as with all terms relating to organized religion, Cochrane used them either by comparison or by analogy for things with which people were familiar. They do not refer to the superficial rules and regulations of "conventional" practice in organized religions. His Clan teachings make his actual understanding very clear on these matters. People easily forget that a genuine spiritual tradition is more than what is known in the public. That is merely a drop in the ocean.[139] This is often referred to on the Clan's website as "dual practice."[140] It is also interesting to note that although Cochrane refers to God in a manner which is reminiscent of Christianity, his own perception of the Divine Intelligence took the form of a woman riding naked on horseback, and he said that her name was Truth.

But what techniques did Cochrane use to work the path of these last three phases and obtain union with the Divine? In our social milieu, we customarily think of union with the Divine as something achieved through meditation, which we customarily associate with Eastern paths of wisdom.

Robert Cochrane showed little or no interest in Hindu or Buddhist spiritual practices. Even Tibet, which had become very popular through the works of Helena Blavatsky, Alexandra David-Neel, and the publication of Evans-Wentz's translation of *The Tibetan Book of the Dead* by Carl Jung, seems to have held no interest for him, and Eastern spiritual practices are never mentioned in his letters to Bill Gray, Norman Gills, or Joe Wilson.

There are, however, Western techniques of meditation which fit in well with Cochrane's Western orientation. As I remarked in the beginning of this book, I am not a member of the current Clan of Tubal Cain, but simply a researcher in the field of mythology and magic. I certainly cannot assert that any of the meditations I describe below were used by him or by other early members. However, given the respect accorded to the Sufi writer Idries Shah (whose work Cochrane and his colleagues knew thanks to the ubiquitous influence of Robert Graves) and the common belief that mystical Islam played a large role in the development of traditional witch beliefs during the Middle Ages, I have felt it to be in the spirit of Cochrane's legacy to include a few Sufi meditations aimed at union with God, as well as two very important meditations from the hesychastic or Eastern Orthodox tradition of meditation.

One common meditation among Sufis and hesychasts alike is the repetition of a divine name. It establishes an inner connection with

---

139 Shani Oates, personal communication, April 2024.

140 A good example of dual practice can be found in an article by Ian Chambers, entitled "The Lady of the Rose Garden," on the Clan of Tubal Cain website, clanoftubalcain.org.uk/roselady.html. The author compares use of the so-called witch's cord with the rosary and Hindu *malas*.

the divine and results in bliss. In Sufism, the name for this type of mantra meditation is *zikr* (sometimes written as *dhikr*), which means "remembrance." The essential aspect of this practice is the continual remembrance of the Divine Intelligence. The names or phrases most commonly repeated are simply *Allah* (God), or *Allah hu* (God, only He), or *La ilaha illa 'llah* (There is no God but God).

The goal is to merge the name of the Divine with your heart. Eventually, the name lives within your heart and illuminates your entire being. The ideal practice of *zikr* should be to repeat the divine name constantly within your heart at all times. Those who lead busy lives may also practice this meditation simply by setting aside some time to sit in silence and repeat the *zikr*. Sit in any way that you please. There is no particular posture for Sufi meditation.

Usually, this practice is done while focusing on the solar plexus or on the spiritual heart, which takes us to the next practice.

HEART MEDITATION

This practice, which might be described as awareness of the heart, is yet another type of *zikr*.

For Hindu yogis, the heart chakra (*anahata chakra*) is in the center of the chest, under the sternum. But according to the Sufis, the spiritual heart is at the same place where the physical heart is (on the left).

Begin by gathering all your disparate energies, bringing them back from the outside world to their home within you. Still the mind and the senses so that you can directly experience the inner reality of the heart.

Focus your attention intensely at the place where the physical heart is located. Forget yourself and your worldly concerns. This state of inner absorption is regarded as a direct path to the Infinite.

Try to listen to your heart beating with the name of the Divine Intelligence that you have chosen to repeat. Keep your attention focused on the heart while cultivating feelings of love for the Divine. In time, one may begin to perceive the sound of the heart beating with the divine name even during the most ordinary instances of daily life.

This practice can be done seated or lying down, and the recommended length is at least half an hour. There are a number of ways that this meditation may be practiced.

PRAYER OF THE HEART

The Prayer of the Heart (sometimes called "the Jesus Prayer") very much resembles the Sufi prayer above. It comes from the Eastern Orthodox tradition of hesychastic meditation and enjoyed a time of popularity in the early 1970s, when the book entitled *The Way of a Pilgrim* became popular with a New Age readership.[141] This meditation is still widely practiced in Russia, and while I was there, a good friend of mine who was a hesychast taught me to perform it as follows:

Practice deep breathing to clear the mind while focusing your attention on what Eastern Orthodox tradition calls "the spiritual heart." Its precise location varies from one individual to another, but is usually just a bit higher up than the physical organ of the heart and is sometimes to one's left side, like the physical heart, or sometimes in the middle of the sternum, like the *anahata chakra* of Hinduism.

When your consciousness is firmly centered in your spiritual heart, begin adding words to your inbreathing and outbreathing. In Orthodox Christianity, the full prayer is: "Lord Jesus Christ, Son of God, have mercy on me, a sinner." The last phrase "a sinner," however, does not appear in very early versions of the prayer.

Those who do not consider themselves Christians in any way, shape, or form may substitute any kind of magic phrase or mantra they please. Shani Oates, currently the Maid of the Clan of Tubal Cain, has written of her use of the Hindu Gayatri Mantra in spiritual work.[142]

The basic idea is to keep repeating your chosen phrase while breathing in and out and focusing your meditative attention on the spiritual heart. In time, the correspondence between your breathing and your attention upon the spiritual heart will cause you to feel as if the heart itself is repeating the mantra. That is the goal of the Prayer of the Heart: to reach a state of mind wherein the heart itself is praying.

Do it for as long as you like or as long as you can. In *The Way of a Pilgrim,* the aspirant achieves a state of mind where the prayer is within his heart unceasingly.

---

141 Toumanova, Nina, trans., *The Way of a Pilgrim* (Dover Publications, 2008).

142 The article "Musings on the Sacred" by Shani Oates describes the way in which she incorporates the Gaytari Mantra of Hinduism with her Western practices. Retrieved from www.clanoftubalcain.org.uk/musings.html.

SUFI BREATHING MEDITATIONS

Close your eyes. Breathe normally a few times, once again focusing your attention on the location of your actual physical heart while contemplating the presence of the Divine within your heart and your daily life. This presence is often perceived as light.

As you inhale, feel God's light shining in your heart, then exhale while feeling God's light striking your heart powerfully, like a lightning bolt. Among Sufis who use Arabic words for the Divine, *Allah* is typically repeating during inhalation and *hu* during exhalation, though of course you may use any names you please.

Gradually increase your breathing rate to three to four times its normal speed while keeping the same visualization and the same mantra. Take shallow but rapid breaths. The inhalation should be longer than the exhalation, while the exhalation should be a bit short and forceful.

Practice this meditation for ten minutes.

Here is another breathing meditation which may be of special interest to the aspirant in Traditional Witchcraft, for it includes the five classical elements of the Western magical tradition (as well as ancient Greek physics), which were also known to the Sufis.

Begin by breathing naturally, in and out through your nostrils, for five full breath cycles. (A "breath cycle" is defined here as one inhalation and one exhalation.) This first series of five breaths purifies you with the element of Earth. As you inhale, imagine that you are drawing the energy and magnetism of the earth into your body. The Earth energy circulates through your own subtle energy systems, restoring and renewing the vitality and strength of your body.

As you exhale, imagine that the magnetic field of the earth draws all the heavy, gross elements or energies that are trapped within you down into the ground, where they are purified and released. With each breath, you will feel revitalized, lighter, and more clearly aligned with the free flow of breath, life, and energy.

Then, with a second series of five breaths, purify yourself with the energy of Water. Inhaling through the nose and exhaling through the mouth, envision a waterfall of pure, clear energy pouring down upon you and within you from above, flowing through you, and dissolving and purifying anything that might block the flow of life-energy that should be moving through you. With each breath, feel that you are washed clean and clear, as this stream of energy and light flows through you in the form of Water.

With the next series of five breaths, purify yourself with the element of Fire. Inhale through the mouth and exhale through the nostrils, letting the flow of the breath focus in your solar plexus as you inhale. Then, let your breath rise up and radiate as light from your heart, shining forth from between your shoulder blades into the world and up through the crown of your head like a fountain of light. While inhaling Fire and exhaling light, envision and affirm that this energy is a purifying fire that gathers up any impurities or congestion that remains within you and burns them into radiance and light in the fires of your heart.

With the next cycle of breaths, purify yourself with the Air element. Inhaling and exhaling through the mouth, imagine the element of Air sweeping through you like a wind, blowing through every part of your body, purifying any density or obstruction that may remain.

Finally, breathing very gently through your nostrils, envision yourself being purified by the most subtle element—sometimes known as "ether" and called the quintessence of all the elements by Greek philosophers, but known to many of us in present times as Akasha. Let this most subtle element dissolve any remaining sense of heaviness or density, and let your heart and mind become open to perfect clarity and the vastness of the sky—the very universe itself.

Energized and purified, sense the subtle yet profound shift that has taken place in the course of these twenty-five breaths. Carry that sense of focus, calm, and connection with the Divine into your daily life.

ICON MEDITATION

Icons are a great deal more than a style of art or an adjunct to Christian piety; the folk tradition surrounding them is a species of archetypal therapy and a form of magic; in legends, images, and folklore of some of the "saints" who form the subject matter of the icons, we may glimpse the lineaments of the ancient goddesses and gods who reigned in the collective mind of many European peoples. The saints who inhabit the world of the icons are archetypes, which, according to Plato, means that they are primal ideas in the mind of the infinite; hence, the legends and lore of the saints may have little or nothing to do with the historical facts surrounding the long-dead human beings who were canonized by the Byzantines so many centuries ago.

St. Paraskeva spins the web of human destiny while St. Elijah brings the rain; St. John the Baptist and St. George attend the fertility of the earth, while St. Nicholas wanders through a magical landscape working his wild miracles. All of this has little to do with Christian doctrine and a great deal to do with the mythic world of Pagan Europe.

The use of icons entered Slavic folklife through Byzantium, and though there are some "Eastern" European countries (for example, Poland) where Catholicism predominates, we could say that one of the principal differences between "Western" and "Eastern" Europe lies in the influence of the Byzantine or Greek Orthodox Church over the cultural development of the Slavic world. Icons are still venerated throughout the Orthodox tradition, though seldom with as much fervor as in Russia, where they are regarded in much the same way that the people of India or Tibet might regard a mandala—which is to say, as a meditative tool to open doorways into the infinite.

In the Eastern Orthodox mystical tradition called hesychasm, adepts meditate upon icons in the same way that Hindu yogis or Tibetan Buddhists meditate upon the divine figures that inhabit their own cultural art. If you don't find Christian symbolism troublesome, meditation upon icons is a powerful way of uniting with the archetypal forces of the Divine.

The same hesychastic friend in Russia who taught me the Prayer of the Heart also taught me that this is how one ought to meditate upon icons:

First, become familiar with the icon you have chosen. Spend some time learning all its details.

When you sit down to meditate with the icon in front of you, don't focus upon it intently with wide-open eyes, but let your eyes be half open and half closed. You have already studied the icon when you acquired it, and now you know its details, but with the eyes half closed and a soft focus, your attention will be drawn unconsciously to different parts of the image. These are the parts which are important to you spiritually.

Imagine that the icon in its totality is being drawn into you, entering inside of you through the soft focus of your half-open eyes. Let it merge with you and take up residence in the energetic center in your body with which the icon resonates. With your eyes partly closed, the entire iconic image will be softer, and therefore it is planted "softly" within you.

When the image has taken up its place inside of you, begin to chant. In classical hesychasm, the chant is almost always a Greek or Russian Orthodox prayer, although my hesychastic friend says you can use any type of chant you want, from a simple "om" to a much more complex mantra.

Keep doing this until it is the inner image within you rather than your own voice which seems to be chanting. In terms of ordinary reality, it is, of course, your own voice, but in the depths of your imagination—and imagination is one of the most powerful forces contained within human beings and one of the primary sources of magic—it will seem as if the image, now planted inside of you, is actually doing the chanting.

Different images are used for different purposes:

In Russian folklore, St. Nicholas is a wanderer like Odin. He roams the countryside and is called Nicholas the Miracle Worker, for his primary function is to make magic—again like wandering Odin, who, in the Norse sagas, often appears unexpectedly, carrying his staff and garbed in his hat and gray cloak, to touch the lives of mortals with a sudden stroke of his magic. Russians pray to this saint for protection while traveling.[143] They also pray to him for healing and success in any risky adventure—whenever miraculous intervention is needed. Russian students often carry an icon of St. Nicholas with them when they take their exams, for this saint is said to aid our studies. Odin was also a god of wisdom and knowledge, master of the runes.

Mary, holding the Christ child next to her breast, is the principal archetype of the Heart Center. There are more purely symbolic icons in which the image of the Christ Child is seen *within* the heart of Mary, which is reminiscent of the birth of the Divine Child who was so important in Robert Cochrane's rituals. The child is an archetype

---

143 St. Nicholas is sometimes regarded as the special patron of those who journey by sea, although this aspect of the tradition appears to come from Byzantine Greece, where St. Nick doubles for the sea god Poseidon.

of the Self—the essential beingness of who we really are—emerging as a newborn because the Self, like a child, must experience changes and grow before it can manifest itself fully. Thus, the image of Christ within the heart of Mary tells us that it is in the heart that our true essence, our Self, is born and nurtured until it grows into maturity.

Pagan Russian magic recognized a center of power in the lower abdomen, which we can translate as the Life Force Center and was the source of a shaman's power. In the icon tradition, this center is often associated with a figure known as St. Demetrius of Thessalonica; all his icons include a warrior's breastplate worn low, beneath his chest, drawing our attention to the Life Force Center. Icons which embody a very strong focus upon this center are relatively scarce. Christianity appears to have been more than a little bit afraid of the magical powers associated with the Life Force Center.

WALKING MEDITATION

This next practice is basically the principles discussed in previous meditations applied to the simple act of walking.

In Sufism, there is a practice called *Nazar bar Kadam* (Watch Your Step), which is about walking mindfully and consciously. Do not perform any actions which may obstruct your spiritual progress. Avoid looking here and there aimlessly, as this distracts the mind from its connection with the Infinite. Sufi masters ask their followers to look at their feet while walking.

Many descriptions of Cochrane's rituals describe the participants walking in a circle while focusing only upon one's footsteps, though this was a technique he acquired not from Sufi writings but from Evan John Jones, who later became the Magister of the Clan of Tubal Cain and who had learned it from a traditional group into which he had been inducted during his youth.[144]

---

144 Shani Oates, personal communication, January 2024.

CHAPTER THIRTEEN

SIGILS AND RUNES

WHEN YOU HAVE SPENT TIME EXPLORING your dreams and past lives and have meditated deeply upon union with the Divine Intelligence, then surely you will know yourself better than you did before. You will have a sense of where you want to go in your life and the kind of magic which is uniquely yours and is now awakening within you.

It is now time to explore the tools you can use to bring your conventional workaday self into harmony with your mystical self and begin living your own magic.

A sigil is a symbol or image which is used in magic to obtain a particular goal or outcome. The term itself derives from the Latin *sigillum* (plural *sigilla*), meaning "seal." The use of symbols for magical purposes has likely been practiced since the Neolithic era, and the marvelous spirals and other symbols which decorate ancient sites like Newgrange may very well be sigils.

It is, of course, the practitioner's mind—their consciousness—which accomplishes the real work of creating magic and realizing goals. As a symbolic representation of the practitioner's desire or goal, the sigil is simply a tool.

Combining symbols with their magical correspondences builds up a telesmatic image of a certain quality (typically reflecting the quality or achievement which the magical practitioner desires). Though the practitioner's consciousness is the primary force that accomplishes a goal, a sigil is believed to call various elemental forces, which assist or empower the practitioner's desire, into action. Sigils were often used in the making of talismans.

In times past, sigils were carved or painted on doors and walls, perhaps to ensure prosperity for the home or good fortune for its inhabitants. In the current day and age, such a practice would be likely to bring a lawsuit from your landlord for defacing his property. A sigil may be drawn by hand on paper, carefully and with precision, and placed in a magical place—your altar, for example.

Robert Cochrane used a fairly large number of sigils; these can be found in his letters to Bill Gray, Norman Gills, and Joe Wilson. Here are a few of them, as interpreted by Robin the Dart, former Magister of the Clan of Tubal Cain.[145]

The Star-Crossed Serpent.
Devotion to the Quest for Gnosis.

Mind exalted above the Star-Crossed
Serpent of Devotion. Love Under Will.

The Castle which forms the axis mundi
or world center. Completion.

Broom and Sword.
The gate opened by Love.

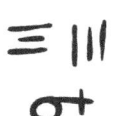

Two sigils for sex magic.

The Triple Goddess as Three Moons. Inspiration.

---

145 Robin the Dart, "Ciphers and Symbols Used by Robert Cochrane," www. clanoftubalcain.org.uk/cyphers.html, retrieved November 5, 2023.

RUNES

At the present time, we think of the runes primarily as tools for divination, and the *Germania* of Tacitus informs us that runes were in fact used for that purpose by early German tribes. But the runes are more than a medieval alphabet used to carve inscriptions in Northern countries; they were an entire body of knowledge and a form of magic in their own way, including the use of runes for sigils. Odin, the king of the gods, hung upside down on Yggdrasil, the World Tree, for nine days and nights—a sacrifice of "himself unto himself," as the poem "Havamal" from the *Poetic Edda* would have it—to gain knowledge of the runes. Runes were a form of high magic among Vikings, Anglo-Saxons, and other Northern peoples.

When Cochrane called himself "Odin's Man," it was this particular aspect of the old shamanic god—the master of knowledge—to whom he seems to have been referring. To the best of my knowledge, Cochrane himself used the Tarot as his principal instrument of divination—his letters suggest that his outlook on the Tarot was somewhat Kabbalistic, after the manner of the Golden Dawn or the Builders of the Adytum. He seems not to have used the runes as a divinatory tool, but he often used them as sigils. I have not been able to ascertain where he learned it, but this practice continued among Nordic peoples until quite recently. My father grew up in a rural region of Minnesota where most of the population still spoke Swedish; when he was a boy (c. 1925), runes were often painted or carved on barns, usually as talismans for a good harvest or for protection of one's property and health for one's family.

On the opposite page is a list of the runes with their simplest meanings, which can be used as sigils.

Sometimes elements from different runes were combined to create a single symbol, which helped the practitioner accomplish goals more complex than the simple ones listed here. These compound symbols were known in Viking times as *bindrunes*. There are now any number of books which deal with this aspect of runelore and rune magic. As noted earlier, your magical altar is a good place for a sigil or runic symbol.

ᚠ	Fehu	Wealth
ᚢ	Ūruz	Aurochs (Wild Ox, Strength)
ᚦ	Thurisaz	The God Thor (Protection)
ᚨ	Ansuz	God (usually Odin, Magical Speech)
ᚱ	Raidō	Ride, Journey (Safe Travel)
ᚲ	Kenaz	Torch (Light)
ᚷ	Gebō	Gift
ᚹ	Wunjō	Joy
ᚺ	Hagalaz	Hail (Trouble)
ᚾ	Naudiz	Need
ᛁ	Isaz	Ice (Binding)
ᛃ	Jēra	Year (Fruitfulness, Harvest)
ᛇ	Ihwaz	Yew Tree (Strength and Wisdom)
ᛈ	Perth	(The meaning is unknown)
ᛉ	Algiz	Elk (Protection)
ᛊ	Sōwilō	Sun (Light)
ᛏ	Tiwaz	The Norse God Tyr (Protection)
ᛒ	Berkanan	Birch Tree (Birth)
ᛖ	Ehwaz	Horse (Power)
ᛗ	Mannaz	Man (Human Dignity)
ᛚ	Laguz	Lake or Leek (Healing)
ᛜ	Ingwaz	The God Ingwaz (Freyr, Abundance)
ᛞ	Dagaz	Day (Light)
ᛟ	Othala	Possessions, Household

CHAPTER FOURTEEN

SACRED POETRY

Poetry can be a marvelous teacher of wisdom, and indeed, much of the world's mythology is conveyed to us through that medium—a fact we are likely to miss if we read "prose translations" or "re-tellings" instead of the original sources. Greek myth comes to us from Homer's *Iliad* and *Odyssey,* as well as Hesiod's *Theogony,* the *Homeric Hymns,* later poetic ventures such as the *Argonautica,* and—a source we have already explored—the mystical *Orphic Hymns.*

Snorri Sturluson summarized Norse mythology in his *Prose Edda,* but before Snorri, there was the *Poetic Edda,* from which we have already quoted a few passages. The mythology of the Baltic nations, such as Latvia and Lithuania, is preserved almost entirely in the form of folk songs, and the great Hindu epics like the *Mahabharata* and the *Ramayana* are poetic achievements of the highest rank.

When it comes to the British Isles—and Cochrane was thoroughly British in his love for Celtic and Anglo-Saxon myth—we also find a great deal of poetic expression, of which the best known is, of course, *Beowulf.* But Cochrane found great wisdom in two special pieces, one of which is contained in the Irish *Book of Invasions* and is commonly known as *The Song of Amergin,* presented in myth as the work of the great magician Amergin himself, though it is also said by some sources to be the work of the renowned bard Taliesin.

In the *Book of Invasions,* a fleet of sea-borne nomads called the Milesians reaches the shores of Ireland, which is ruled by the demi-gods who go by the name of the Tuatha Dé Danann (Children of the Goddess

Danu). When the ships of the Milesians land, their magician (the text does not use the word Druid) leaps onto the Irish earth and intones the following invocation:

> *I am Wind on Sea,*
> *I am Ocean-wave,*
> *I am Roar of Sea,*
> *I am Bull of Seven Fights,*
> *I am Vulture on Cliff,*
> *I am Dewdrop,*
> *I am Fairest of Flowers,*
> *I am Boar for Boldness,*
> *I am Salmon in Pool,*
> *I am Lake on Plain,*
> *I am a Mountain in a Man,*
> *I am a Word of Skill,*
> *I am the Point of a Weapon (that poureth forth combat),*
> *I am God who fashioneth Fire for a Head.*
> *Who smootheth the ruggedness of a mountain?*
> *Who is He who announceth the ages of the Moon?*
> *And who, the place where falleth the sunset?*
> *Who calleth the cattle from the House of Tethys?*
> *On whom do the cattle of Tethys smile?*
> *Who is the troop, who the god who fashioneth edges*
> *In a fortress of gangrene?*
> *Enchantments about a spear? Enchantments of Wind?[146]*

The Milesians, though mere mortals, go on to defeat the Tuatha Dé Danann and gain control of Ireland. The Tuatha Dé Danann retreat inside the *sidhe,* which technically means "hills" but refers to the prehistoric burial mounds which dot the landscape of the British Isles, and the Tuatha Dé Danann themselves become known as the *sidhe,* which takes on the meaning of "the faery folk."

---

146 Macalister, R. A. S., trans. and ed., "The Book of Invasions" in Celtic Literature Collective (Irish Texts Society, 1941) www.maryjones.us/ctexts/lebor5.html, retrieved Oct. 17, 2023.

In his deep appreciation for *The Song of Amergin,* Cochrane departed from the ideas of his usual inspiration, Robert Graves, who saw the poem as a complex metaphor for the Irish Ogham alphabet—a notion now universally rejected by scholars. Cochrane seems to have realized that the poem was, in fact, involved with the attainment of magical states of consciousness and the inner transformations which accompany them.

In the middle 1960s, the terms "shaman" and "shamanism" had not gained the popularity (or the misuse) which they enjoy today, but many modern readers would immediately recognize *The Song of Amergin* as the incantation of a shaman regarding the transformations he has undergone in his journey to the Otherworld and back, and the powers he now possesses as a result of his experiences.

Cochrane recommended that his students meditate at length upon the poem. Indeed, there are few texts that bring the powers acquired through shamanic transformation closer to one's spirit than *The Song of Amergin,* a poem to be studied, repeated, and perhaps even committed to memory to inspire a sense of the many different states of magical consciousness we can acquire in our quest for gnosis.

But if *The Song of Amergin* is relatively simple and direct, the other ancient Celtic poem which Cochrane regarded as deeply significant to the study of Traditional Witchcraft is difficult to interpret—even professional scholars in Celtic literature and myth differ in their opinions about it.[147] It is entitled *Preiddeu Annwn,* or "The Spoils of Annwn." The poem recounts an expedition by King Arthur to Annwn, the ancient Welsh Otherworld.

> *I praise the Lord, Prince of the realm, King.*
> *His sovereignty has extended across the world's tract.*
> *Equipped was the prison of Gweir in the Mound Fortress,*
> *throughout the account of Pwyll and Pryderi.*
> *No one before him went into it,*
> *into the heavy blue/gray chain; a faithful servant it held.*
> *And before the spoils of Annwfyn bitterly he sang.*

---

147 Higley, trans., "Preiddeu Annwn: The Spoils of Annwn" *op. cit.,* retrieved Oct 18, 2023.

And until Judgment shall last our bardic invocation.[148]
Three fullnesses of Prydwen we went into it.
Except seven none rose up from the Fortress of the Mound.

I am honored in praise. Song was heard
in the Four-Peaked Fortress, four its revolutions.
My poetry, from the cauldron it was uttered.
From the breath of nine maidens it was kindled.
The cauldron of the chief of Annwfyn:[149] *what is its fashion?*
A dark ridge around its border and pearls.
It does not boil the food of a coward; it has not been destined.
The flashing sword of Lleawch has been lifted to it.
And in the hand of Lleminawc it was left.[150]
And before the door of hell lamps burned.
And when we went with Arthur, brilliant difficulty,
except seven none rose up from the Fortress of Mead-Drunkenness.

I am honored in praise; song is heard
in the Fortress of Four-Peaks, isle of the strong door.
Flowing water and jet are mingled.
Sparkling wine their liquor before their retinue.
Three fullnesses of Prydwen we went on the sea.
Except seven none rose up from the Fortress of Hardness.

I merit not the Lord's little men of letters.[151]
Beyond the Glass Fortress they did not see the valor of Arthur.

---

148 *Yn bardwedi* is somewhat unclear. The most common use of prefixed *yn* is "our." But this could also be the preposition "in": "in bardic prayer," or even an error for *ym*, "my" or *y*, "his." If no error is assumed, then are Gweir and Taliesin (the speaker) identified? Are they singing together? Are they similarly incarcerated? Do they speak for all bardic (and divine) prisoners and singers?

149 Annwfyn is an alternative spelling of Annwn, and seems to be preferred by the translator, Sarah Higley.

150 The names Lleawch and Lleminawc are a mystery even to scholars of early Celtic literature.

151 Here, the master bard Taliesin appears to be remarking that lesser writers are without skill and unworthy of his regard.

Six thousand men stood upon the wall.
It was difficult to speak with their sentinel.
Three fullnesses of Prydwen went with Arthur.
Except seven none rose up from the Fortress of
Guts [Hindrance?].[152]

I do not merit little men, slack their shield straps.
They do not know which day who was created [or: created whom?];
what hour of midday Cwy[153] was born.
Who made him who did not go [to the] meadows of Defwy?
They do not know the brindled ox, thick his headband.
Seven score links on his collar.
And when we went with Arthur, dolorous visit,
except seven none rose up from the fortress of God's Peak.

I do not merit little men, slack their will.
They do not know which day the chief was created,
what hour of the midday the owner was born,
what animal they keep, silver its head.
When we went with Arthur, sorrowful strife,
except seven none rose up from the Fortress of Enclosedness.

Monks howl like a choir of dogs
from an encounter with lords who know:
Is there one course of wind? is [sic] there one course of water?
Is there one spark of fire of fierce tumult?

Monks pack together like young wolves

---

152 The original word here might be either *golud* or *colud*. *Goludd*, "hindrance," "impediment," or "frustration" makes good sense in the context of this stanza about a glass castle and an uncommunicative sentinel. But it is also possible that the original word should be *coludd*, "guts" or "bowels." Other scholars have translated this word as "Fortress in the Middle of the Earth," "impediment," and "concealed fort."

153 Once again, the wording is obscure, and a character by the name of Cwy is unknown elsewhere in Celtic literature. The remainder of the poem is filled with unusual and archaic terms; a proper translation is anyone's guess.

from an encounter with lords who know.
They do not know when midnight and dawn divide.
Nor wind, what its course, what its onrush,
what place it ravages, what region it strikes.
The grave of the saint is hidden [or: lost, vanishing, in the Other-
world], both grave and ground [or: champion].
I praise the Lord, great prince,
that I be not sad; Christ endows me.

In the final couplet of every stanza except the last, a perilous journey into the old Celtic Otherworld of Annwn is mentioned, a feat accomplished by King Arthur and three boat-loads of men (of whom only seven returned). Several fortresses which appear to be located in Annwn are mentioned, notably the "Mound or Fairy Fortress," "Four Peaked or Cornered Fortress," and "Glass Fortress," though it is possible that these are separate locations—stations along the road to the Otherworld.

Prydwen is the name of Arthur's ship. The most obvious translation of *preideu* is "spoils" or "plunder," which is what Arthur's men are seeking. This plunder seems to be a cauldron, but *preideu* can also mean "cattle" or "herds," and though this meaning seems not to fit the context, magical beasts are mentioned further on in the poem.

In the Welsh original, the Mound Fortress is Caer Sidi. Caer Sidi is like Gwales in the Second Branch of *The Mabinogion*, where the bereaved retinue of Brân rests for eighty years in pleasant forgetfulness. *Sidi* may come from Old Irish *sidhe*, which is derived from the noun *sidh*, the "gods" or "fairy-folk," or the mound or dwelling place of such folk. These otherworldly abodes were often submerged. Reward and punishment alike are doled out in the fairy fortress.

In the first stanza, a character named Gweir is encountered imprisoned in the fort's walls. This personage appears to be the same as Gwair, one of "Three Exalted Prisoners of Britain" known from the *Welsh Triads*. He is imprisoned in chains, apparently until Judgment Day, singing before the spoils of Annwn. Lundy, an island off the coast of Cornwall, is known as *ynys weir*, "Gweir's Island," a detail that reinforces the sense of his importance as a resident or prisoner of an island fortress. The first stanza also mentions Pwyll, the legendary prince of Dyfed who, in the first branch of *The Mabinogion*, becomes the Chief of Annwn after helping its king, Arawn, and who was credited with ownership of a cauldron.

The second stanza describes the cauldron of the Chief of Annwn, finished with pearl, and how it was taken. The speaker may be intended to be Taliesin himself, for this stanza refers to "my poetry, from the cauldron it was uttered, from the breath of nine maidens it was kindled, the cauldron of the chief of Annwn." Taliesin's name is connected to a similar story in the legend of his birth. Gweir was imprisoned in perpetual song before a cauldron that first gave out poetry when breathed upon by nine maidens, reminiscent of the nine muses of classical thought.

The cauldron is a very complex image with a complex background. There is the cauldron of Cerridwen, famous in Celtic magical lore, in which the enchanted brew that will confer poetic and magic power is stolen by the young Taliesin. It is to this story that the poet in *Preiddeu Annwn* clearly refers. But the cauldron is also an object wrested by Brân in the Second Branch of *The Mabinogion,* as we have seen in Chapter Eight.

This cauldron has the property of bringing slain warriors back to life. There is also an Irish cauldron in *Culhwch and Olwen,* a story in which Arthur is directly involved. Having promised to help Culhwch complete a number of impossible tasks—one of them being the attainment of the cauldron of the giant Diwrnach—Arthur sails in his ship to Ireland and comes away with the cauldron after a successful battle. (Ireland may have been a poetic or metaphorical term for the Otherworld in Welsh lore.) Furthermore, an Irish tale, "The Phantom Chariot of Cuchulain," contains a poem called "Fortress of Shadow." It has a sea voyage, a raid upon an island stronghold with iron doors, a subterranean chamber, magic cattle, a cauldron which is filled with treasure, and an escape in common with *Preiddeu Annwn.*

The third and fourth stanzas describe the difficulties involved in the confrontation with the forces of Annwn. The Fortress of Glass is an interesting term. Sometimes Celtic poetry associates glass with "otherness." Nennius describes the Milesians on their journey from Spain, encountering a glass tower in the middle of the sea whose people do not respond to their hails. They attack the castle with thirty ships, all of which sink but one; the people of that ship populate the whole of Ireland, landing upon the island as their magician Amergin chants his magical song.

The fifth and sixth describe a great ox that may also be among the "spoils" of Annwn. The last two stanzas are obscure, and various translators have treated them quite differently.

Those who find the difficulties associated with interpreting such mystical and mysterious poetry challenging and rewarding, as Cochrane did (rather than frustrating and incomprehensible), may enjoy immersing themselves in the magical world of *The Mabinogion, The Welsh Triads,* and the Irish Mythological Cycle.

CHAPTER FIFTEEN

THE
SACRED EARTH

IN THE EARLY DAYS OF WITCHCRAFT'S REVIVAL, back in the mid-1960s, one significant difference between Gardner's Wiccan followers and the Traditional Witchcraft movement spearheaded by Robert Cochrane was that Wiccans held their sabbats indoors while the Clan of Tubal Cain always worked outdoors, in nature.[154]

According to Evan John Jones, who succeeded Cochrane as Magister of the Clan of Tubal Cain, Cochrane strongly preferred a specific landscape: a wooded area at the top of a hill on the edge of fast-flowing water and, if possible, a waterfall. The Clan regarded such places as a liminal space or boundary between this world and the Otherworld. As we have seen in Chapter Three, all witches fashioned their own Otherworld for themselves through craft and imagination, a special place to which their souls would travel after death, but Jones asserts that most such Otherworlds contained a river with a waterfall. The river was equated with Lethe, the river of oblivion in Greek mythology where one's memories of earthly life were purged from the spirit, though the spiritual knowledge gained during that lifetime remained. The Clan regards finding such a landscape in which to hold its ceremonies as

---

154 Wiccans seldom work naked anymore. Though such a practice suited the late 1960s and the 1970s, the shift to more conservative sexual and social mores during the 1980s largely put an end to that particular era and its "sky-clad" form of ritual expression, and now they often work outdoors.

vitally important and has always recognized the vital connections that can only be experienced in the wild.[155]

Evan John Jones remarks:

When you locate your sacred enclosure on the crest of a hill among a few scattered trees, you are really taking the 'Faith' back to where it started. When you continually work indoors, you lose touch with the spirit of nature which is the very foundation stone upon which the Faith was built. Even working in someone's yard or garden is not really quite the same thing — it usually is far too tame, neat, and tidy, something that nature definitely is not. When you work outdoors, you work among nature's visible cycles, feeling them in a way that a mere calendar-based ritual cannot compare to.

February, the close of one vegetative year and the start of another, with its empty fields and bare trees alerts the keen eye to the signs of new life. May Eve, and those self same trees are garlanded with leaves and blossom and the tides of life are flowing strong. Lammas is the time of plenty when the harvest ripens, yet in the very air we feel the ebbing flow of life. Hallowe'en, the time of the dead, when the circle under the oak is covered with fallen leaves which should never ever be swept away, and dead though they are, beneath their cover there is still life, which turn serves the wellbeing of the soil on which stands the sacred oak.

Yes, the Faith is rooted in nature as well as in the interplay between the natural and the supernatural. So by working our magic where the deadening hand of the urban dweller has only lightly touched, we are linking up with the spiritual genius from whence the Craft first sprung.[156]

Cochrane's passion for nature went far beyond the selection of an attractive landscape in which to perform ritual. At the time of this writing, the topic of Earth Mysteries and ley lines is interwoven with the lore

155 Howard, Michael and Evan John Jones, "Interview with Evan John Jones" www.clanoftubalcain.org.uk/bonafides.html and personal communication with Shani Oates, January 2024.

156 Jones and Oates, *Star Crossed Serpent I: Origins, op. cit.*

of UFOs and aliens, though such an outlook originated with the first publication of John Michell's *The View Over Atlantis* in 1969 and would therefore have been unfamiliar to Robert Cochrane, who died in 1966.

Cochrane's primary inspiration was Alfred Watkins, author of *Early British Trackways* and *The Old Straight Track*, who passed away in 1935 when Cochrane was only four years old but whose influence remained strong, as he is commonly acknowledged as the founder of the Earth Mysteries movement. Watkins identified what he believed to be a number of ancient straight-line roads on the British landscape; he called them "ley lines." They were notable because of the number of stone circles, menhirs, hilltop fortresses, and so on which lay upon a straight track, as if they had been deliberately bound together. To Watkins, these straight-line roads must have been built for practical purposes; he believed that Neolithic and Bronze Age farmers had constructed them for the transport of livestock, agricultural products, precious metals, and other items.

It was only later that his followers began to speculate that ley lines marked powerful and magical currents in the earth itself. Various and sundry investigators developed methods which they alleged were able to measure the quantum of energy at any given location, and they concluded that the landmarks bound together by ley lines, as well as the lines themselves, were abundant in such energies. Cochrane's letters make it clear that he held similar beliefs about ley lines and their power.

But what did these energies mean?

Though many suggestions—including Michell's extraterrestrial speculations—have been made, Evan John Jones calls the ley lines "spirit paths or ghost roads," and there are many reasons to believe that this interpretation is correct.[157]

There are some concepts found throughout the world with such remarkable similarities that scholars recognize them as having been derived from a single source. In Chapter Three, we have already discussed such a concept—that of a fourfold or four-directional world. How, then—setting aside, for the moment, speculations about lost continents or loquacious aliens—can one explain such a phenomenon?

Joseph Campbell, a scholar of world mythology, suggested that such ideas all have their origin in shamanism. They most likely developed in Siberia, before some ancient wanderers began the long walks which

---

157 Howard and Jones, "Interview with Evan John Jones," *op. cit.*

led them west to the European continent and east into the Western Hemisphere. For example, the Italian historian Carlo Ginzburg has demonstrated that the fairytale we call Cinderella is world-wide and originated in the story of a young woman's encounter with the old shamanic Bone Goddess, the initiator.[158]

Likewise, straight line paths are a concept known throughout the world. As well as the ley lines of Europe (for they are not limited to the British Isles), straight lines—much more clearly visible than the trails hypothesized by Watkins and his successors—are known in North and Central America as well. Among the Maya, they are known as *sacbeob* ("white roads"), for they are constructed of white stone and link various sites for reasons which many scholars regard as obscure. Farther north, there is an entire network of straight line roads in what is now the state of New Mexico, all of them leading to the well-known Anasazi site of Chaco Canyon. While they may run for many miles across the open desert, these roads never take the easy way around when they encounter hills or mountains. Instead of circling round the hill, they sustain the straight line by going over the hill, which must have been a difficult (as well as impractical) mode of travel for the ancients. While some of the Chaco roads are visible only from the air, others are quite clear on the ground (I have hiked one of them, near the ruined Anasazi tower of Kin Ya'a).

A ground-breaking experiment was conducted by the School of American Research in Santa Fe, New Mexico, during which scientific archaeologists and traditional Hopi elders met on an equal footing to compare their ideas on Anasazi sites. (The Anasazi are acknowledged as the ancestors of the present-day Hopi.) When the subject of Chaco's straight line road system came up, the Hopi insisted that these were paths for the ancestral spirits, who can only travel in a straight line, and that pilgrims bound for important rituals and ceremonies in Chaco Canyon must have walked these paths to honor their ancestors and join with them in spirit.

The dead can only travel in straight lines; the rationale behind "dream catchers," which many Native Americans hang over the heads of their children, is that they prevent the spirits of the dead from approaching by getting them entangled in the dream catcher's web and therefore unable to continue walking a straight path.

---

158 Ginzburg, *Ecstasies, op. cit.*

The American scholar W. Y. Evans-Wentz, best known for bringing *The Tibetan Book of the Dead* to the attention of the world at large, wrote in his early work, *The Fairy-Faith in Celtic Countries,* that many unsuspecting Irish families had inadvertently built their houses partly upon such a spirit path, and, when the family was surprised by the dead marching through their house, actually removed that section of the house and built a new wall, perhaps somewhat askew but at least avoiding the paths of the dead.

The same phenomenon has also been described to me by traditionally raised Native Hawaiians. One woman informed me that the dead often marched in a straight line through her family home, and that the children hid under their beds in fear to avoid them. "But still," she remarked, "hidden though we were, we could see them. I remember the Night Walkers quite clearly."

In Britain, the longest and best-known ley line is the St. Michael alignment, which begins at the town of Hopton on the east coast and heads southwest until it reaches the church at St. Michael's Mount on the tip of Cornwall. It passes through the important Neolithic sites of Avebury and Silbury Hill, continues through another important collection of menhirs known as the Hurlers, and finally reaches St. Michael's Mount at the very tip of the peninsula. It is not difficult to imagine Avebury, Silbury Hill, and the Hurlers as important gathering places for ancestral spirits on their journey through our world, and very little archaeological work has ever been done beneath some of the other village churches that lie upon the St. Michael's Line; what lies beneath these sites is still unknown. A correspondent informs me that working magic at various sites along the St. Michael's Line is an unusually powerful experience.

Ley lines are not the only markers of sacred space upon the earth; indeed, the whole world is alive with magic.

Throughout Europe and the British Isles, I have seen or heard about large flat rocks that slope down. Often, young women seat themselves at the top of the slope then slide down the flat surface. This custom is supposed to promote fertility and bring children into one's life. Such rocks have always been known throughout Europe as "the bones of the Earth Mother." And it is the Earth Mother who brings fertility to the world and those of us who live there.

In European folklore, the tales of mortal men who enter rocks and mountains all include some of the same elements: a mountain opens up, the traveler enters, and they find a goddess within. Russian folklore affirms that large rocks, hills, and mountains are the bones of the Earth Goddess Mokosh—the feminine nature of the spirit in stone is acknowledged in myth.

In 1630, a native of Hesse in Germany confessed that, for several years, he had been traveling in spirit to a mountain called the Venusberg during Ember Days. Here, "fraw Holt" (i.e., the goddess Holda or Holle) had caused him to gaze into a basin of water, where he had seen splendid horses, as well as the spirits of the dead in the form of men sitting at feast or in the flames. A century earlier, in the early 1500s, an Italian peasant also confessed to visiting the mount of Venus where lived Donna Herodias.[159]

The story of "Tonhauser and Donna Venus" was a well-known medieval legend, commemorated in Richard Wagner's opera *Tannhauser*. According to Heinrich Kammann, whose *Mons Veneris* (*Mount Venus*) was published in 1614, Tannhauser was a medieval minstrel who, on his way to a singing competition, passed near the Horselberg, a mountain in Thuringia.

There, he encountered a beautiful woman in the moonlight. The minstrel recognized her as none other than the goddess Venus and followed her into the Horselberg, where he passed seven years in passion and in revelry. In time, however, he became weary, and called upon the Virgin Mary. The mountain split open and Tannhauser emerged. Throughout the world, he went seeking Christian absolution, but no one, not even the Pope, would give it to him. Finally, he returned to the Venusberg to stay.

The presence of Venus inside the World Mountain may remind us that some standing stones are named for women. Usually, we think of rocks as "masculine" because stone is such a dense, powerful thing. The presence of the goddess Holda and Herodias (Aradia), and especially the prominent role in folklore of Venus—soft, erotic, "smiling Aphrodite"—may surprise us. But let us remember the young women who used to slide down rocks in hopes of bearing children, and that, in many places throughout Europe, rocks were once said to be the bones of the Earth Mother herself.

As with stone, so with water. The energy of a rushing stream is often said to wash away all one's sadness and heartbreak, and cleanse the emotions. Some regard the Lakes of Rila in the mountains of Bulgaria

---

159 Johnson, *Witchcraft and the Shamanic Journey, op. cit.*

as the most powerful place in all of Europe for dispensing the positive energies and love of Mother Earth. As we have seen, Cochrane had a strong attraction to waterfalls, and these too may be places of power. Reichenbach Falls in Switzerland (where Sherlock Holmes battled with Professor Moriarty) are considered to be a center of very powerful energy.

Springs that burst forth from the earth, sparkling and bubbling, have also been regarded by many as magical sites. I remember a village in northern New Mexico—which shall remain anonymous—that was served by a natural spring. For centuries, the animals had been taking nurturance there, and, for the last few hundred years, human beings joined as well. There was a magical quality in the spring which had an unusual effect—many of the dogs in the village (and probably other animals as well) had one blue eye and one brown eye. It was also said—and having been there many times, I can attest that it is true—that some of the people who partook had one blue eye and one brown eye as well.

Trees hold a special place in the lore of the sacred Earth. One of my Pagan teachers in Europe used to say: "We are like trees. The difference between us is that trees are more evolved than we are."

Because ancient Europeans lived in a forest environment, the old Pagan mythologies—whether Celtic, Teutonic, Baltic, or Slavic—are rich with the magic and the lore of trees. Ancient and medieval villages and towns were simply places where the forest had been cleared away for human habitation; beyond the village limits, the trees still reigned supreme. Whole groves and individual trees alike were venerated. Many trees were believed to be the homes of the ancestors or departed spirits, while large old oaks in high or isolated places were sacred to the local thunder god, who was present all over Europe under various different names.

Because each clan holding or village community was a cosmos unto itself, whoever and wherever we may be, we are always at the center of the universe. Hence, specific trees were venerated locally as "world trees," the center of the shamanic cosmos in its local manifestation, and folk magic practices involving sacred trees may be found in European folklore from Ireland to Russia. One of the "Pagan" charges brought against Joan of Arc in her witchcraft trial was that she had danced around the "fairy tree" at the village of Domremy when she was a girl. (So did everyone else in the village, though in Joan's trial, which was for the most part political in nature, this fact was conveniently ignored.)

In Eastern European magical traditions, trees are something quite special: highly evolved beings whose energy field, more than all other animals and plants, comes closest to the human condition.

The type of tree that speaks to you—the type of tree with which you will choose to bond—will give you a clue as to the nature of your own spiritual gifts. All trees have positive energy. All trees seek to give us their love; if we reach out to them with love, they will return their love to us.

Oak, linden, birch, maple, pine, and spruce were regarded by the ancestors of Europeans and European Americans as some of the most miraculous trees. Not only do trees come closest to the human condition, more than all other animals and plants, but humans may return to Earth after death in the form of trees. In Baltic lands such as Latvia and Lithuania, the old Pagan philosophy postulated an aspect of the human soul that fades away when the body dies, and another aspect of the human soul that was a living power and did not depart from the earth when a person passed to the next world.

Instead, this part of the human soul was reincarnated—it would leave the body as a breath, a vapor, and find a new lodging not only in other human beings, but also in trees, flowers, animals, and birds. Sometimes, it would issue directly from one's mouth in the shape of a butterfly, a bee, a mouse, a toad, or a snake, or it might grow out of the mouth of a young girl in the shape of a lily. Often, this aspect of the human soul would be reincarnated in trees. At the time of one's birth, a specific tree was assigned to every person, and it was filled with the same life forces as its human counterpart.

Hermetic philosophy and Hindu yoga have instilled within us the idea that incarnation as a human being is the highest form of rebirth that one can achieve. In Pagan Baltic philosophy, we find a very different concept. All of nature is sacred; therefore, no stigma is attached to being reincarnated as a flower, bird, or animal. And since trees are, in many ways, more evolved than mere humans, reincarnation as a tree may be considered a very high level of incarnation.

Even city dwellers may be able to find a state park where they can build a campfire—with friends, if possible, and alone if necessary—to celebrate the four cross-quarter festivals. And even if you feel embarrassed about performing rituals where other people might see you, it is still a ceremony if you honor nature by using the appropriate kinds of wood for your campfire. (In some regions, the "appropriate" kinds of wood might be a bit hard to find, but finding them is part of the magic.) Evan John Jones names the trees as follows:

> *For Imbolc (Candlemas) burn yew wood, for yew is often found in graveyards the death or passing of the previous year. On Beltane (May Eve), burn a mixture of birch, hazel, willow and hawthorn. Birch has a feminine spirit and symbolizes birth and rebirth, while hazel is symbolic of fertility, fire, divination and knowledge. Though our ancestors often thought of willow and hawthorn as trees of bad luck and mourning, both are considered lucky on Beltane, as long as they are not brought into your house.[160]*

Lughnasa or Lammas is the thanksgiving for all the year has delivered to us, and the appropriate plant is grain stalks. Samhain or Halloween is, of course, the time to remember our ancestors, and therefore yew is once more the correct wood to use. But yew is more than just a symbol of graveyards and death. It can also stand for rebirth because it can grow new trees from a pinned down branch. Therefore, it can both represent mourning and the rebirth that follows, and all the magical things that we pray will happen to us when the time comes for us to pass.[161]

When the church ladies went knocking at my grandfather's door to inquire as to why he was never seen at church on Sunday, he replied:

> *"Ladies, I've been a builder all my life and I have built many churches. You say the church is the House of God, but there's just as much dishonesty, quarrel, and financial chicanery involved with building a church as there is with any other structure.*
>
> *Do you see that forest behind my house? Who built all those trees? Only God. Ladies, when I'm in the mood for worship, that is where I shall go—to the true House of God."*

---

160 Howard and Jones, "Interview with Evan John Jones," *op. cit.*
161 *Ibid.*

The supremacy of nature in Traditional Witchcraft cannot be underestimated. Cain was a wanderer in the wild places of the world, and when Robert Cochrane had his own vision of the Divine Essence, it appeared to him as a naked woman who emerged from the trees of the forest. The early Clan of Tubal Cain always practiced their rituals outdoors, often in the wild (or as near as one can find to wildness in modern Britain). Cochrane himself preferred the tops of hills and locations near waterfalls.

Nature is not merely a sacred place; it is the essence of the sacred.

LEGACY

THOUGH ROBERT COCHRANE was sometimes perceived as a rival to Gerald Gardner, he believed that Wicca had "the makings of something greater," and I personally have no quarrel with Gardner or his vision of witchcraft.[162] A gentle religion of nature had survived from Pagan times and rested upon the twin polarities of Goddess and God—though historians may raise a skeptical eyebrow, it is a peaceful vision and one that does more good than harm. It certainly suited the era in which it began to flourish: the "free love" and "flower power" epoch of the mid-1960s.

Why, then, is Robert Cochrane's vision of Traditional Witchcraft—in many ways a harsher, more ascetic, more uncompromising vision—growing in importance at the present time, some sixty years after it first emerged?

We no longer live in a world of love and flowers. The world of the present day is more violent, darker, and filled with uncertainty and fear. Cochrane may have been some years ahead of the times. His uncompromising outlook on spiritual life nearly mirrors the concerns of today, more than those of sixty years past.

More and more frequently, those who seek enlightenment—or at least something they can believe in—wander upon a "crooked path," one which leads them from one mystical philosophy or spiritual path to another, always hunting for something that fits. Cochrane's path to

---

162 Shani Oates, personal communication, January 2024.

gnosis—which included mythic figures from Genesis; goddesses and gods from Greek, Norse, and Celtic Paganism; a dose of Sufism; mythic figures like Odin and King Arthur; and an insistence that witchcraft was a path which led the seeker to gnosis—a word which literally means "knowledge" but which is commonly regarded as esoteric or spiritual knowledge—makes sense now. Cochrane even insisted that one could be a traditional witch and a good Christian at the same time.

It all makes more sense to us now as we pursue our own "crooked paths" in search of mystery, magic, and supernal light.

Cochrane's legacy is only now being realized by those outside his own tradition.

BIBLIOGRAPHY

"A Letter to the Editor" (On Michael Kirkham on Robert Graves). Minnesota Review, 1967, 7(1).

Anonymous. "The Second Battle of Magh Turedh," *Celtic Literature Collective,* edited by Mary Jones celt.ucc.ie/published/T300011.html.

Apollonius Rhodius. *The Argonautica.* Translated by R.C. Seaton. G. P. Putnam's Sons, 1919.

Apuleius, Lucius. *The Golden Ass.* Translated by Robert Graves. Farrar, Straus and Giroux, 1971.

Blake, William, and Lessing J. Rosenwald Collection. *Jerusalem, the emanation of the giant Albion.* Printed by W. Blake, 1832.

Ben Isaiah, Rabbi Abraham and Rabbi Benjamin Sharfman. *The Pentateuch and Rashi's Commentary, A Linear Translation into English: Genesis,* S.S.&R. Publishing, 1949.

Chambers, Ian. "Tubal Cain and the Dolorous Spear." www.clanoftubalcain.org.uk/spear.html.

—. "Siren Song — quid Sirenes cantare sint solitae?" www.clanoftubalcain.org.uk/sirensong.html.

—. "The Lady of the Rose Garden." http://www.clanoftubalcain.org.uk/roselady.html.

Claudian. *The Complete Works of Claudian.* Translated by Neil W. Bernstein, scholar.archive.org/work/nhunstvozncfjnqm37p5cxzo54.

Cochrane, Robert. "Letters to Robert Graves," docplayer.net/52612115-Robert-cochrane-s-letters-to-robert-graves.html.

Cochrane, Robert. "Letters to Bill Gray." clanoftubalcain.org.uk/the_letters/letters_Bill_Gray_lk.pdf.

Crawford, Jackson, trans. *The Poetic Edda*. Hackett Publishing Company Inc., 2015.

—. *The Saga of the Volsungs: With the Saga of Ragnar Lothbrok*. Hackett Classics, 2017.

Crowley, Aleister. *The Rites of Eleusis*. rahoorkhuit.net/library/libers/lib_0850.html.

Ginzburg, Carlo. *Ecstasies: Deciphering the Witches' Sabbath*. Pantheon, 1991.

—. *The Night Battles: Witchcraft and Agrarian Cults in the Sixteenth and Seventeenth Centuries*. Johns Hopkins University Press, 1983.

Goethe, Johann Wolfgang von. *Faust: A Tragedy*. Translated by Martin Greenberg. Yale University Press, 2014.

Graves, Robert. *The White Goddess: A Historical Grammar of Poetic Myth*. Farrar, Straus, and Giroux, 2013.

Green, Miranda. *Animals in Celtic Life and Myth*. Routledge, 1998.

Grimm, Jacob. *Teutonic Mythology: Volume III*. Translated by James Steven Stallybrass. Dover, 2004.

Guest, Charlotte, trans. *The Mabinogion*. Global Grey, 2018.

Harrison, Jane Ellen. *Prolegomena to the Study of Greek Mythology*. Princeton University Press, 2021.

Hesiod. *Theogony*. Translated by Hugh G. Evelyn-White. theoi.com/Text/HesiodTheogony.html.

Higley, Sarah, trans. "Preiddeu Annwn: The Spoils of Annwn." d.lib.rochester.edu/camelot/text/preiddeu-annwn.

Hippolytus Romanus. *The Refutation of All Heresies*. Translated by J. H. MacMahon. Self-published, 2015.

Howard, Michael. *The Children of Cain*. Three Hands Press, 2011.

Howard, Michael and Evan John Jones. "Interview with Evan John Jones." clanoftubalcain.org.uk/bonafides.html

Hutton, Ronald. *The Triumph of the Moon: A History of Modern Pagan Witchcraft*. Oxford University Press, 2019.

Jackson, Laura (Riding). *The Person I Am: The Literary Memoirs of Laura (Riding) Jackson*. Trent Editions, 2011.

Johnson, Kenneth. *Witchcraft and the Shamanic Journey*. Crossed Crow Books, 2023.

—. *Flight of the Firebird*. Crossed Crow Books, 2023.

Johnson, Kenneth, trans. "Hymn to Proserpine," Orphic Hymns XIX.

Johnson, Kenneth, and Anita Garr. *Jaguar Medicine: An Introduction to Mayan Healing Traditions*. Mystical Jaguar Productions, 2013.

Johnson, Robert. *Inner Work: Using Dreams and Active Imagination for Personal Growth*. HarperCollins, 1986.

Jones, Evan John and Shani Oates. *The Star Crossed Serpent I: Origins*. Mandrake of Oxford, 2013.

Jung, C. G. *Man and His Symbols*. Bantam Books, 2023.

—. *Memories, Dreams, Reflections*. Vintage Books, 1989.

Kerenyi, Karl. *The Gods of the Greeks*. Pickle Partners Publishing, 2016.

Leland, Charles Godfrey. *Aradia, or the Gospel of the Witches*. Global Grey, 2023.

Lindop, Grevel, ed. *Robert Graves: The White Goddess: A Historical Grammar of Poetic Myth*. Carcanet Press, 1997.

Macalister, R. A. S., trans. "The Book of Invasions," in *Celtic Literature Collective*. Irish Texts Society, 1941. maryjones.us/ctexts/lebor5.html

Nagy, Gregory, trans. *Homeric Hymn to Demeter*. uh.edu/~cldue/texts/demeter.html

Oates, Shani. *The Hanged God: Odinn Grimnir*. Anathema Books, 2022.

—. *The Search for Odinn: From Pontic Steppes to Sutton Hoo*. Anathema Books, 2022.

—. *The Star Crossed Serpent III: The Taper that Lights the Way*. Mandrake of Oxford, 2016.

—. *The Star Crossed Serpent IV: The Devil's Crown*. Mandrake of Oxford, 2017.

—. *Tubal's Mill: A History of the Robert Cochrane Tradition*. Mandrake of Oxford, 2018.

—. *Tubelo's Green Fire: Mythos, Ethos, Female, Male and Priestly Mysteries of the Clan of Tubal Cain*. Mandrake of Oxford, 2010.

—. *Wolf's Head: Odinn, The Ecstatic God of Tethers and Skin-Turning*. Anathema Books, 2020.

—. "Musings on the Sacred." www.clanoftubalcain.org.uk/musings.html

—. "12th Night: Hunting the Wren," in "Meanderings of the Muse." clantubalcain.com/page/4/.

Oates, Shani, and Michael Howard. "An Interview with Shani Oates." clanoftubalcain.org.uk/shani-interview.html

Patai, Raphael "Lilith," in *The Hebrew Goddess*. Wayne State University Press, 1990.

Plato. *Phaedrus*. Translated by Alexander Nehamas and Paul Woodruff. Hackett Classics, 1995.

Porphyry. "On Images." Translated by Edwin Hamilton Gifford. classics. mit.edu/Porphyry/images.html

Radhakrishnan, S., ed. and trans. *The Principal Upaniṣads*. Humanity Books, 1992.

Robin the Dart. "Cain: An Agricultural Myth?" clanoftubalcain.org. uk/cain_ag.html.

—. "Ciphers and Symbols Used by Robert Cochrane." clanoftubalcain. org.uk/cyphers.html.

Shah, Idries. *The Sufis*. ISF Publishing, 2018 edition.

Shakespeare, William. *The Merry Wives of Windsor*.

—. *King Lear*.

—. *Macbeth*.

Taylor, Thomas, "Orphic Hymn to Prothyraeia." 1792.

Tolkien, J. R. R. and E.V. Gordon, trans. *Sir Gawain and the Green Knight*. Oxford University Press, 1960.

Toumanova, Nina, trans. *The Way of a Pilgrim*. Dover Publications, 2008.

Valiente, Doreen. *The Rebirth of Witchcraft*. Robert Hale, 2007.

Virgil, *The Georgics*. classics.mit.edu/Virgil/georgics.html.

INDEX

H

46, 48, 51, 56–57, 59–60, 62–64, 72–73, 75–77, 80–81, 88, 93–95, 97–99, 101, 105–107, 111, 113–114, 116, 122, 124, 127–130, 148, 159–160, 165, 177, 184, 198, 200, 206, 208, 211–212

N

O

P

Y

Z